D1637096

CONVERSATIONS WITH ERIC SEVAREID

INTERVIEWS WITH NOTABLE AMERICANS

WALTER LIPPMANN   WILLIAM O. DOUGLAS

HUGO BLACK   DEAN ACHESON

GEORGE KENNAN   JOHN McCLOY

ROBERT HUTCHINS   LEO ROSTEN

ERIC HOFFER   MARY PEABODY

MARIETTA TREE   FRANCES FITZGERALD

DANIEL PATRICK MOYNIHAN

Public Affairs Press, Washington, D.C.

Published by Public Affairs Press
419 New Jersey Ave., Washington, D. C. 20003
Copyright, 1976, by CBS News
Printed in the United States of America
ISBN 0-8183-0248-8

INTRODUCTION

By Eric Sevareid

Television programs spin by on their kaleidoscopic wheel of time. They can have influence but usually of short duration. The best programs in the areas of culture or news and public affairs are invariably followed by hundreds, sometimes thousands of letters from viewers who ask if they might have a printed transcript of the program, to read at their leisure, to think about at their own pace.

Few individuals, in the present state of technology, can afford the reels of film or video tape involved, to screen in the privacy of their homes and offices. Organizations, more and more, are doing this. Some of the interviews or "conversations" in this book — those with Justices Black and Douglas and John McCloy in particular — have been widely re-played in colleges and professional associations. Still, the type of TV program represented here cries for the ancient, permanent and convenient form of print.

Television cannot take a picture of an idea. It can transmit by sound the words expressing the idea. Personality does emerge from the conjunction of voice and thought, but it emerges in fullest degree if the face and expressions of the personality are added, as television can do. This is important for anyone seeking to understand history by understanding the individuals who have helped to make history. Few people, I should think, could watch and listen to John McCloy for two hours without comprehending completely why so many American Presidents trusted this man with so many high and delicate tasks. Who could watch the huge and rough-cut figure of Eric Hoffer without absorbing the almost elemental passion of the man, his love of ideas, his guileless romance with America?

It may be asked if the men and women of these conversations think and talk in their natural way while confronting the artillery of three whirring cameras and the interviewer who was, in the case of two or three, a stranger to them? The answer is that they do, to a remarkable degree — when the subject matter is of an impersonal nature. It would have been quite different had I wished to question them about their private lives in the now popular exhibitionist vogue. They "sat" for me; they talked for me because, I think, they had a measure of trust in me. Indeed, had they not, they would not have agreed to the ordeal in the first place. None was possessed by any frivolous desire or need for publicity. None was page-one news at the time of the conversations. I deliberately chose individuals who were just below the surface of the news, but persons of lasting influence. I was not trying to "make news" but to reveal what truths we could by this means. My own style as an interviewer is not that of the remorseless prosecuting attorney barking trip-hammer questions. I had not chosen personalities I suspected, but those I respected. For me, at any rate, the way to get the man to remove his cloak is to be, as in the fable, the sun, not the wind.

But this does not satisfy a certain breed of critic, those who think there must be deception behind every statement, clay in every eminent foot. Why had we not made more of Justice Black's early membership in the Ku Klux Klan? Why not more of Justice Douglas' association with the Parvin Foundation which had some unsavory gambling connections? The reasons were simple: The Black story was an ancient one, freely admitted long ago as a blunder by an overly ambitious and very young Alabama politician and long ago lived down by the man's tremendous record as a humanitarian free of bigotry. The Parvin affair had left no personal taint whatever on Justice Douglas, re-hashed as the matter so often was.

In any case interviews of this kind are not part of the exposé function of television news, indispensable as that function is. They are not designed to corner a man but to let him out; to reveal the meaning of his life and the nature of his thought as fully as one can; to inform and educate; even, where possible, to inspire.

The general audience understood, if various press critics did not. A river of letters followed each of these broadcasts. A common theme was detectable in this mail: surprise at the privilege of listening to the free play of first class minds, a sense of excitement at spoken insights that seemed to drill to the very core of so many of the baffling difficulties of our collective life and our international confusions. And relief that these were not the familiar abrasive, adversary interview confrontations.

I had deliberately selected personalities who had been long on the scene, some who had been intimately associated with the seminal events that have shaped our politics, domestic and foreign. I wanted the new generation to hear men like Acheson, McCloy, Hutchins and Kennan, who "were there when it happened." What these men knew at first hand to be true about the past has been blocked off in degree by young, revisionist historians who can study the documents but who cannot know the atmosphere of those times.

Older Americans were gratified by the discussions, but grateful letters from very young people arrived in surprising numbers. Some said that their cast of thought about the past had been altered. Some were astonished to find that the personage was still alive. Many had never heard of Leo Rosten or Eric Hoffer and were excited by their discovery.

Hoffer, indeed, came as a resounding revelation to millions of living rooms. I had been warned by one or two superiors at CBS that "only the intellectuals will take to him." My answer was that it would be the ordinary people of the workaday world who would respond to him as one expressing their own un-articulated feelings about life and this country. And so they did. Every CBS station switchboard on the network lit up like a Christmas tree when the hour was over. His books sold out within a day at every bookstore in the country; he was an instant celebrity. America has had other thinkers and writers of first rank who came from the class of manual workers. But Hoffer is the only one I can think of who remained working class throughout his life, in his surroundings, friendships, ways of thinking. He is their authentic spokesman and therefore a national resource.

Of the personalities in this volume it would be Hoffer and Lippmann who represent the opposite poles of personal style, cast of thought and use of the language. Hoffer — epigrammatically spare in his writings — talks with flowing force and sometimes fury. In public or in private he is the "natural man." The ascetic, austere Lippmann was as lean and precise in his speech as in his person, his passions only the passions of the mind and those under iron control. He had paid little attention to television in his disciplined daily life and I was astonished when Fred Friendly of CBS persuaded him to sit before the cameras. There was something hilarious about the loud-voiced, ham-fisted Rabelaisian Friendly, master of sales and showmanship, arguing with the soft-spoken, Puritanical Lippmann. But it was their very oppositeness that attracted each to the other. One of their meetings ended with Friendly, in mock despair, saying,

"After all, Walter, I made you a celebrity!" Lippmann murmured, "I made you respectable."

Even the masters of the language cannot use it with total precision in extemporaneous conversation. In these conversations, Lippmann, Kennan and Acheson came the closest to that. Yet when Lippmann read the taped transcript of his first filmed conversation he said, "My God, my syntax!"

For me, these encounters, even under the remorseless lights and camera eyes were much more pleasure than pain. The real pain came later. We would "shoot" with three film cameras for at least two hours, sometimes three. Then some poor soul had to transcribe the talk from the sound track to the typewritten page. Then others had to edit transcript and then the miles of film, re-arrange sequences, fashion it all into a compact whole that would open strongly, hold interest throughout and end with strength. This is no mean art, if one is to respect the integrity of the subject's line of thought, as we tried very hard to do. The worst agony was in the cutting-out process. Occasionally one felt he was cutting away living flesh.

Words as spoken are one thing. Spoken words put to print must be slightly different, the syntax put to rights without distortion of meaning. Indeed, the editing done for this volume clarifies the meanings. It is surely a service to speaker and reader alike. This delicate work has been left to the sensitive hands of M. B. Schnapper, editor of the Public Affairs Press.

So he — and I — offer these pages of speech as a kind of *aide-memoire* to the reader who is trying, like the rest of us, to comprehend more clearly where America has been and where it seems to be.

CONVERSATIONS WITH

Conversation With
Walter Lippmann

April 8, 1964

Sevareid: You have been writing and with great influence for some fifty years about the affairs of this country. I can't think of any record to match it in American journalism — not even Horace Greeley's. You have been personally acquainted with Presidents, Cabinet officers, military people, many people of high rank. In fact, Presidents have come to see you. How do you maintain a relationship with them that is intimate enough so that you can go to them when you want information and yet write critically about it if necessary? Do you restrain yourself in any fashion to keep that relationship?

Lippmann: No, I think there are certain rules of hygiene in the relationship between a newspaper correspondent and high officials, people in authority, which are very important and which one has to observe. Newspapermen cannot be cronies of great men. Once a man, even if you have known him more or less as a crony for years and he becomes something like a Governor, much less a President, it's all over. You can't call him by first name anymore.

Sevareid: Well, to go to something more impersonal and more important, Mr. Lippmann, a couple of years ago you said that we were achieving a superior position in terms of power in the world vis-a-vis the Russians, but a year ago you felt that our alliance was coming somewhat unstuck. How do you feel about this general balance now?

Lippmann: I think we're living in the aftermath of the threat of nuclear war between the Soviet Union and the United States. That threat has for a time been dissipated as a result of the fact that the United States achieved superiority in nuclear weapons but, of course, not omnipotence. In other words, we're in no danger of a

1

threat, of an attack, by the Soviet Union. On the other hand, we're in no position to order the Soviet Union around. This stalemate with our own superiority was demonstrated in the Cuban crisis and is, I think, enshrined in the test ban treaty. The test ban treaty is really, if you look at it from here as to Russia, is an acceptance by Russia of our existing superiority and an admission that, while we are superior, they can live with that. We can't use it as a threat to their existence.

Sevareid: Well, now, what is the result of all this in world politics? Are the great powers paralyzed by this thing?

Lippmann: The result is that the military alliances and military arrangements (I'm not talking only of NATO but of the alliances in Asia too) which were based on the fact that the world had only two powers that might go to war, are coming apart. You see, when we had the terribly dangerous confrontation of these two nuclear powers everybody was so frightened that they crowded into one or the other. Now that the fear has been lifted, they tend to their own ambitions and troubles. That's why the world is much more disorderly but it is much less dangerous.

Sevareid: Are you then less disturbed by reason of what has been happening with the North Atlantic alliance?

Lippmann: Yes, I agree with General de Gaulle. The alliance's agreement, a very solemn agreement that if one of us is attacked we will all go to the help, that is not coming apart. What is coming apart is the military structure of the integrated forces that General Eisenhower originally commanded as Supreme Commander and which is called the NATO establishment. That, General de Gaulle believes, is obsolete because it was devised to prevent a Soviet or Red Army invasion of Western Europe.

Sevareid: Then NATO succeeded?

Lippmann: It succeeded and it has outlived the necessity for it. That's why the Europeans no longer really give it any great support.

Sevareid: Well, the depolarization of the world, so-called, what is it going to mean in other terms?

Lippmann: Europe is recovering, of course. It has recovered economically in Western Europe remarkably. In fact, it has entirely recovered, you might say. But Europe, as a whole, is still split down the middle and the full recovery of Europe won't have taken place until that fissure is over — in other words, until Germany is reunified and Eastern Europe becomes part of a larger European community.

Sevareid: Is that happening in small ways?

Lippmann: Yes, there's a great deal of evidence showing that it is happening. For instance, Western Germany, the Bonn Republic, has now entered into relations which are formal in everything but name with an increasing number of Eastern countries — Poland, Hungary, and so on. The trade economic ties between Western Germany and Eastern Europe are growing very rapidly, more rapidly than any other, and the old day of absolute division is over.

Sevareid: Mr. Khrushchev has just talked about a good dish of goulash as better than revolution. Does this mean in your mind a fundamental change in the Russian pattern of approaching the world?

Lippmann: Basically, yes. Marxism is a dying creed in Russia. Mr. Khrushchev wouldn't admit that but it's a dying creed because it doesn't fit the kind of industrialized modern economy the Soviets have begun to develop.

Sevareid: Well, Russia has become, as far as communism goes, the "established church", in a sense, with China the "church-militant." Is this change really good for our interests? How serious a matter is China for us?

Lippmann: She's not nearly so serious as Russia was 5 years ago. She is not a nuclear power and therefore she's not capable of the kind of thing that Russia was capable of.

Sevareid: You don't feel very concerned about what China is trying to do?

Lippmann: I feel very much concerned about her influence, but it can't be done by sheer nuclear force. She doesn't have it. I think China can be contained peaceably for another ten or fifteen years and then she will be very much like the Soviet Union today.

Sevareid: You sound as though we have very little to worry about.

Lippmann: If you want to have a great big worry to worry about, I can't think of it at the moment.

Sevareid: You're not worried about what may happen in Southeast Asia in terms of our interest?

Lippmann: I think we have in Southeast Asia a very serious thing for which it's hard to see any satisfactory solution.

Sevareid: President Kennedy said he believed in the "domino theory" — that if one part of Southeast Asia falls the rest will go. Do you believe in that?

Lippmann: I don't think it's all going to go like dominoes. I mean, if the worst happened in Vietnam it would be overthrow of the government by Vietnamese — by South Vietnamese — who would then proceed to negotiate what would amount to a surrender to North Vietnam. Part of this would be ordering us to leave the country. We would lose our influence in the whole Southeast Asia, which includes the Southeast Asia peninsula and Indonesia. And loss of influence for a great power is a very serious thing.

Sevareid: Well, how do you explain to people why the United States is involved in the Vietnam war? Ought we be in it?

Lippmann: There was a vacuum. The old empires — the British empire, the French empire, the Dutch empire — broke down. They were conquered by the Japanese and the Japanese empire broke down. There was no government and we were involved in all these places. We allowed ourselves and maybe had to — there are some differences of opinion about that — get sucked into Vietnam because the French had to get out. I believe in the old-fashioned American strategic doctrine which was, before Korea, never to get engaged in a land war on the mainland of Asia. Sea power, air power, yes, but never land. I've heard it said by a very eminent American soldier that any American who committed American troops to a land war in Asia should have his head examined. That's the prejudice with which I approach this thing. I would never have gotten in as deeply as we did into Vietnam but we're in and you can't cry over spilt milk. The question is: how do you finish with it?

Sevareid: Is General de Gaulle and his proclamations about that helping us or harming us now?

Lippmann: I think it's very difficult to say. The proclamations don't make a great deal of difference to us. We have had a government in Saigon which was corrupt and reactionary, the Diem government, and we did our best to hope it would disappear, which it did. That government was probably getting ready to negotiate some kind of an arrangement with North Vietnam. It certainly wasn't fighting the war very vigorously in South Vietnam.

Sevareid: Do you really feel it's possible to negotiate some neutral status for Vietnam?

Lippmann: I don't. I think it may be too late. I think it has been possible. I think the French, from what I know of them, wonder if it isn't too late. But if anything is negotiated that does make a settlement there short of the actual military conquest of Indochina by the Chinese, it'll have to be done with China. General de Gaulle, at least,.

has analyzed this correctly. Whether he can pull it off, I don't know.

Sevareid: There are a number of people who call him a mischief-maker and say he's broken up all the grand designs for the postwar world in Europe, in relation to us. Is his recognition of China mischief for us?

Lippmann: Well, of course, if you have a frozen position and somebody breaks out of that and does things that don't accept the assumptions you've accepted, that always is mischievous and a nuisance. All your plans get thrown into confusion, but we have to open our minds to the possibility that on a lot of things de Gaulle may be right and we may be wrong.

Sevareid: But he, by saying that certain things are the real realities, may be bringing them about.

Lippmann: Let's take an example from Southeast Asia. He may be right that it's impossible to stabilize Southeast Asia without coming to terms with China. We may not be able to do that. I know we can't because we have commitments to the Nationalists and Chiang Kai-shek, but de Gaulle doesn't have those commitments. The fact that he doesn't do what he would have to do in the period when we were practically omnipotent in the world should not disturb us.

Sevareid: Can he do these things because he personally is a very powerful figure in a country that is essentially weak in relation to us? He is not picking up the responsibility in Indochina.

Lippmann: Yes he is. Only he knows from nine years of warfare that the French conducted in Indochina that you cannot get a military solution of Southeast Asia.

Sevareid: But if there were a neutrality agreement, it would be American power, not French, that would have to guarantee it.

Lippmann: Certainly, certainly. He'd be the first, I think, to admit that. But it won't be done by American power of people flying around in helicopters in South Vietnam. I don't wish to be misunderstood. We have to try and stabilize a government before we can do anything else, but the great power that we have is economic, sea, and air power. That's our power in Southeast Asia. Otherwise it's way beyond our reach.

Sevareid: Doesn't de Gaulle suffer from what Senator Fulbright called mythology?

Lippmann: I don't doubt that everybody has his myths. He undoubtedly has his, which is about the grandeur of France. But de Gaulle's positive side — the thing that will make him regarded, I think, as a genius in history — is his ability to foresee what is happening now and in the near future. He's the first head of state who has realized and acted upon the realization that the postwar period has ended. That's the meaning of de Gaulle in Europe.

Sevareid: Do you agree with his prophecies about Russia and her gradual move back into the Western world?

Lippmann: Yes, I think that's happening and the Russians are very conscious of it. In Eastern Europe, in Hungary and Poland, where I was not long ago, the interest in being Western is very extraordinary.

Sevareid: Would you say then that the Cold War in relation to Russia, if not China, is really over?

Lippmann: The Cold War in its dangerous and malignant phase, which was when nuclear weapons were the ultimate thing, that's over. The rivalry of the political systems, the social thing, is not over and probably won't be over for a generation.

Sevareid: The world has changed. Maybe our policies and thinking about it haven't changed very rapidly but aren't we really overextended in too many ways and in too many places? Would we be wiser if we concentrated our foreign aid efforts in fewer places?

Lippmann: Yes, I think so. Foreign aid is, in a sense, very unpopular with Congress because it's an awful phrase. We've used such aid as a kind of "slush fund" around the periphery of Asia. We support armies, give them arms they don't need, give them planes they don't know how to fly, just to keep the officer-class happy because they're the people who control the government and they threaten that if we don't subsidize them they'll go over and join the Communists. Now, that part of it I think we have to do. Every big government has a "slush fund." There's no use fooling yourself about this and we musn't be too moralistic and serious about it. But serious foreign aid of the kind which is really intended to develop an underdeveloped country should be concentrated in those places where there's some chance of success.

Sevareid: We are not deeply involved in Africa yet. We are in Latin America, we are in Asia. Is the trend now to try to pull back or ought we be further into Africa?

Lippmann: I think the trend is to limit our commitments abroad rather than to extend them. I would say that Africa south of the Sahara is a place where we should never get in and be the primary power. We are in for a number of reasons, partly because we are overcommitted and partly because we ourselves have an African problem in this country, but we are not well suited to take a leading part in Africa south of the Sahara. So I think we should always be the second man, the third man, not the first man in these issues.

Sevareid: Is Cyprus the kind of place where this country ought to be involved?

Lippmann: Our country has to be involved there but not actively. It isn't actively involved in the sense we have troops there. I think Cyprus is a good example of how we should proceed in places where we don't want to get involved except through the United Nations or some other alliance organization. We are not in the front of the thing. We're not responsible for who gets killed and who doesn't get killed in a Cypriot village.

Sevareid: Are we learning a little sense of reticence now?

Lippmann: I think that, yes. There are signs of it. I think we're increasingly realizing that we are not, as we were apparently at the end of the Second World War, omnipotent. We had everything, everybody was prostrate but the United States. We had the only nuclear weapons there were. We had all the money that was disposable, that could be lent to anybody. Russia was prostrate; all of Europe was prostrate. Eastern Europe didn't exist. China was in terrible condition. Also Japan. From that we developed an illusion that our omnipotence would last forever. The great thing we're having to learn now, have had to begin to learn, in the past three or four or five years is that that period is over. That's what's meant by the postwar period ending.

Sevareid: Is this what you take Senator Fulbright to mean when he talks about the persistence of a mythology in our thinking about the world?

Lippmann: Yes. When he speaks about myths persisting he means what we believed — and what was probably true when we believed it well back to the Second World War — about Russia, about China, about various countries. Our conceptions of what these countries are like and what they're up to stay frozen while actual events move on; that's what he's talking about.

Sevareid: But how do you unfreeze the given practical position we have on our problem in Cuba, for example? What can be done?

Lippmann: I don't think we're doing badly about Cuba. The Soviet people are withdrawing there. They are down to very few people now and all the military people will probably be gone in a few

months. In fact, there's a little subsidiary worry in our minds, now
that they've left and are not manning the anti-aircraft guns. Those
guns are now in the hands of Castro, which may be more dangerous
than when the Russians were there. However, we'll get by that. This
is not a problem which will have a quick solution. If it has a peaceful
and satisfactory solution over a number of years that's good enough
for us. I think that the time will come when Castro will feel the
pressure enough and is pushed by the Soviets into negotiations, not
necessarily with us, but with some of the Latin American countries
for readmission to the Organization of American States and a lifting
of the severity of the embargoes and the boycotts. I think that's
probable.

Sevareid: You don't think it's for us to voluntarily lift the embargo?

Lippmann: No, we can afford to wait. Castro can't threaten us.
He's no danger to us, as Senator Fulbright said, and we're in no
hurry. He'll be the one who will have to be in a hurry.

Sevareid: I think you said sometime ago that if Castro were successful in what he's trying to do with Cuba this would really be
dangerous in the rest of Latin America.

Lippmann: If he were able to produce a brilliant Communist state
in spite of us, in spite of everything, it would, of course, be a
very dangerous example. It's only as an example that you have to
fear Castro. The agents and a certain amount of arms are really a
trifling matter compared to the other. The example is what counts.

Sevareid: Suppose other Latin American countries turn Communist in the meantime?

Lippmann: Well, things could go very badly but we have to cross
that bridge when we come to it — if we do.

Sevareid: Since you last talked into these cameras five years ago,
this country has experienced a couple of historic things at least —
the beginning of what some people call a Negro revolution and the
abrupt ending of the Kennedy era. I wonder if you think enough
time has gone by now so that one can judge John F. Kennedy and
how history may judge him thirty years from now. How do you feel
about his time in the White House?

Lippmann: Well, I don't think enough time has gone by. The
shock of his murder is still so close to us and the people now are
still either grieving deeply or missing something that fascinated them
tremendously. They are in no position to make an appraisal.

Sevareid: What was it about Kennedy that so fascinated people?

Lippmann: His looks, his way of dealing with things, the fact that he was a new kind of American politician. I'm not sure how much the country was at home with this new kind, but he was new and a whole new generation sort of pinned their hopes on his success.

Sevareid: Was he successful during his three years as President?

Lippmann: That is something nobody can answer today. This is the reason why any genuine historical judgment is quite impossible. We have yet to see how a lot of the things that he is identified with come out. For example, he may have brought to an end the threat, for the foreseeable future, of nuclear war, but it's awfully early to be sure that this is true. Then, he initiated certain things at home, such as a new fiscal policy, a really serious attack on the problem of Negro rights, civil rights, that President Johnson is now carrying on, and he was preparing the campaign against poverty. Until we know how those come out we won't know what historians will say.

Sevareid: Certainly his style, so-called, was very different. How important do you think this matter of style is in a chief executive?

Lippmann: I think it's very important. But this doesn't mean that there's only one style. I mean a man must be true to his own style, not to somebody else's style. The Kennedy style was something that the country had never seen before in a President.

Sevareid: What have been your own impressions of President Johnson's method of conducting this office?

Lippmann: My feeling about that is this: When President Kennedy was murdered the situation abroad and at home was in a state of crisis. His own policies were blocked at home and they were frustrated abroad. The country was very deeply and bitterly divided about him. There was sectional feeling. There was class feeling. There was racial feeling. President Johnson is by nature a healing man, a man who heals. That's been his function, his mission, in his first hundred days.

Sevareid: Are you saying, in effect, that while Johnson may not have the fervent phalanx of admirers in the country that Kennedy had he has fewer enemies?

Lippmann: Oh, very many fewer. And the country is far more united and at peace with itself, except over the issue of Negro rights, than it has been for a long time.

Sevareid: You attribute this to the accession of a new President?

Lippmann: I attribute it to the accession of President Johnson. Not any man who succeeded Kennedy could have done it. But this man's genius in politics, which he's tried out for fifteen years in the Senate, and thirty years in Washington, has been finding the point at which a consensus, an agreement, is possible. That's a very broad area that he takes in. The country feels this about him, somehow, and he has responded to it.

Sevareid: The President has done pretty well with the Congress. Perhaps better than Kennedy.

Lippmann: He's done extremely well. He's done, I think, what President Kennedy could not have done had he lived.

Sevareid: You felt a very few months ago that the Congress was almost conducting a sit-down.

Lippmann: Oh, I spoke before of the crisis that existed when Kennedy was killed. The Senate had deliberately brought the Kennedy administration to a standstill, and they wouldn't even appropriate, perhaps, the appropriation bill. That's as near an absolute confrontation as you can get in our system of government. Well, that's broken up, partly by the shock of the assassination and partly by the skill of President Johnson.

Sevareid: Every political leader has some flaws and faults. When you watch President Johnson at work do you detect any particular weaknesses that may catch up with him?

Lippmann: Well, I suppose, yes. It comes out of his background and experience. He is so much the product of the legislative branch of the government that his executive action is, and rightly most of the time, deeply attuned and extremely sensitive to what Congress wants. Now, you can't conduct foreign affairs wholly in that method. I feel, for example, that the difficulty over Panama arose not over the words which were quarreled about but over the perhaps excessive fear that if a revised treaty is negotiated, as undoubtedly it will have to be sooner or later, it will be very difficult to pass it through the Senate. I think President Johnson has done extremely well with this problem, except now and then one sees, I think, an excessive deference to the prejudices — and what Senator Fulbright called the other day, the myths — which exist in the Senate.

Sevareid: Would it be a fair generalization at this point to say then that whether policies are wiser or not, at least the machinery is better oiled and is working better.

Lippmann: Well, the policies are the same. There's no difference in policies between the two Presidents. This should be known not as the Johnson administration, but as the Kennedy-Johnson administration. It is a continuation. Every important measure and every important policy continues from President Kennedy. He would have had to do what Johnson is going to have to do before he gets through — revise some of those policies. But they started as Kennedy policies.

Sevareid: So far this is more continuity than transition, is it?

Lippmann: This is continuity.

Sevareid: At some point President Johnson must have a Johnson stamp on all this, must he not?

Lippmann: But not for the sake of his pride or anything. Of course if he's re-elected and has a substantial majority, not a hairline majority such as Kennedy had, he will be able to do in a sense what Eisenhower was in a position to do when he came in. He was able to revise some of the old standards, old stances, old myths of his own party and of the Congress and of the country. And that's going to be Johnson's work if he's re-elected.

Sevareid: Are you one of those people who worry about the extreme pace of his personal activity, particularly in view of the fact that he has had one heart attack?

Lippmann: I'm going to leave that to his doctors and his wife. I don't think I'll answer that.

Sevareid: Are you willing to make any prediction about who will be the Republican nominee?

Lippmann: Oh, I can't make a prediction. I think it lies between Nixon and Lodge and conceivably William Scranton. The man I think has the greatest promise as a public man in the coming years is Scranton but he's not known. He's not experienced at all. If I were his campaign manager I'd run him for Vice President and get him well-known, even though he was beaten.

Sevareid: How do you account for the Lodge phenomenon? After all he's 10,000 miles away, saying nothing, and yet he's winning primaries.

Lippmann: There are a number of things to explain it. "Nature abhors a vacuum." "Absence makes the heart grow fonder."

Sevareid: Yes, but there's another old saying, "Out of sight, out of mind."

Lippmann: But Lodge is not out of sight, what with modern means of communication. He's very visible. Besides I think there's a genuine feeling that he is a moderate, that he belongs to the wing of the party that has to be dominant if it's ever going to win. It's the Eisenhower wing of the party, really.

Sevareid: Are there some romantic trappings in his present setting?

Lippmann: He's out there doing a hard job, which people admire — public service at considerable risk to his reputation and even to his self, physically, and all these things work in his favor.

Sevareid: What works against him?

Lippmann: The politicians who worked with him in 1960 don't think he made a good campaign and don't like him. I think the straight machine politicians don't want to nominate him. That's his greatest difficulty.

Sevareid: What about Mr. Nixon? Is he deeply entrenched in the affections of this party or is he rather shopworn by now?

Lippmann: Well, he's not entrenched in the affections of the party. His nomination would be the nomination of a caretaker for the party in a bad year. Nixon has, as a candidate, certain qualifications. He has a reputation for knowing a great deal about foreign affairs and his party will talk about foreign affairs a great deal. And he is an infighter. They undoubtedly will have to try to do something to weaken President Johnson's personal standing in the country. Nixon is more willing to do it than almost any candidate.

Sevareid: Do you think that Goldwater and Rockefeller have pretty well run their course?

Lippmann: I think they've run their course.

Sevareid: What's the trouble with Governor Rockefeller? He's had a lot of federal government experience, he's been Governor of the biggest state in the country. Why hasn't he done better in this campaign?

Lippmann: Apart from the problems of his private life and his marriage, he was the man best suited by background and training to seize the middle ground for the Republicans but he hasn't done it. He has conducted a campaign in which he never quite knows whether he's trying to be like Senator Goldwater or whether he's trying to be not like him. He has underestimated the American voter, which I think is what the New Hampshire primary vote shows. That's probably the most dangerous thing a politician can do. He's tried to get down to a level which is below the level of the people who really make opinion and decide elections and they don't want to be talked down to. They know he's talking down. They know that Rockefeller isn't as folksy and palsy-walsy as he says he is. This has been, I think, fatal to his campaign. He's done what a really good politician cannot do — he's stooped to conquer and he's not conquering.

Sevareid: About a year ago in one of our discussions you said, I think, that perhaps the Republicans ought to nominate Mr. Goldwater and put to a test, finally, an idea that has persisted in the party at least since Taft's time — that if you nominated what they call a real Republican he could win. That you would bring out a lot of voters who normally don't come out. Have you changed your feeling about this?

Lippmann: Oh, yes. I wasn't really anxious to have Goldwater a candidate but I thought, as against John F. Kennedy, it might have cleared the air very much. The real objection to nominating Goldwater is that it would wreck the Republican party for maybe two presidential elections. It would put the party in the control of a far-out extremist wing which never can win in this country. There aren't the votes there. New Hampshire was a good measure of this. Senator Goldwater got less than twenty-five per cent of its vote. I think that with Kennedy's death and with the very fragile character of Goldwater's support once he was exposed in front of television and in public meetings, that the unsuitability of his candidacy has become so evident that I don't think we need the test.

Sevareid: Do you wish to speculate about who might have the best chance on the Republican side?

Lippmann: I wouldn't say that any of the candidates we hear about has a much better chance than any other one. The Republican problem is to rebuild their party, which is in very bad condition due to their division between the far right and the moderates.

Sevareid: Is it a terribly important question just whom the Democrats nominate for Vice President?

Lippmann: My feeling is that President Johnson's position is unique in that he cannot be helped by anybody who is named as a possible candidate.

Sevareid: Which of the various gentlemen mentioned for Vice President would be the greatest help to President Johnson?

Lippmann: That's not a good question, Eric, because I'm not that kind of a political dopester.

Sevareid: You said that nobody who is now named would be of great help. I don't quite understand you.

Lippmann: I mean that Johnson can win with one of the people mentioned and he won't win more because he has one of them on the ticket than if he didn't have them. Now, there are choices among them as to who would make the best President. That is the real consideration in this case. That's the point I'm trying to make. For Johnson the only real consideration is who would be a good successor.

Sevareid: Well, since I'm not talking to the President of the United States, but to Walter Lippmann, who do you think would be the best Vice Presidential candidate?

Lippmann: It lies between two men in my mind — Senator Humphrey and Secretary McNamara. I think we'll have to wait a little longer to see how McNamara makes out in Vietnam and how Humphrey makes out in civil rights before we need come to any conclusion.

Sevareid: McNamara as a Vice Presidential candidate presents an interesting problem. He's a Republican, isn't he?

Lippmann: I suppose he was a Republican but, of course, that's the way the Kennedy administration was constructed — putting Republicans in key points. It was an attempt on Kennedy's part to create something like a coalition government.

Sevareid: You don't think that McNamara's party identification would present a real problem at a convention?

Lippmann: I suppose there'll be Democratic politicians who may object but I wouldn't think it would make any difference if President Johnson decided that McNamara is the man he wanted.

Sevareid: You haven't mentioned among possible Vice Presidential candidates Attorney General Robert Kennedy. Do you think he's going to play a part in this?

Lippmann: Well, he'll play a part. He's a political power in the Democratic party, but I don't see any reason why he should be nominated for Vice President.

Sevareid: You make it sound as though President Johnson would be a very hard man to defeat next fall.

Lippmann: I wouldn't like to have the job of trying to defeat him. Of course, if things go very sour and we have an economic breakdown or some catastrophe abroad, which nobody can foresee today, everything said today would change. It's conceivable that something terrible will happen and that it would be easy for a Republican to win. But it isn't easy today and I think all Republicans know that.

Sevareid: If something were to happen that really made trouble for President Johnson wouldn't it almost have to be something of a domestic nature? Foreign affairs, unless they're totally catastrophic, normally haven't affected incumbents so much, have they?

Lippmann: I agree. As long as the country is united and trusts the President he can suffer a great many setbacks abroad and not necessarily lose by it at all. After all, President Eisenhower accepted a good deal less than a victory in Korea. That was certainly a peace without victory if ever there was one. And the people liked it — they were really glad it was over. It didn't hurt him politically.

Sevareid: Do you think it might not be possible that the civil rights demonstrations in the streets of this country this spring and summer might not get out of hand and provoke a reaction among white people to the extent that President Johnson could really be hurt next November?

Lippmann: The whole civil rights affair — the bill and the situation which it springs from — are explosive under our society. That's one of the catastrophies I had in mind when I said something terrible might happen. Yes, it's conceivable. It's conceivable that a long filibuster over the civil rights bill will produce race riots in which whites, in the North as well as the South, will join. Yes, it's possible.

Sevareid: Do you think of the filibuster as a legitimate form of check and balance against the will of the majority?

Lippmann: I've always defended the filibuster or opposed easy cloture. I've always opposed them when the issue was one which would be better dealt with if you could get the consent of the minority. I don't want to override Southerners. I don't want to override the South, for example, by a fifty-one per cent majority. On the other hand, I'm sure we've reached a point where holding up the civil rights bill indefinitely is intolerable. You can't have filibusters in time of war. You can't have a filibuster which denies this country the right to promote the internal peace of this country, which is what the civil rights measure is about. So I think that after they've had a good, long talk about it (it shouldn't be hurried) I'd like to see a cloture passed, if that is necessary, but I hope none will be. The value of the filibuster is that in a crisis it could be a very great defense of liberty in this country.

Sevareid: There seems to be nothing of a mighty and dramatic nature that the United States can do abroad now. We have reached a period of a great slowing down of the cataclysmic events we've lived with. What is the task of this country? A great country must have some great enterprise. What ought it to be? I presume it's here at home, is it not?

Lippmann: Yes, it is. We had to fight World War II. We had to fight the Cold War. We had to conduct the race of armaments. We had to nullify and neutralize Soviet nuclear power and we've done that. We've succeeded. We're out from under a terrible threat, but doing all this has been frightfully costly. It has cost over half the federal budget. It has also cost the time and energy and emotional concern of our people for twenty years. The result is that we've had to neglect the development of our vast country. And the result is seen in the condition of our schools, in the condition of our cities, in the backwardness of our transportation system, railroad transportation, and in a lot of other things. Now that the critical danger is past we can turn our attention to our own affairs without neglecting our responsibilities elsewhere.

February 22, 1965

Sevareid: We seem to be surrounded by a lot of paradox. We're the most powerful country in the world and we can't seem to find either victory or peace in a small Asiatic land. There's almost a feeling that this is a pre-war period. What do you think the President's real choices are now in Vietnam?

Lippmann: The President has a very hard choice to make. He's really in a dilemma. Either horn of the dilemma is extremely uncomfortable and unpleasant.

One horn is to escalate — that is to widen and increase the war, which is a very terrible choice because it almost certainly would lead us into a war with China before it ended. And we can't tell what Russia would do in the case of a war with China. Anyway the risks of widening the war are incalculable. The President, of course is doing his best to avoid that.

The other dilemma is to negotiate a truce in Vietnam. We're not sure we can because the interior situation in South Vietnam is breaking up, crumbling, and that is what the victory of the Vietcong is feeding upon. We're not sure that the Chinese or the North Vietnamese, who think they're winning and have good reason to think that they're winning, would be willing to negotiate something that stopped them short of complete victory. Complete victory would be a collapse of the Vietnamese government and a setting up of a new government which would invite the United States to leave. This would, of course, be exceedingly embarrassing and humiliating.

Whether we ought to have been in Vietnam in the first place is a separate question, but, having got in there, a great many Vietnamese have become dependent on us and the chances for their future if we leave are very slim. I don't know that they'd all be liquidated. Some of them would certainly have to flee the country. We have a debt of honor to these Vietnamese who have thrown themselves on our side in this civil war. Therefore, it's very hard for the President to choose disengagement. He's trying to find something between the two extremes I've mentioned.

Sevareid: You've called this a civil war. The administration talk is always about intervention from North Vietnam, another state. Do you really think it is just a civil war?

Lippmann: I think it is but, like all civil wars foreign outer powers intervene in them. That's been true of every civil war you can think of — including our own, beginning with the French intervention in it. Intervention from the outside is very important but it isn't the same thing as revolution. The American Revolution wasn't made by the French, it was made by the Americans. All recent revolutions — the Russian revolution, the Chinese revolution, etc. — were made by the people of the country itself. That's also true, in my view, in Vietnam.

Sevareid: What is the most we can hope for as the outcome of negotiations, however it takes place?

Lippmann: The most we could hope for is that there will be a sufficient political truce in the civil war for a period of some years so that the people can adjust themselves to each other. I mean, of course, the people who have been fighting on opposite sides in the civil war. Negotiations can heal their wounds and that's about all. We can't make South Vietnam or Southeast Asia an American outpost. We don't want to; the President says we don't want to. And we can't do it. What we can do is see that Vietnam doesn't become a Chinese military outpost, which is quite a different thing from saying that it will eventually be within the Chinese sphere of influence.

I don't know of any man living who thinks that 35 years from now, when the Chinese are one half of the whole human race, that they aren't going to be the dominant power in Southeast Asia. Of course they are but they're not there now, and we have to protect the people who would be liquidated, killed, really persecuted if we suddenly disappeared. That's our problem.

Sevareid: Isn't much of the dilemma whether we actually can get the negotiations going?

Lippmann: It is a real question whether we can rally enough world opinion and enough diplomatic support, particularly from the Soviet Union, from Japan, and India and other Asiatic countries, to induce negotiations. We have to find ways of going behind the scenes. And there are many ways behind the scenes — to China, to Moscow, to Tokyo, to London, to Paris — to create a situation which diplomatically nobody in the world can define today, which will make it advantageous and necessary for the Communists to negotiate.

Sevareid: What's needed is a cease-fire from the Vietcong before negotiations.

Lippmann: It's necessary to do the diplomatic exploration I've been talking about, not a conference, before there's a cease-fire. One of the terms I would think indispensable to a negotiation or any kind of talk, back and forth, would be that we would not withdraw while the thing was going on. You see, we have been faced with an ultimatum from Hanoi and Peking that we must get out and then talk. Now, that we can't do because that means abandoning all our friends and all our interests and that would be scuttling the ship.

Sevareid: There are complaints in the press that this is not only an undeclared war we're conducting, but an unexplained war. The President is criticized for not talking to the public about this involvement. Do you think he should?

Lippmann: I think he's in a very difficult position. An irresponsible journalist can tell the truth but if the President of the United States tells it morale will probably collapse in Saigon. That government would just blow up. If he tells what he wants to do, on what terms he would be willing to consider negotiating, they'll immediately reject them publicly, which makes it impossible for them to accept it in the end. And there'll be a great outcry from our war hawks that he's appeasing. So he's caught in a jam. I don't think he can explain the war more. Because of the nature of our involvement he has to work through what amounts to secret diplomacy.

Sevareid: Do you find here in Washington a really serious war party, war hawks so to speak, who want to make a big roar out of this war in Vietnam?

Lippmann: They're very strong and powerful. I don't think they're a big camp, but I think they're quite influential.

Sevareid: Do you care to say in what areas they would be found?

Lippmann: I think they would be found in the military area and to some degree in the diplomatic area. But they're not found in the interior and at the top of the White House. I feel sure of that.

Sevareid: Well, in the White House there's only one top man, so I assume you mean that you're convinced that the President —

Lippmann: I mean that the President is not a war hawk. The war hawks want to bomb Hanoi and all the industries. They want to knock out the whole industrial system of North Vietnam. If anybody says the Chinese will come in, intervene, if that's done, then the bombing of China is urged. The President's policy in bombing is a very strictly controlled and regulated policy. We're not bombing North Vietnam, we're bombing the borderland above the Seventeenth Parallel, which is a rather empty country. We signal our attacks and they know when we're coming. There's no surprise attack. They're really public relations jobs much more than they are military jobs. They're political bombings, they don't kill people. I don't think they kill anybody. There's no evidence that they do because what we bomb is wooded sheds. Now, I don't think there's any doubt at all that if we bomb North Vietnam the way the war hawks want it bombed and make it uninhabitable, the North Vietnamese Army — which by the way is the largest land army in eastern Asia, except China's — will move right down into South Vietnam where they can't be bombed and where there are rich prizes. I don't think South Vietnam will resist them. They couldn't.

The war hawks answer to that is: Yes, South Vietnam is so important that we must send troops in. When you really press them they talk in terms of hundreds of thousands of American troops to hold the line. If we were in the position in Vietnam that England was in 1940, if they were on our beaches, we'd have to do that but we're 8,000 miles away. I don't think we have to do that and I hope we won't.

Sevareid: Suppose, in the showdown, the war hawks, so to speak, have their way. Then what happens?

Lippmann: At first, if the war hawks prevail and we become involved in a big war, they will rejoice, but in the end the people will weep.

Sevareid: You don't agree, then, with those who say that South
Vietnam is another Berlin or Korea?

Lippmann: No. It's not a Korea because it's not an invasion as
in Korea. That was an open, old-fashioned invasion by an army that
crossed a frontier and there were battles in the open. This is not the
situation. This is like a flood, like water spreading. You can't beat
it back or shoot it with a shotgun. It won't go back.

Sevareid: One would suppose the war hawks learned their own
lesson, a military lesson, from Korea when the Chinese came into it.

Lippmann: Well, they say the Korean syndrome — that's what
they call it — has frightened the Americans. I don't know if they've
learned from experience.

Sevareid: There are many people here who think that if we do
withdraw from that part of Southeast Asia, however it happens,
that we will have suffered an enormous and historic American defeat.

Lippmann: I think we made a mistake to involve ourselves in a
war on the land in Asia. It's contrary to all previous American military teaching and doctrine. We have to expect to pay some price
for it. We can't expect to get out gloriously from a mistake. But if
you mean that the United States will cease to be a power in Asia
because it negotiates itself out of Vietnam eventually, the answer to
that is it's not true. The United States controls the whole Pacific
Ocean, all the water, all the air above it, and all the air over the
way into the interior of China and so on. This is a situation that has
never existed before in American history and that will continue
to exist.

Sevareid: I take it you're not concerned about any immediate
toppling of dominoes in the rest of Southeast Asia.

Lippmann: Not immediate, but I never deceive myself. I never
believed in going into Southeast Asia. I've said this many times. But
as long as we are there I believe what we have to do is to stay there
long enough to make the process orderly rather than disorderly and
violent.

Sevareid: Does our government have an overall policy for Asia?

Lippmann: We have objective commitments which I do not believe
is policy for the long run. I'm not talking about tomorrow but about
five, ten, fifteen, twenty years from now. We have these commitments
as a result of our victory over the Japanese Empire in the Second
World War. We find ourselves in places where we can't expect to
stay for the rest of time. We aren't going to stay forever in South

Korea and we aren't going to stay forever in South Vietnam, nor forever in Taiwan, nor in Okinawa, which is part of Japan. If we have any sense, any maturity, we will adjust our minds to the fact that over the generations, the tide is going to recede to something more normal and natural.

Sevareid: What you're saying then, as I understand it, is that in the long run, we must be prepared to live with Chinese Communist domination of Southeast Asia.

Lippmann: The situation for us in the Pacific is very like what happened in Europe with the Russians. We have lived with Soviet domination of Eastern Europe since 1945 and look at it now. It's dissolving. If we can hold China, in a great military sense, from building a navy like the Japanese Navy was at Pearl Harbor, from becoming a real threat to our peace, if we wait as we've waited with the Soviet Union, the same forces will in the end work in China that have worked in the Soviet Union. She'll relax her grip.

Sevareid: But East Europe is confronted with a countervailing force in the sense of the great weight and prosperity of West Germany and the rest of West Europe is pressing close on East Europe's very borders. You wouldn't have that, really, would you, in the Far East? Where would the other force come from?

Lippmann: The best I would expect, in looking at the long run, is that we can get the same kind of pause and interlude—that, I think is the best we can hope for. I think, for instance, that Vietnam, which was always anti-Chinese, will follow the same line that Tito has followed in Europe as against the Soviet Union. It will be Socialist or Communist in a manner of speaking. Those words don't apply very well in Asia but it'll be tending to be anti-Chinese and independent and that will be, from our point of view, quite satisfactory.

Sevareid: Do you fear the Chinese possession of the bomb?

Lippmann: I certainly do. I fear it very much. I'm not having hysterics about it because it's a long way off before it can be a threat to us. I haven't absolutely made up my mind about it but I think we probably could afford to offer the nations that are threatened by the bomb — India and Japan, the two important countries — a guarantee not that we'd defend them with troops and ships and airplanes but that if they were hit with a nuclear bomb we'll hit back with a nuclear bomb. While I'm not sure that that's the right policy, I think we ought to consider it very carefully.

Sevareid: Wouldn't that make a full circle of American commitment? We have made this commitment for Europe, for Latin America under Mr. Kennedy at the time of the Cuban missile crisis, and now you would include Asia, too.

Lippmann: That is a commitment which we are able to fulfill. Holding villages in the jungles of Vietnam is not a commitment that American troops can really fulfill.

Severeid: Do you think what's happened recently in Vietnam, including our bombing, has altered the relations between Moscow and Peking?

Lippmann: Moscow is forced to align itself with Peking but the underlying differences between those two powers are so deep that I don't think they can, in the long run, become one power again. I think, therefore, we can count on the diplomatic offensive I was talking about before, on quiet Russian support. First of all, they'd have a territorial conflict over the longest frontier in the world and the most badly defined. It stretches 4,000 miles across Soviet Siberia and China, with territory in dispute all along the way. That doesn't make for peace. There's been a lot of fighting going on that never got reported on this frontier.

The other thing is that they're in different stages of development. The Russians have passed the revolutionary stage in their own development. They have a going society with big industry and they don't have to keep the country in a state of war alarm, war tension, in order to get the people to endure the hardships that the regime requires. China doesn't want a war any more than Russia does but she wants a state of war feeling because she needs it for her own affairs. Russia needs the opposite; she needs intercourse and commerce with the West. That's the original root of the quarrel between Khrushchev and Mao Tse-tung and it continues with Khrushchev's successors. They have an irreconcilable difference.

Severeid: Well, when China is a highly industrialized country isn't she apt to be much more cautious? She'll be more vulnerable to atomic attack and destruction, for one thing, than she is as a nation of villages.

Lippmann: She'll go through the same evolution that every revolutionary society goes through. She'll become middle class, which is what the Russians are becoming. And when they're middle class, they don't like to have their property destroyed, their families broken up, and their savings lost. In other words, they become soft. That softening process has happened in Russia and it will happen if we can hold off war long enough — for say fifteen, twenty years — in China.

Sevareid: Let's turn to our relations with Europe. There's a sense here in Washington that President Johnson has changed the terms of reference in our relations with the NATO alliance countries. What is this change?

Lippmann: He has changed them, I think, for the better. After the World War and up to President Johnson's time the United States was not only the military protector of Europe but it was also the banker and the general political and moral boss — superintendent at least — of Europe. In the course of this period we got ourselves very badly entangled, first with the British, who thought they were our special friend. This resulted in their being excluded from the Common Market by General de Gaulle. Then we got into a tangle with the Germans, who thought they were our special favorites. In those days, when Chancellor Andenauer was the Chancellor of Germany, he was our chief advisor on European affairs.

We oughtn't to have special favorites among our allies. President Johnson, who has kept on excellent terms with the British and with the Germans, has ended that. Problems arose over the proposal to create a multilateral mixed-manned nuclear fleet in which the Germans would have owned 40%. That aroused fury all over — among all the people in Europe who still fear Germany and in the Soviet Union. Johnson put that proposal on ice; he suspended it.

Sevareid: Is that what you once called masterly inactivity?

Lippmann: Masterly inactivity. You see, when you are no longer needed as the leader of Europe then the right thing to do is to stop trying to lead it. Let Europe develop in its own way, which is, I think, going to be quite satisfactory.

Sevareid: Is it going in the direction of a more cohesive united Europe?

Lippmann: Yes. It's going in the direction of breaking down of the Iron Curtain between the two halves of Europe. This is a process of trade and sport and cultural communication between Europe's two halves.

Sevareid: Do you think we could have arrived at that rather favorable point had we not taken the great leadership for many years, had we not had all those troops of ours in Europe?

Lippmann: We had to do it. It was under our protection and with our financial help, Europe recovered. It's like a family. You have to recognize that the child has grown up and you can't treat it as if it were a baby.

Sevareid: In Germany there now seems to be a revival of interest in its reunification. Do you see this coming about?

Lippmann: I think it's going to come. I'm not surprised at the revival of this interest. Germany, divided as it is, not even in possession of its own capital, is a sick country. It's done very well economically but politically it's sick. It will never be well until it's reunified. The reunification can come about, I think, only by the process I was talking about — by the gradual weaving together of the two parts of Europe. When that takes place Germany will be reunited in the process.

Sevareid: President de Gaulle is now the last of the great wartime leaders of the West and the most powerful political personality in Europe. Why don't we get along with him better? Who misunderstands whom?

Lippmann: I don't doubt that there's a good deal of misunderstanding both ways. He and President Roosevelt didn't get on. He and Churchill had difficulties but they got on better than President Roosevelt and de Gaulle. The basic difficulty is that de Gaulle is like a man who can't see very clearly what's right in front of him. But he sees absolutely perfectly what's in the distance. He has the farthest vision, he can see further than any man in our time and I don't even exclude Churchill. De Gaulle foresaw, at the worst moment in the fall of France, how in the end the war would be won — namely by the coming in of Russia and the United States. That kind of vision is very annoying to public men who don't see that far.

On the other hand, the fact that de Gaulle doesn't see very clearly in front of him and stumbles over the furniture is very annoying too. He kicks shins as he goes. That's the problem and the genius of his vision. For instance, he has foreseen — we are following the same policy by the same logic but we didn't take it from him — that the reunification of Germany and of Europe would have to come about through increasing connections with Eastern Europe, between East and West Europe. He's doing that. He's been much closer to the East Europeans than anybody.

In the Far East it is very annoying to us that he recognized China. It was a sign of great vision — to see that there'd never be peace in the Far East until it was made with China. It can't be made with anybody else but that kind of thing is the cause of difficulty.

Sevareid: Do you think President Johnson ought to personally meet with President de Gaulle any time soon?

Lippmann: I'm in no hurry for that. I don't think they're built to understand each other too well. I think they had better meet through very skillful ambassadors.

Sevareid: Apparently the President wants to go to Europe and to Russia some time soon. Do you think the time is really ripe for that?

Lippmann: Well, if he asked my advice, which he hasn't, I would not advise him to go.

Sevareid: Why not?

Lippmann: I'd advise him to get the Great Society going in this country and we have something in the bank to talk about. His style isn't the style that Europeans naturally understand. It's an old-fashioned American style and I wouldn't think he'd do too well. I don't think you can accomplish anything by face to face talk with a man like de Gaulle or with a man like Kosygin.

Sevareid: It's just a mass public relations exercise.

Lippmann: It would be public relations — too many reporters, too many cameras, and too many everything, and it wouldn't work. They'd all say things that they wish they hadn't said when it's over. So I'm in favor of the President staying home. If he wants to travel I think he might go to South America. That might be useful.

Sevareid: If the President does go to Russia he'll find a new regime now. Mr. Khrushchev has gone since we last had our conversation. Why do you think he did go? What's different about the new regime?

Lippmann: I don't know. I haven't been to Russia. I don't think the cards are face up on the table. We can't read them. But if you look at the underlying forces, Kosygin has just as great an interest as Khrushchev had in avoiding nuclear war with the United States and also an interest in getting better relations with Eastern Europe and the Western world for economic reasons.

I'm told by everybody I've talked to — and I've only talked to one relative of one of the new rulers of Russia who was here on a scholarship — that they got tired of Khrushchev's inefficiency and his wildness. He promised things that he hadn't the authority to promise. That was the reason they said let's get things more organized and more orderly. The very noticeable fact is that they've divided Khrushchev's jobs into two jobs. Khrushchev was both Secretary of the Communist party, which was considered the most powerful job, and Prime Minister of the Soviet Union or Chairman or whatever they call it. Now they have two men, Kosygin and Brezhnev, and it's very interesting that they no longer travel together. They don't go to foreign countries together as in the early days before Khrushchev got both jobs. He used to travel around with Bulganin.

Sevareid: Well, I suppose one of the two present men must be the prevailing one eventually.

Lippmann: Unless there's been a change and Russia is evolving — unless the evolution is that the Communist party is no longer the militant world party that it was when Khrushchev first came into power.

Sevareid: The established church instead of church militant, in other words.

Lippmann: Yes.

Sevareid: About Great Britain, I think you were there recently. There seems to be a feeling of deep crisis about that country. Financial crisis for one thing and a government with a bare majority in Parliament. What is really happening?

Lippmann: There is a deep crisis in Britain. It may be that historians will say that it was the Labour Party's misfortune to come into power too soon. The things that prevent the Labour Party from doing what it says it wants to do and may be able to do is to revivify Great Britain from within — its industrial life, its technology, and its education. This is postponed because they're still dealing with the remnants of their empire out in Malaya, all the way from Aden to Singapore, and with the remnants of their old sterling area, remnants from the days when London was the banker of the world. Now Labour has the job of dealing with these things. It's a job that should be done by Conservatives. That's their business.

Sevareid: Did you follow the Churchill funeral ceremonies on television? What was the real significance in your mind of the enormous emotional impact of this? Was it merely due to the man as a personality or was it a turning point in British history? What was it?

Lippmann: I think the fundamental emotion here — at least the one I felt and I assume other people felt — was one of immense gratitude to this man who had saved the world from Nazism and Fascism. That's one of the great achievements of a single man in modern history. Without him there was no reason to think that Great Britain could have or would have resisted.

Sevareid: Did the funeral of this man represent in a sense the burial of the British lion that the world has known for three hundred years?

Lippmann: I've heard people say that but I don't think we're in a position to reach any such conclusion. I remember a song of Beatrice Lillie, "There's Life in the Old Girl Yet." We'll probably see that.

Sevareid: Were you particularly upset about the fact that Vice President Humphrey did not go to the funeral?

Lippman: No, I think the President made a mistake about this. He couldn't go himself; I think he was too sick. His head wasn't clear enough to have done the obvious and right thing — which was to appoint General Eisenhower as his personal representative. Eisenhower was already invited by Lady Churchill to come to the funeral; he should have been the American representative. He was the man who was Supreme Commander under Churchill, he had been President twice, he was the man. There was too much confusion in the White House to think out the right thing. I don't blame the President for not wanting the Vice President to leave when he himself was sick.

Sevareid: A moment ago you said that President Johnson, before he goes abroad, ought to get the Great Society program really working. How do you define this program, the Great Society? What's the essence of it?

Lippmann: I think the best way to answer that is to say how it differs from the New Deal, the Fair Deal or the Square Deal — those deals that preceded it. All of those older deals were based on the assumption that the amount of wealth in the country was more or less fixed and that in order to help the poor or to educate people or to do anything, you had to divide the wealth, take away from the well-to-do, and give it either to the government or to the poor or somebody. That's why it's called a New Deal. It's the same pack, but you deal it differently.

Now, the Great Society is a result of a revolution that's occurred — a silent and beneficent revolution that's occurred in our generation, under which we have learned, not perfectly because it's very difficult, it's a new art — how to control, regulate and promote the production of wealth in an advanced industrial society like our own. We are able to produce more wealth by putting on taxes, interest rates and all the budgetary arrangements that we use to make things grow. We finance the new developments, education and everything that we talk about in the Great Society, the beautifying of cities, and everything of that sort out of the taxes on the increase of wealth that we're able to produce. We increased the wealth, the product of the United States, by perhaps thirty billions last year. The taxes on that will pay for the whole of the Great Society. Nobody is any poorer, everybody's richer. That's the basis of the Great Society.

Sevareid: What's the single most important aspect of the President's program?

Lippmann: It's education because it's like a vestibule from which all the corridors lead out. Unless you have education you cannot take away from the poorest part of the population the thing which keeps them poor. They haven't learned enough and been trained enough to do a good job, to keep a good job. Education also leads to research, to production of people, to increase of scientific knowledge and technical knowledge. It's the basis of making the democracy work.

Sevareid: Do you agree with the claims of some people in the press that President Johnson, in trying to govern by consensus, so to speak, is refusing to spend any of his political capital, that he doesn't want to lose any of his mass public support, that a great President ought to be more courageous on that score? Do you feel that way?

Lippmann: On the contrary, I am in entire sympathy with him. It applies internally. Now, when you get abroad that's another question. Within the country the only real way to solve a problem like, for instance, the racial problem, is by having an overwhelming majority in favor of enforcement of civil rights. A consensus really means that between 65 and 75 per cent of the people are in favor of the policy. Not everybody's going to be in favor of it and that's what the President is trying to conserve. And he's quite right to conserve it. If anybody can solve the civil rights problem in the United States, it will be done that way, having the law, enforcing the law, by getting observance of the law by consent, voluntary consent, by a great mass of people.

The same is true of capital and labor. You can't solve their problems except by a consensus. The same is true of the whole argument we heard so much about in regard to the welfare state, what do you do for the poor, and what do you do for the rich, and all that. Consensus politics is possible only in a society which has reached the kind of revolutionary condition that we have, where we can control the output of wealth.

Sevareid: Most of us don't think of President Johnson as a philosopher in any formalized sense or an ideologist in any sense. What's the secret of his appeal to the people?

Lippmann: The root basis of it is that he is really one of them, to a degree, which very few Presidents in recent times have been. He doesn't have to be told what simple Americans, farmers, businessmen, are thinking. He already feels it himself. It's in him, and they know he feels it. That's what creates the relationship between them.

Sevareid: Does he have that quality of appreciation instinctively — more than President Kennedy or President Eisenhower?

Lippmann: He does indeed. If you think of their careers, as compared with his, you'll see that they were, as compared with Johnson, outsiders coming into the political life of this country. But he's right in the heart of it, where it grows, and the thing is in him. He doesn't have to be taught it.

Sevareid: Since our last conversation we've had quite a considerable national election. The Republican party, in terms of offices held at all levels in the country, is at its lowest point in about thirty years. Are we in danger of a one party system?

Lippmann: We're in no danger of having a one party system. We may have a condition which we've had several times before in our history when one party was predominant for a generation. But the party system always revives in a free country. We're a free country, so there's no danger. The problem is for the other party to mean something and correct its mistakes. The great mistake of the Republican party since the time of Theodore Roosevelt is that it has quarreled with the intellectual community in the United States, and alienated them and, then, under McCarthy's regime, persecuted them. They all went over to the Democrats and that gave the Democrats an intellectual capacity for dealing with issues that the Republicans simply didn't have.

Sevareid: Is that a more serious alienation than the alienation, in recent times, of Negroes or labor?

Lippmann: The alienation of the Negroes is a very serious thing. It probably cannot be corrected by this generation of Republican leaders. I mean by leaders men like Dirksen and Nixon and that level. They participated in this process, they connived at it, and they will not be able to recover. But the younger people who are not burned in that fire may be able to do it. Obvious examples are Congressman Lindsay of New York and Congressman Taft of Ohio. Taft was just beaten because of the Johnson landslide; otherwise he would have been elected. Men now around 40. Republicans will never reconstitute their party with the old war-horses who ran it into the ditch last year.

Sevareid: This happens to be the twentieth year since the birth of the United Nations. President Kennedy, I think, once called it the keystone of our foreign policy. Most people in the world seem to have great hopes for it. What do you think about its present condition and its prospects?

Lippmann: I think it's in great difficulties. It's going through a crisis. The League of Nations and the United Nations, these two versions of the same idea, required, before they could operate successfully, that peace should be made. The reason the League of Nations failed was that it couldn't make a peace; it needed to have a peace to keep. The same is happening to the United Nations. It's in grave difficulty because there's been no peace in Europe since the Second World War — Berlin, the occupation, division. There's no peace in Asia and I don't expect that the United Nations can make that peace; the great powers have got to make the peace.

After peace is made, and on the basis of its being made, the United Nations can function to keep it from tipping over, keeping order and balance. I think that the crucial question, not merely for the United Nations but for the world, is whether we can bridge the next ten or fifteen years without war. The survival of the United Nations and the peace of the world depends on that.

Sevareid: But surely there will always be in this revolutionary time outbreaks of one kind or another in many, many places.

Lippmann: There'll be outbreaks. Of course, the world is in ferment and moving very rapidly but the great power confrontations, which are a very different thing from rioting in the Congo or a place like that, in some balance that is acceptable to the great powers.

Sevareid: Would any institutional reorganization of the United Nations be of much value?

Lippmann: I think we made a great mistake about the United Nations in, I think, 1948. We had wanted to use the United Nations to prevent wars and troubles breaking out but the Soviet Union vetoed everything. We wanted to get around the veto and so we decided let's give the power to keep the peace to the General Assembly where we then had a perfectly clear and certain majority. Now that is the decision which the Soviet Union is rebelling against. That's why they won't pay their dues, that's why they won't admit that the General Assembly ever had the right to raise an army and use it for peace-keeping purposes. We admit in theory that actually we don't want to have the General Assembly commit us to go into war anywhere. Theoretically we're not really arguing with the Russians. We're just saying these were the rules. The UN is bankrupt. Congress won't appropriate money for it because Russia won't pay up. That's the situation as I understand it.

Sevareid: Would there be any great advantage in putting the decisive power back in the Security Council?

Lippmann: The only advantage of this is that that's the only place you can put decisive power. When you have decisive power you have to give a veto. The Senate of the United States would never have ratified the UN Charter if we hadn't had a veto. And if the Senate were asked today would you be willing to go to war because 75 of the 112 nations in the General Assembly voted you to go when you didn't want to go, would you go? Well, of course you wouldn't go.

Sevareid: The whole affair in the Congo since 1960, when the UN tried to intervene and stabilize things has damaged the UN in more than financial ways certainly. But what about Africa and the central part of it, the Congo? How far ought we go in trying to stabilize that place?

Lippmann: We knew back in 1960, whenever it was that the Congo was liberated or made independent, that we didn't want to get in there. We were afraid that the Russians would come in and therefore we turned to the United Nations and asked Dag Hammarskjold to take care of the Congo, keep it in order so that we wouldn't get involved and the Russians wouldn't get involved. That's how the United Nations got in there and was fairly successful for quite a long time. The original idea of leaving things to the United Nations was correct. The United States has no business becoming militarily involved in Africa. It's bad enough to be involved in Southeast Asia but to be involved in Africa too would be the height of absurdity. We couldn't do everything at once.

Sevareid: Then you're not terribly concerned about what happens in the middle of Africa?

Lippmann: I'm rather concerned but I don't take the thing ideologically as seriously as some people do. I think the war and trouble in the eastern Congo with the Chinese mixing in is tribal fighting and not really a question of communism or anti-communism. Even if it were, what difference does it make in that corner of the middle of Africa? If it does make a difference, what can we do about it and why should we have to do it?

Sevareid: There is a great argument again this year, and it gets more critical every year, about just how far we ought to go in many places of the world in terms of our involvement, even our economic involvement. Why is there disenchantment about American economic and diplomatic interventions around the world?

Lippmann: I think it has basically come about because we have involved ourselves in too many places. We couldn't fulfill the promises we made when we went in and it's reacted against us. So our involvement causes not friendliness to the United States but unfriendliness. We have to concentrate and focus our effort.

Sevareid: One manifestation of our trouble has been the great wave of riots, burnings of our information offices and libraries, attacking of our embassies. How far can a great power tolerate this? Do we continue to stand by and just ask for apologies?

Lippmann: What we ought to do, in a place like Cairo, if they burned down our library, is leave it burned down. Just leave it there. Don't rebuild it, don't even clean up the street. Let it stand as a monument to what happened. I think they'll soon want to clean it up themselves.

Sevareid: Indonesia is another problem. It would appear that foreign aid from this country is becoming a political instrument in the hands of the recipients rather than the donor.

Lippmann: I think Sukarno told us to go jump in the lake or something like the equivalent of it about our aid to Indonesia. I would just stop the aid.

Sevareid: Nasser also said we could take our aid and jump in the lake.

Lippmann: I would stop the aid. I'd send him a formal note telling him he is reported as saying he doesn't want our aid. Let him say what he wants.

Sevareid: Then why don't we stop it?

Lippmann: Don't ask me why we don't stop it. I think I would stop it if I had anything to say about it.

Sevareid: The brunt of much of what you've said in this hour is to the effect that we are overextended in the world, we are in too many places, we will have to pull in our horns to a considerable extent. Is it fair to say that Walter Lippmann has become an isolationist in 1965?

Lippmann: I don't think those words mean anything or at least I don't care whether anybody uses them. I don't care about the word isolationism and I don't care about the word appeasement. I'm interested in the rights and needs and responsibilities of the United States. We are not the policeman of mankind. We are not able to run the world and we shouldn't pretend that we can. Let us tend to our own business, which is great enough as it is. It's very great. We have neglected our own affairs. Our education is inadequate, our cities are badly built, our social arrangements are unsatisfactory. We can't wait another generation. Unless we can surmount our present crisis and get going on to the path of a settlement in Asia and a settlement in Europe, all of the plans of the Great Society here at home, all the plans for the rebuilding of backward countries in other continents, will be put on the shelf because war interrupts everything like that.

Conversation With
Justice William O. Douglas

September 6, 1972

Sevareid: We're in Goose Prairie, Washington. Elevation: 3,400 feet. Permanent population: 8 people.

This June, Supreme Court Justice William O. Douglas was counseling a reporter friend on the dry fly preferences of Bumping River trout. In this adversary proceeding the trout won. The reporter was there to talk with the 73-year-old Justice about the Supreme Court, the Constitution, the country.

Goose Prairie has no public electricity, no telephone, no television. It doesn't seem to miss them in the middle of the Cascade Mountains.

Douglas has been on the Supreme Court for 33 of his 73 years. He has been called the fastest working Justice in the twentieth century and a legal genius. He has been called many less flattering things because of his unflaggingly liberal views. He has written more books, traveled more, hiked more than any Justice ever. He has also married more.

His present wife is Cathleen Heffernan. When they married in 1966 she was 23 years old; he was 67. Cathleen has just finished law school, high in her class, with no private help from her husband. It's Douglas' fourth marriage, the last three to women much younger than he. Republican congressmen have made indignant speeches about this. Douglas replies that his private life is his own business.

If Douglas serves out two more years he will break all records for longevity as a Supreme Court Justice. He has already served with nearly a third of the one hundred Justices in the history of the court. Many of his rulings — the latest is on the Ellsberg case —

are intensely controversial. But some of his dissents are now the law of the land. We talked about them in our conversation.

Douglas: America abroad is not any one single thing. America is greatly admired for many things. I don't think we're admired so much for our B-52 bombers and for our atomic stockpile. We're really admired for the First Amendment and the freedom of people to speak and believe and the right to have a fair trial. The really great thing about our Constitution that people don't generally appreciate is that it was designed to take government off the backs of people, designed to make it difficult to do things to people.

Sevareid: A whimsical sign saying "Absolutely nothing happened on this spot, September 6, 1859" stands at the entrance to the mountain home of Justice Douglas in Goose Prairie. He used to camp on this spot as an 11-year-old hiker from Yakima, 49 miles away. He has battled all his life to save the wild places. On June 29th of this year something did happen here. The Justice spoke publicly about the court, his convictions, his long and stormy career.

I'd like to ask you, Mr. Justice, about some of the well-known people of the last generation you've known very well. After all, you've been around a long time now — 33 years on the court alone. Were you close to Franklin Roosevelt, who appointed you?

Douglas: I got to know him pretty well.

Sevareid: Why do you think he appointed you? You were just 40 years old and had some brief experience with the Securities and Exchange Commission at that time.

Douglas: I have no idea. I was not a candidate. I had no ambition to be on the court. I had no ambition for any public office. I had, as a matter of fact, been elected Dean of the Yale Law School and I was going back there in a few months. I often wonder what would have happened if I'd become Dean.

Sevareid: I suppose Roosevelt just liked your general approach to things, your general cast of mind. You made quite a record on the SEC. Joseph Kennedy brought you into it in 1934, I believe.

Douglas: I didn't know him but he had heard about me. I'd been active in the securities field. He brought me down to head up the reorganization of the SEC.

Sevareid: You were out to reorganize business. You didn't like big business. He was a business operator. He took over companies and he got out of them.

Douglas: I was talking to him one night. "You know," he said, "I must be nuts." And I said, "What is your evidence?"

He said that "the only two people in the world that I really like and enjoy being with are my son Jack and you. And you're utterly different. I disagree with everything you stand for. How do you explain it?" I said, "I guess maybe you're nuts." He was Irish and he was a great outgoing man and a great friend.

Sevareid: And why would a man like that want you in on reorganizing finance?

Douglas: Because he knew I knew something about it.

Sevareid: Let's talk about the Kennedys a minute. I remember you went off on a long trip through Russia with Bobby Kennedy, who was pretty young then. He'd been with the McCarthy Committee and all that in the Congress. Now I've heard people say that it was Bobby Kennedy's being with you all that summer that changed him from a kind of Joe McCarthyite type in his political thinking to a more liberal humanitarian type. Do you put any credence in that?

Douglas: Well, I don't know. I knew Bobby for some years prior to that. Joe called me and said, "You're going to Russia?" I said yes. "Could you take Bobby?" I said I'd be delighted. He said, "I think Bobby needs some education in the world." So Bobby came along and he learned a lot. He was rather antagonistic. He wanted to argue the merits of communism with everybody he met. He wore himself out. He carried a Bible in his left hand when he was in Russia. "Bobby," I said, "this is not the time, you can't convert anybody. This is the time to find out how people live, how much they make, about the status of women and the conditions in prisons and so on." By the end of the trip he had passed off his more-or-less aggressive, antagonistic role and was beginning to see the Slavic civilization in a different perspectve. He grew. Bobby had a great factor of growth in him. I think he was on his way to the White House when he was assassinated.

Sevareid: You're now 73. Once a horse rolled over you and crushed your chest. I well remember that. You've got a pacemaker in your heart and you're still hiking and riding. Do you get a feeling you're living on borrowed time?

Douglas: No, no, I don't. I have no worries and concerns. I early adopted the theory that the most dangerous thing a person can do at any time is to be alive.

Sevareid: So you just go through the same way of living?

Douglas: I don't do exactly the same. I used to walk, on a Saturday or Sunday in Washington, 25 miles. But I confess that I've cut it down to 15.

Sevareid: The whole Supreme Court situation now would be considerably different if Justice Abe Fortas hadn't resigned over the Wolfson business. He was an old and intimate friend of yours and a good friend of mine.

Douglas: I was sorry to see Abe resign. I spent two nights with him, practically all night talking to him, urging him not to resign, because he hadn't done anything that was unethical. He was associated with a foundation Wolfson had started. But on all the Wolfson cases before the court he always withdrew and never participated. The Justices have been very meticulous about not sitting in cases where they have any direct or indirect influence.

Sevareid: You didn't feel that what Abe Fortas did in the Wolfson thing was even an impropriety? Of course, this is an area where everybody makes his own judgement.

Douglas: Well, it depends on what you do with your spare time. I don't think it's anybody's business as long as it doesn't interfere with court work or collide with duties or create conflicts of interest.

Sevareid: Do you think Fortas could have fought that out?

Douglas: I urged him to because there was no substance at all to the claims that were made. I think the sad part of it was that Abe — who I think would have been one of our great judges of all time — didn't want to be on the court.

Sevareid: At the beginning he didn't.

Douglas: Lyndon B. Johnson twisted his arm and put him on. There was political pressure to get him off.

Sevareid: You've been around the fringes of party politics a lot. Some people who know you have felt that you really, at one time, did want to be President, that you did want the nomination. Were you serious about it at any time?

Douglas: No, I had never wanted to run for anything — in Yakima, in the State of Washington, or in the country.

Sevareid: Back in 1944, when the question of the Vice Presidency was coming up at the Democratic convention, Roosevelt wrote a letter to Bob Hannegan, the party chairman, listing two men as acceptable to him for the second spot: Douglas and Harry Truman.

Douglas: It was in that order, yes.

Sevareid: I understand there's a letter in existence, the original Roosevelt letter, that listed your name above Truman's name but that Hannegan, when he sent copies to party leaders, turned the names around because he wanted his fellow Missourian, Truman.

Douglas: Right!

Sevareid: Was that actually the case, then?

Douglas: That's the whole story, I think. It was unknown to me at the time. I'm happy that it happened that way. I didn't have any desire for the office. I would have taken it, I suppose, if I had been drafted.

Sevareid: You'd have been President instead of Harry Truman.

Douglas: Well, a lot of different things would have happened. There would have been no bomb dropped on Hiroshima.

Sevareid: What else do you think you'd have done?

Douglas: I have no idea.

Sevareid: I guess there's never been any Supreme Court Justice as outspoken about a lot of things off the court as you've been. You criticize American foreign policy quite often publicly. The objection to this by a lot of people, as you well know, is that a Justice shouldn't do that. This somehow affects the separation-of-powers principle and you really musn't cross that line.

Douglas: Well, I grew up in that tradition, getting it from college and law schools and getting to know some of the Justices like Brandeis. But something happened that changed my view. This happened in my first week or two on the court. One of the first cases argued was whether or not our salaries as Justices were tax-able. The old court held that they were not because there's a pro-vision in the Constitution that says Congress shall not reduce the salary of a federal judge during his term of office. The old court held that when Uncle Sam pays you $10,000 and then takes $5,000 back in a tax that's a reduction. There was, I think, a 6 to 3 de-cision. Holmes dissented and Brandeis dissented. I thought that they were right so I voted to tax myself in 1939.

In conference each of us has a sheet, a docket sheet, for every case. After discussion the youngest Justice in service votes first. Chief Justice Hughes turned to me and said, "Douglas, how do you vote?" I said, "I vote to reverse." And that's the way the court went. As I made the little entry in the docket sheet I said to myself, "Young man, you've just voted yourself first class citizenship." I decided that if you're going to pay taxes like everybody else that you should be a citizen like everybody else, except and unless the thing you're doing interferes with the work of the court.

Sevareid: You've traveled an awful lot—more, I think, than any other Justice ever, much of it in the so-called Third World. What do you find in terms of the reputation of this country because of the Vietnam war?

Douglas: I'm afraid that, as a result of the Vietnam war, in the eyes of many people in the underdeveloped nations we're the new Genghis Khan, the great destroyer, which is very, very unfortunate.

Sevareid: There was an effort to have the court decide the constitutionality of the Vietnam war. I think you and Potter Stewart wanted to hear the case.

Douglas: We've had three votes at various times—Potter Stewart, Bill Brennan and myself. I wrote some opinions on this.

Sevareid: I believe you said, when the court refused a writ, that Vietnam was a Presidential war. That sounds as though you really made your mind up that it's unconstitutional.

Douglas: The Constitution says that Congress has the power to declare war. It doesn't say Congress and/or the President or the Congress and/or the Supreme Court. It just says Congress shall have power to declare war. And historically that has been the case. This is not just a little episode like Jefferson sending a fleet off to the Barbary Coast after some pirates. Vietnam is an all-out effort.

Sevareid: Obviously we're not going to get a judicial ruling on the war. But you, Justice Douglas, a private person sitting here, believe it is unconstitutional. What has happened?

Douglas: Well, I'm inclined to think it is. I haven't heard arguments. I might change my mind.

Sevareid: If the Supreme Court said the Vietnam war, while it's going on, is unconstitutional, what would happen?

Douglas: It would mean, practically, that the boy who didn't want to go wouldn't have to go. The war would probably go on with volunteers. Drafting boys would be out.

Sevareid: You wrote once that we're losing so much privacy to government intrusion that unless there's some kind of rebellion against this we're going to be suffocated. What kind of rebellion? What did you really mean?

Douglas: I think people, instead of succumbing and assuming everything the government does is right, should object, protest, write letters to the editor or make a speech or form a committee. The greatness of this country is reflected in the Constitution that was designed to take government off the backs of people and make it difficult for government to do anything to the individual. The electronic age makes it easy.

Sevareid: You must feel good about the recent decision against wiretapping and bugging domestic dissidents without a court order.

Douglas: I voted with Justice Powell—as might be expected.

Sevareid: The Army surveillance of domestic dissidents has been thrown back to the Congress. Didn't you want that decided by the court?

Douglas: Right. The Army has no business, in our system, fooling around with political ideas. The Army should be on its bases, marching men up and down, on the firing range, and so on.

Sevareid: I'd like to wheel back to ask you something I should have asked before. I was personally concerned about the impeachment effort two years ago and the Parvin Foundation of which you were, I think, an officer. You were cleared by the House Judiciary Committee of anything illegal or wrong, but why did you resign from the Parvin Foundation if you had won the argument that you hadn't done anything wrong?

Douglas: Well, you see the idea of the foundation came out of a book I wrote called "America Challenged." I was proposing in that book not that we send jet planes to Ethiopia—the only thing they could be used for would be to put down the peasants—but to spend the money bringing people here and giving them courses about government, the First Amendment, fair trials and so on and then sending them back to their country as new leaders. Our effort should be educational. The foundation was formed to effectuate that. We established at Princeton ten fellowships that brought men from Africa, mostly from the Middle East. It was a great success, I thought, because many of the men on their return ended up in jail, which meant that they were doing a good job.

Sevareid: But you resigned from the foundation. Why?

Douglas: Because we were expanding to South America and it was going to take a lot of time. I realized that somebody would have to take over who could travel a lot and spend a lot of time searching out people. I decided, long before, that in about another year I'd have to get out. So I just did.

Sevareid: A lot of the criticism of your behavior, speeches, and activities has been that you really have not been sensitive to the public sense of reverence about the court. There was a story somebody told me of some man saying at a cocktail party that at least Douglas has proved that Supreme Court Justices are human beings. Somebody else said, "Yes, isn't it a pity?" Isn't there something in this—that people want to think of the court as a temple with rather disembodied great wisdom residing there?

Douglas: It may be that there are some people who think that is the best way, that the court is a symbol of authority. We're all human. The decisions we make and the reasons we give are profoundly important to the people. I think that the person who stays in the court 10, 20, 30 years should be very active in life. Otherwise he'll end up a dried husk, unrelated to anything that's going on in the world except his own personal experience that may be wholly irrelevant.

Sevareid: You don't feel you're echoing Commodore Vanderbilt who for different reasons said "The public be damned?"

Douglas: No. I'm very respectful of the public. I'd like to educate them on what judges are, what judges should be, what civic affairs should be. I'd like to see our people very stoutly independent of judges, of bureaucrats, of presidents, of congressmen and governors. I'd like to see our people very assertive and not submissive. The great danger is the surveillance and other pressures for conformity. The data banks run through: How many times was Eric Sevareid arrested? Out it comes and he's denied a job.

Sevareid: But on the other hand, it seems to me that I've never seen such freedom of speech, of theater, of books, of demonstrations as we've seen in recent years. That's resulted in a kind of backlash, a fear of fragmentation and anarchy in the country.

Douglas: I think that's good—not the reaction to it but the fact that it's going on. I have great hope in the young people. I've been criticized. I wrote a couple of articles for Playboy. The reason I wrote for Playboy was that it reaches 18 million youngsters. They're the minds I'd like to reach. People of my generation are bankrupt, politically bankrupt. They're philosophically bankrupt. Look at what they've produced—a system that makes war the alternative, a system that's highly stratified, that pays off great sums of money. This is socialism for the rich. I'd like to reach the minds of the youngsters because it need not be that way.

Sevareid: I'd like to talk to you a bit about the court system as a whole, not just the Supreme Court. To a great extent it's bogged down, almost broken down, in one area after another—fantastic delays, congestion, backlogs. It seems to a lot of us who've gone into this, that it has quite a bit to do with the crime problem. How do you resolve this problem?

Douglas: One of the reasons is that we, as a people, have had a great propensity to make everything somebody objects to on some moral grounds a crime. A lot of the stuff that's going on in our courts involves only people but no victims.

Sevareid: Crime without victims—like vagrancy, drunkenness. Do you think too much has been loaded on the courts?

Douglas: Yes, too much minutia of the lower things. The courts should save their energies for the big things. Now, on the big things, the problem has been greatly exaggerated. Roughly 90% of all criminal cases in federal courts are disposed of on pleas of guilty.

Sevareid: Is that your answer to the complaint that various Supreme Court decisions protecting defendants have contributed to court congestion and difficulty for prosecutors?

Douglas: They haven't contributed. The FBI works under the Constitution. It's the best police force in the world. Miranda is cursed and denounced by local police. The FBI lives under Miranda: It's highly trained and efficient.

Once they decide to hold a man, that's the start of criminal prosecution. Our Constitution says a man has a right to a lawyer, he is presumed to be innocent, the government must prove beyond a reasonable doubt, there must be an indictment, a right to jury trial. Those are all very important safeguards because once a powerful government—I don't mean this administration but a government that is as powerful as ours is at the present time—gets after the individual, he's cooked unless he has an Edward Bennett Williams or Clarence Darrow to defend him.

Sevareid: Chief Justice Burger said that criminal trials take twice as long, on an average, now as they did ten years ago. Is this a good thing?

Douglas: I don't know if that's true, generally, or not. In New York State about 95% of all criminal cases are disposed of on pleas of guilty. In California, last year 74.4% were disposed of on pleas of guilty. We're talking about a relatively small number of cases, although they are important cases. There's a great rush on in some areas to get rid of the jury to speed things up. But to send poor devils down to trial by a judge against their will is a horrible thing. I think judges get to be calloused. They've become sort of law-and-order automatons.

Sevareid: You've been worried about the rights of minorities and what courts can do under the rules. But look at all the cases involving Angela Davis, the Berrigan brothers, and others. They've been getting a pretty fair deal from juries in this country.

Douglas: That's right. The jury reflects the conscience of America, not every jury. By and large, that's a much better testing ground, I think, than the testing ground of a judge.

Sevareid: Well, the Supreme Court decided recently that state courts don't have to have unanimity on a jury to find guilty.

Douglas: That was a very tragic decision.

Sevareid: I don't know what exempted the federal courts.

Douglas: That's a mystery because of the Sixth Amendment.

Sevareid: Well, if a jury splits and a minority of, say, two, three, or four members say they don't think a man is guilty then you'd assume there's reasonable doubt. What happens to the principle of beyond reasonable doubt?

Douglas: You've been reading my dissenting opinion.

Sevareid: As a matter of fact, I really didn't. It just occurred in my own stupid head.

Douglas: You're interviewing the wrong judge. I don't know the answer.

Sevareid: The principle is abrogated in a way.

Douglas: The principle is, well, not perhaps abrogated—it's eroded.

Sevareid: I think Chief Justice Burger said that a lot of things like environmental cases, consumer class actions, ought not to come to the courts. You'd take more of these things, as I understand it.

Douglas: If Congress should redesign the jurisdiction of federal courts so as to leave out of them the environmental questions we'd go down the drain really very fast. We'd then be victims of the administrative agencies. These agencies, though they're high-minded and not venal, are very oppressive. There must be some check on them. There must be unless they're going to be abolished. I always thought that they should be abolished. I told FDR he should never create an agency unless he abolished it in ten years. At the end of ten years it becomes a monster.

Sevareid: A lot of people around the court talk very differently on this subject. The court has more money this year; you have more clerks per Justice and so on. You've got a great big backlog. There's this talk of too big a load of overwork.

Douglas: We have a bigger backlog in the sense of more case filings. When I went on the court we had 1800 cases a term. Now we have about 4200 that we have to screen. Of those 4200, most come from prisons; 98 or 99% of them are frivolous. We read them all because they produce classic situations like Gideon and Miranda. We're actually hearing and deciding fewer cases now than we were when I went on the court.

Sevareid: Why is that?

Douglas: The selective process has changed. The judges have changed and the idea of what is important has changed in the minds of the judges. There are highly subjective considerations: Is this case fit to take? Should we take it? And so on. We take fewer and fewer cases. When I went on the court we sat six days a week. Under Warren we sat five days a week with a conference on Friday. Now it looks as if our trend will be to sit three days a week with a conference on Saturday. The job takes about four days a week.

Sevareid: It does for you, but some of the other Justices complain they're working 18 hours a day every day to keep up.

Douglas: You need the week to think about these problems, but you can be hiking too. You don't need to stop thinking.

Sevareid: Can you keep the facts of a specific complicated case in your head as you're walking through the woods?

Douglas: Oh sure. It's the best way to solve a problem if you're confused. When I talk to lawyers, I tell them that you're never confused if you read the Constitution the right way.

Sevareid: You said a moment ago that you don't need clerks. Now you have more clerks than ever. Why don't you need clerks?

Douglas: Because we make highly individual decisions. Nobody in my office can tell me or should tell me how I should vote.

Sevareid: Don't you have somebody look up precedents?

Douglas: Oh, I assign them to do research and they submit research to me in addition to the briefs. They're helpful in that way. But we're surfeited with law clerks. We don't need them.

Sevareid: You mean you're prepared to do the looking up of all the precedents yourself?

Douglas: Oh, sure.

Sevareid: You're not going to sell that to many judges.

Douglas: No. But I'm entitled to my First Amendment rights.

Sevareid: Well, you've turned out, I guess, just about more formal written opinions than anybody in the court or you must be close to that record. But there has been criticism by legal scholars that you're too hasty, that you don't pay enough attention to precedents.

Douglas: That means they don't like my decisions.

Sevareid: They're saying that you think sociologically, politically, that you decide what's fair in those terms in your mind and then you find precedents to suit them. That's been a running criticism.

Douglas: I've always thought, on Constitutional decisions, that *stare decisies*—that is, established law—is really no sure guideline because what did the judges who sat in 1875 know about, say, electronic surveillance? They didn't know anything about it. Why take their wisdom? That's why I once said, to the consternation of a group of lawyers, that I'd rather create a precedent than find one. The creation of a precedent in terms of the modern setting means adjustment of the Constitution to needs of the time.

Sevareid: You know, there's been a lot of talk, scuttlebutt around Washington for months, and articles in papers, about a lot of abrasiveness inside the court — unhappiness, conflicts, and whatnot. I don't expect you to talk about personalities but there is a different atmosphere now, isn't there?

Douglas: There's no abrasiveness. There's no discord or ill will. It's just a different group of men with different habits.

Sevareid: There's always a cycle of philosophical differences. The majority goes this way and that.

Douglas: The distinctive thing about the court and its history is that it's a circle of men with fierce ideological differences—with every man willing to die for his point of view. But as a group, they're harmonious, which is unusual to find.

Sevareid: President Nixon said he wants strict constructionists on the court. Justice Black regarded himself as the strictest of constructionists, but he was not Nixon's kind of judge.

Douglas: I told Hugo, when we read that in the papers, "He's talking about us—about you and me." Hugo laughed and said, "I don't think so." "Well," I said, "Congress shall pass no law abridging freedom of speech or press. You and I take it to mean what it says. That's strict, strict construction. "Other members of the court over the years have said that when the Constitution says Congress shall make no law abridging freedom of speech or press, it really means Congress may make *some* laws abridging freedom of speech and press. Now, if you go off on that tangent it takes a long time to make your decision. You have to do an awful lot of research. You work 18 hours a day, and write 58-page opinions.

Sevareid: Would you say that's an absolute, as Black said?

Douglas: Yes, in terms of whether it's good or bad.

Sevareid: Is that phrase "strict constructionist" confused with judicial restraint—meaning that the courts ought to leave more things to Congress and the administration? What's the difference in the two phrases?

Douglas: I think it means that the gut reaction of the speaker indicates that he disagrees with the court. The Constitution is not designed to leave things to Congress. In certain areas, yes. Should the President send a man to the Vatican as Ambassador? That's none of the court's business. But as I said before, if the President or a Governor or a General or anybody takes somebody by the neck and says, "Go to jail!" or "Go to Vietnam!," that's the business of the courts. That's not for the President or the Governor or the General alone to decide. You have a justiciable controversy. And if you intrude as a judiciary, as we did in the steel seizure case involving Harry Truman, you upset a President. Harry Truman was very upset. He was so upset that Hugo Black gave him a party. We all went and poured a lot of bourbon down Truman.

Sevareid: Did he change his mind at all?

Douglas: He didn't change his mind but he felt a little better, at least for a few hours.

Sevareid: You said once that the court must not be bound by the fears and illusions of the past. What about the fears and illusions of the present? You can go too far with that, can't you?

Douglas: Sure.

Sevareid: Wasn't there some truth in the past?

Douglas: Sure. These are values that the oncoming justices have to weigh. It's very difficult to know what a new member will be like until he's there for five or ten years, because very few new members have been free and independent before. All the layers of prejudice in clients and whatnot have been peeled off and there the man is.

What does he basically think in terms of constitutional values? It takes time. Once he finds out what it is he either embraces the old precedent or he overrules it.

Sevareid: But Black said the law changed because the justices changed.

Douglas: That's right.

Sevareid: There is now a pretty sizeable general mood not only against impersonality of government, big institutions, but a move towards decentralization. Let people in the local communities take more into their hands and so on. Communities feel differently about school prayers or obscenity. Haven't you been against diversity on the local level?

Douglas: Obscenity is a separate and distinct problem in my point of view. I don't think that the First Amendment gives the states or the Congress any power to legislate as to what is poor literature.

Sevareid: Not even by communities that may be Puritanical in outlook? Shouldn't they have power to decide this for themselves?

Douglas: Maybe so but then we need a Constitutional amendment because the First Amendment applies to the states as well as the federal government. At the time the First Amendment was adopted obscenity was practically unknown in this country. It all came later on. In 1859, as the 19th century developed, we had federal legislation on obscenity. So you can't say, historically, that speech and press excluded obscenity. The human race has been obscene from the beginning. This is a matter of taste and culture. What would pain you and me might be a lyric to somebody else. To get in this field, I think, is a great mistake unless we have a Constitutional amendment. If the people want to suppress obscenity then you can have your big Constitutional argument and vote it up or vote it down. But I don't think judges should fool around with obscenity. I think, with Hugo Black, that it's barred by the Constitution. Is the "Song of Solomon" obscene? Some people think it's very, very suggestive.

Sevareid: Well, what about the big 1954-55 school desegregation decisions? Do you have any cause to regret the way the court went on this? I think Mr. Justice Black said that "all deliberate speed" probably could have been left out. What have been your thoughts since then? It's an awful mess now.

Douglas: The "all deliberate speed" phrase is an old, conventional equity term. If I should tear down your fence, the judge would direct me to restore the fence "with all deliberate speed," which meant I could wait until the ground thawed out. We didn't give much thought to it. As things worked out, it wasn't a very happy choice because the resistance was great. Furthermore, the President in the White House at the time, Dwight Eisenhower, didn't think very much of the decision. It took him some time to move into action. If he had sold off some of his great prestige by going to the people, by saying this is the law whether you agree with it or not and we're going to have one nation out of many diverse people and we're going to start with the schools, we would be much further along. But no President did that.

Sevareid: Now the Nixon Administration is moving against the decision in many ways with new messages to Congress which attempt to have prohibitions against court moratoriums, court actions, and whatnot. Is this a serious threat to the independence of the judiciary?

Douglas: The court has a great tradition for independence, what-ever the background of a Justice may happen to be. I think the court will remain independent. In my years there's been no President who has ever talked to any member of the court about any case or any problems. It's just not done.

Sevareid: Do you feel at all, in the dark of the night, that the desegregation decision you approved, like the other Justices, got us in a mess no one can find a way out of?

Douglas: Well, there is nothing that works perfectly. It's working pretty well in most places; it's sticky in other places. We hear mostly about the trouble spots. Busing is an old problem here at Goose Prairie, Washington. A bus comes down the road here and picks up children and drives them about 42 miles to a consolidated school where they get a better education.

Sevareid: That's how busing started—in consolidated schools.

Douglas: The children are bused back at night. These kids of Goose Prairie ride 80-some miles a day in a bus. Now the black schools have notoriously been inferior. The school boards in this country have never had blacks on them to any great extent.

Sevareid: A lot do now.

Douglas: Well, you'd be surprised if you looked at the national statistics. Things are moving in the right direction but what I'm trying to say is that the financing of black schools has been inferior. The result is inferior staffs, inferior library facilities, and so on. I think probably the most important thing is association of children with a competitive group where there are some children of their own age setting a pace. That's probably the most important factor. That's why I think — from an educational point of view, not a Constitutional viewpoint — the mixture of the races is very good.

Sevareid: Let's get back to the Bill of Rights. Do you have any ominous feelings about what's going on? You've just had a decision on the rights of reporters. They can be compelled to testify about their sources in certain cases. People in my business are getting their backs up very high on that.

Douglas: I was opposed to this decision. I think it was wrong. As poor as our press is, I think it should be independent of government, completely independent, for all the reasons stated by Jefferson. When government can say what you can publish or what you can't publish, then the press is no longer free and independent. Then the people don't know. Then the press depends upon the handout of some information that the administration in power thinks is suitable for the people to know. That's not healthy.

Sevareid: Is broadcasting part of the free press?

Douglas: I think so.

Sevareid: But the court has now put us in practically a second-class citizenship category. The Red Lion decision has done this. Why should the most pervasive medium of information and ideas not have full protecton of the Bill of Rights?

Douglas: I think they should.

Sevareid: On the strength of what you've said, maybe we'll go back and try this one again?

Douglas: Well, I have only one vote.

Sevareid: Your feeling is that the Bill of Rights has a real priority in the Constitution?

Douglas: A priority in the sense that it's filled with "thou shalt nots" that are absolutes. No person shall be compelled to testify against himself. That's in the self-incrimination clause. Everybody in every criminal prosecution shall be entitled to a lawyer.

Sevareid: What's the basic picture in your mind of what society ought to be like? Or are you just instinctively on the side of the poor and those who haven't had the good chance in life?

Douglas: I think of this country ideally as a nation of very independent, vigorous, non-submissive people sticking to their own ideals, their own religion, their own political beliefs and so on. I look upon this nation as a place for free enterprise to flourish. That means the absence of monopoly, the non-growth of conglomerates that are bigger than European nations.

Sevareid: The sort of thing you tried to stop in your early career?

Douglas: Right. What's been going on can't go on without the people eventually rising up and taking things over and becoming a socialist state. Maybe we're doomed for that. I think there's something better if we stick to small private enterprise and break up the conglomerates.

Sevareid: You think bigness is really a curse, don't you?

Douglas: Yes, because there's nobody smart enough to be able to run twenty, thirty, forty different industries that are pulled together. Separately these industries have great values. Brandeis used to lecture me on this and I believed him. He said that if we continue in the way in which we're going this nation will become a nation of clerks, submissive clerks, rather than independent, free men. He was right.

Sevareid: You want responsive government. You believe in the one-man-one-vote principle, the majority rule principle. Yet the court is the great exception to this. Nobody elects people like yourself. Justices can hardly be removed. Should there be a different way of choosing the Supreme Court?

Douglas: I've thought about that a lot. I don't know how members of our court would run for office and campaign. I shudder to think of it. I don't know what kind of a court you'd get. I'm sure you wouldn't get a Hugo Black or an Oliver Wendell Holmes. I don't know what you'd get. The court is really the keeper of the conscience. The conscience is the Constitution. It's very important to have a keeper of the conscience, an independent group, above the storm, free from political influence. I think that might be lost if everybody was running for office.

Sevareid: You have now been in the court 33 years and in another couple of years you will have been there, I think, longer than any man since the founding of this Republic. Is that your ambition?

Douglas: No, I have no such idea. Longevity has never been part of my plans. Good health has been. My doctor says I'm in better shape than he is.

Sevareid: I haven't seen him but you look pretty good. So we shouldn't expect your retirement any time soon?

Douglas: Right.

Conversation With
Justice Hugo Black

December 3, 1968

Sevareid: In the old city of Alexandria, Virginia, George Washington's town, stands the lovely old house of Hugo L. Black, senior Justice of the Supreme Court of the United States. If you come by on a fair day you're likely to see the 82-year-old judge at his chief avocation—tennis with Mrs. Black. He uses a new steel racket, he still shows traces of his old form, but he doesn't chase the shots much any more.

Associate Justice Black has served on the court 31 years—as senior Justice for 23 of those years. When President Roosevelt appointed Senator Black to the court there was a national uproar and not for the first time, nor for the last in the court's history. Roosevelt and the country learned, though it was common knowledge in Alabama, that Black, as a young politician, had for a short time been a member of the Ku Klux Klan.

In the midst of the uproar in 1937 Black made a radio address to the nation explaining the Klan business and said he would never again publicly discuss the matter.

Only Justice Black's closer friends prophesied correctly that he would stand against racism and in the front ranks of those who believed that the constitutional requirement of equal protection of the laws for all citizens means just what it says.

The Supreme Court has been a powerful force in drastically changing human relations in this country over the last generation. The present court is called "the Warren Court," after its Chief Justice. Some think it ought to be called "the Black Court," after

51

its chief philosopher. So far as we know there is no precedent for a television interview with a sitting Justice about the law, the Constitution, and the Supreme Court.

It was late in September when my CBS colleague, Martin Agronsky, and I talked with Justice Black in his Alexandria house.

Agronsky: Mr. Justice, you have dedicated your life in many ways on the court toward the application of the Bill of Rights to all of the states. You said once: "It's my belief that there are absolutes in our Bill of Rights, and that they were put there on purpose by men who knew what words meant — and meant their prohibitions to be absolutes." What are your reasons for saying that?

Black: I'll read you the part of the First Amendment that caused me to say there are absolutes in our Bill of Rights. I did not say that our entire Bill of Rights is an absolute. I said there are absolutes in our Bill of Rights. Now, if a man were to say to me out on the street, "Congress shall make no law respecting an establishment of religion" (that's the First Amendment) I would think: Amen, Congress should pass no law. Unless they just didn't know the meaning of words. That's what they mean to me. Certainly they mean that literally. I see no reason to attribute any less meaning than they would have had then or would have now. They might not have that meaning now because of the general idea that there can be no absolute anywhere. I don't agree to that.

They (the authors of the First Amendment) wanted to mark boundaries, because there were some things they did not want government ever to have the power to do. With some things they didn't feel that way. They felt that they should have power to do something within what they called "reasonable limits." The Fourth Amendment says, "The right of the people to be secure in their persons, houses, papers and effects against unreasonable searches and seizures." Now, I assume if they had wanted to make all searches and seizures illegal, so that no government at all could ever have searches and seizures, they would have said so. But they said "unreasonable." Turn on down to Amendment Eight. It says, "Excessive bail shall not be required." It says "excessive." The people who wrote it knew that it did not set specific boundaries.

I subscribe to the doctrine that the Fifth Amendment, which says that no person shall be compelled to be a witness against himself, means no person shall be compelled to be a witness against himself.

Now I don't, of course claim any right to keep the Constitution up-to-date. I've sustained laws as constitutional that I was bitterly against, didn't agree with. I think that's my obligation. I don't care what anybody has decided—that's immaterial. Our system of government puts different people on the Supreme Court, people with different views.

Some people have said that I'm either a knave or a fool because if I was not dishonest I couldn't say that there are absolutes. Well, I just don't agree. I think I can—and I do.

Agronsky: I would think you'd know the Constitution by heart by now. Why do you always carry around that little book containing the Constitution?

Black: Because I don't know the Constitution by heart. My memory is not that good. When I say something about it, I want to quote it precisely.

Agronsky: Do you think people understand the Constitution?

Black: I think most of them do not although I'm sure they feel they do. Some seem to feel they know it better than the court. That's evident in letters I get from people who don't have a good idea of grammar and certainly aren't good writers. Some tell me "you ought to get off the court and—" Some tell me to go back to Russia. Well, that's too far for me to go back. I've never been there.

But they think they know the Constitution. And their idea is all the same. You can trace it to the same thing. It doesn't make any difference what it is, what their experience is, or why they're mad with the court. It's all because each of them believes that the Constitution prohibits that which they think should be prohibited and permits that which they think should be permitted.

Sevareid: I don't think the Constitution says a member of the Supreme Court has to be a lawyer but they all are. Could a non-lawyer possibly be a judge of the Supreme Court?

Black: I don't see why he shouldn't. Not at all. I'm not sure that they should all be non-lawyers. If you're going to have a government of law, you've got to have somebody that knows something about the basic fabric of it. I don't see, for instance, why in their day Socrates and Plato wouldn't have been great judges.

Sevareid: There are not many of those around.

Black: We don't know how many good minds are in the world.

Sevareid: What kind of man, in the American scene today, who is not a lawyer, could be a good Justice?

Black: Walter Lippmann. He studied law, knows a great deal about it. He's very familiar with the law and there are many others of the same type.

Agronsky: You indicated that sometimes a judge could be too legalistic, too concerned with the legal approach. Suppose that you were to find in some case which you were considering that there was a difference between what you thought was fair, what the heart says, and what the law provides. How would you decide?

Black: I would follow what I thought the law provided. Undoubtedly. You see, you have laws written out. That's the object in law, to have it written out. I would follow exactly what I thought the Constitution said. And I wouldn't try to amend it. I thoroughly believe in the division of the three branches of government.

Agronsky: Do judges ever reach beyond the law?

Black: Undoubtedly they do. There was one basic thing about the desire for the Bill of Rights. One great urge was that a good many people believed in the natural law concept. Some put it on a religious basis, some put it on a philosophical basis. Some people prefer the natural law concept — what's fair, what's best, what, in some people's language today, is the most decent way to follow a custom in government. And so someone conceived the idea that due process of law meant "according to fairness." It's been my idea that that's not what due process means. That would do something I'm not for and I do not believe the Constitution provides. It would permit the judicial branch of government, which is supposed only to interpret the Constitution and the law, to write it from day to day and month to month and year to year. What best fits the times is a very prevalent philosophy. I'm not sure but what it's the controlling philosophy in this government, so far as lawyers or government are concerned.

Agronsky: You don't feel that judges should judge according to what fits the times?

Black: No. How would they know? Jefferson asked if we want to trust just one man. One man certainly cannot sense what's right and just any better than the whole public.

Agronsky: There was one historic shift by the court that seems to relate to this point. In 1898, in Plessy v. Ferguson, the court held that separate could be equal in interstate transportation. Yet in 1954,

in Brown v. the School Board, it held that separate could not be
equal in the nation's schools. The law hadn't changed. What appears
to have changed is the judges' opinion of how the law should be
interpreted. Did they not relate to the temper of the times?

Black: The judges had changed. That's right. As far as my opinion
is concerned, I would have agreed to Plessy v. Ferguson. My view
is that we had a simple question in Brown v. the School Board. Does
separate but equal give the colored people of the nation equal protection of the law? Were they being treated any better because
they had different, separated schools? Well, I've lived in the South
all my life, practically until I came to Washington. I didn't need any
philosophy, any changing times to convince me that separate but
equal was a denial of equal protection of the law. I never, for one
moment, based my decision on anything except the thought that
it was a denial of equal protection of the law, had been in the past
and will be in the future.

Agronsky: When the 1954 segregation decision was handed down
there was a clause in Chief Justice Warren's opinion that referred
to the implementation of the decision "with all deliberate speed."
What effect do you think that particular reservation has had?

Black: Looking back at it now, it seems to me that it has delayed
the process of outlawing segregation. It seems to me, probably, with
all due deference to the opinion and all my brethren, that it would
have been better — maybe, I don't say positively — not to have
that sentence, to treat the case as an ordinary lawsuit and force
judgment only on the counties affected. Each case would have been
only one case. That fitted into my ideas of the court, not making
policies for the nation.

Sevareid: Let's turn to the workings of the Supreme Court. The
court gets, I think, about 2,500 cases every year and you can take
under consideration only about ten per cent of them. Ought there
be fewer cases sent up or ought there be more Justices? Is this a case
of justice denied because it's delayed?

Black: I don't think it can fairly be said that we give no consideration to all who apply. I think we do. You can't decide each
case, you can't write long opinions on each, but when we meet we
take up the cases on our docket that have been brought up since
we adjourned. Frequently I'll mark up at the top "Denied — not
of sufficient importance," "No dispute among the circuits," or
something else. I'll go in and vote to deny it. I've considered it to

that extent. Every judge does the same thing in conference. So when you take all the cases that are denied this year, or any year, the court did, to some extent, consider them.

Agronsky: What happens in a judicial conference? I know it's so secret that not even the clerks are permitted to come into the room. Could you tell us anything about this?

Black: We just discuss the cases. There's a fiction that everybody always waits for the youngest man to express himself or vote. They may wait for him to vote but they do not always wait for him to express his views.

There's nothing secret about part of the conference. The Chief Justice, if he is with the majority, states the case to the majority and gives his view of what the law should be. He speaks first and then the next man in rank speaks. That would mean, in the present court, Chief Justice Warren would speak first. I'd speak second and then Justice Douglas and so on down to the bottom. Now, when we cast a formal vote, after all the discussion, then is when we let the youngest member of the court express his views.

Sevareid: Does the Chief Justice have any extra power that other Justices don't have in the court?

Black: No power, except the power to run the court. There are certain cases that, so far as the Chief Justice is concerned, he would not argue at all. He thinks they're too simple. The other Justices — through one word, one line, one telephone call, one anything — can put cases back on the list for argument.

Sevareid: The power of the Chief Justice among his colleagues is simply limited by his persuasive powers?

Black: His persuasiveness, as everywhere else practically, is limited only by his integrity, his strength of character, his wisdom, his knowledge. Now some think — it's hard for me to think it because I would never be influenced by it — the Chief Justice assigns an opinion to the Justice on his side. And some think that Justices sort of kowtow to the Chief Justice in order to see that they got good assignments. I don't know. That might be an urge.

Agronsky: Well, when the Chief Justice can pick out somebody on the court and say "You're assigned to write the majority opinion," and "You're assigned to write the minority opinion," wouldn't that have a significant effect?

Black: It certainly would not have with my vote. My vote's mine.

I'm going to vote according to my conscience, not according to what somebody could or had done for me before.

Sevareid: Justice Black, on free speech and assembly and the rights of people to have order, I think you wrote a dissent a couple of years ago. It involved a small public library in Louisiana. You said that no group, however just their cause, has a constitutional right to use other people's property, even the property of government, as a stage to express their dissent. If protestors or demonstrators don't have any inherent right to use streets or any public places then aren't you really infringing the right of protest itself?

Black: Well, that assumes that the only way to protest anything is to go out and demonstrate in the streets.

That is not true. It never has been true. We've had a government where people have been protesting against one another, having elections, having different religions, meeting at different places, having different parties meeting at different places, all through history. But we haven't had to say that freedom of speech gives people the right to tramp up and down the streets by the thousands, saying things that threaten others, with literal language, or that threatened them because of the circumstances under which they do it.

Bill Douglas and I both expressed our view on that about 25 years ago. We said that the First Amendment protects speech, protects writing, protects assembly. But it doesn't say anything that protects a man's right to walk around and around my house if he wants to, fasten my family into the house, make them afraid to go out of doors because something will happen. That's conduct. Now if the First Amendment said that Congress should pass no law regulating conduct then I would have said that it can't regulate any conduct. The amendment doesn't say this. It says you shall not pass a law involving freedom of speech or the press. That's talk.

Sevareid: Is there a way to define the difference or the line between action and speech as protest?

Black: The only way the court has ever been able to define it, as to the First Amendment, is in the decision where they said that the Mormons had a perfectly logical argument if conduct is the same as speech. The Mormons said: This expresses our religious views. We're protesting because the federal government is passing a law suppressing our right to have a dozen wives. Well, the court said: That won't do, that's conduct, that's not speech. Of course it involves speech, partially. Before you get a dozen wives, you've got to do some talking. But that doesn't mean the Constitution protects your right to have a dozen wives. The two are separate. Of course there are places where you cannot sharply draw a boundary.

Agronsky: Let's take a contemporary example — the demonstrators who gathered before the hotels in Chicago and Grant Park this year. Do you think that the demonstrators in this instance were right to assemble the way they did or that the police were right in not permitting them to assemble, in charging them and breaking up the demonstration?

Black: Well, that gets right to cases that we have. We're liable to have that very case. I don't want to say what my view would be because I don't know what the evidence would show. I don't know what they were doing. I don't know how far they went. Mayor Daley says they did so-and-so and the other side says they're just a group of nice young idealists singing sweet songs of mercy and love. That's what the press and the television seemed to think — they were just young, budding idealists who should not be noticed. Now, the Constitution doesn't say that any man shall have a right to say anything he wishes anywhere he wants to go. That's agreed, isn't it? There's nothing in there that says that. It does not say people shall have a right to assemble to express views on other people's property. It just doesn't say it. It says they shall have a right to assemble if they're peaceable but it doesn't say how far you can go in using other people's property.

Agronsky: Do you mean even government property?

Black: Why certainly; that's not theirs.

Sevareid: You can't assemble in mid-air. Whose is government property?

Black: It belongs to the government as a whole. Just exactly as a corporation's property belongs to the corporation as a whole. Now, the government would be in a very bad fix, I think, if the Constitution provided that the Congress was without power to keep people from coming into the Library of Congress and spending the day there, demonstrating or singing because they wanted to protest the government. I don't think they could. They've got a right to talk where they have a right to be under valid laws.

Agronsky: In another very controversial case, the obscenity case in which Mr. Ginzburg was sent to jail by the lower courts, the majority upheld his being sent to jail. You were in the minority. Do you think that there are any times at all when obscenity can be restricted, prohibited, and not come into conflict with the freedom of press and of speech guarantees in the Constitution?

Black: I've said they couldn't. Of course, I understand that pornography sounds bad. But I never have seen anybody who could say what it is. Nobody. Some people say it's way over here and some people say it's way over there. If the idea is to keep people from learning about the facts of life, as between the sexes, that's a vain task. How in the world can you keep people, who mix with others on the street and around various places, from learning. They're going to learn. But that's not the reason I take the view I do. The reason I take this view is that it's an expression of opinion. It refers to one of the strongest urges in the human race. It's something people have not failed to talk about and they will not fail to talk about. People are going to have organizations and write letters and say, "You're letting my children suffer." There's plenty of argument for the idea. But they ought to take care of their children and warn them against things themselves rather than try to pass a law. Obscenity is wholly ambiguous. It means one thing to Mr. Agronsky, another thing to Mr. Sevareid, another thing to these people, and another thing to me. I don't like obscenity. I don't use it. I never have; I've always detested it. But that's no reason, I think, that it's not speech on an important subject. Let them talk.

Agronsky: There's an interesting aspect to your position on the obscenity case in that you refused even to examine the evidence.

Black: That's not peculiar. Why should it be peculiar?

Agronsky: One would think a judge should examine evidence.

Black: Why should he? If I don't think there is such a thing as obscenity why should I go and look at those things? It doesn't make any difference what the talk is. I don't think it violates any law.

Sevareid: Justice Black, Presidents, of course appoint the members of the Supreme Court and they tend to appoint men who share their general philosophy of public affairs. A President in power a long time may appoint several Justices. Does this in any way infringe on the whole principle of separation of powers?

Black: I do not think so. I think that it's perfectly natural that a President would first look to the people he knows best. And he happens to know best the people in his party. Presidents have always appointed people who believed a great deal in the same things that the President who appoints them believes in.

Sevareid: Then, in a sense, the President of the United States is

sort of "ghost at the banquet" up there in the court all the time.
Does his mind, his purposes, play a long influence?

Black: Well, I don't know how much influence he has. Franklin
D. Roosevelt appointed me. He never mentioned a case that was
in the court while I was on the bench. I saw him frequently. He
never indicated that I should decide cases one way or the other.
It was just as though he hadn't appointed me.

Sevareid: But he knew your cast of mind.

Black: Yes, but that doesn't mean I always went with him. I
fought his National Recovery Act. I said it was unconstitutional
on the Senate floor.

Agronsky: You were a close friend of President Roosevelt. What
do you think about him as a man and as a human being?

Black: I thought what most people thought. I liked Roosevelt. I
thought he was magnificent. I don't mean to say that he was the
most learned man in the United States, that he knew more law, that he
knew more about government. But he was such a great expert
in so many fields that you could put him at the top.

I feel about Roosevelt like a man did who wrote a biography
of Thomas Jefferson in which he said the following: "Washington
wasn't our greatest general, that's a mistake. He wasn't our greatest
President, that's a mistake. He wasn't our greatest scholar; if anyone
thinks that he's mistaken. But he was our greatest man." That's
what I think Roosevelt was.

Agronsky: A very different kind of man was President Harry
Truman. Did you have much to do with him?

Black: Oh, I was very fond of Harry. I campaigned for him in
Missouri. Newspapermen who underestimated him certainly should
have known better, as I've told them a number of times. When
we were talking about him I said, "Truman made a speech before
you here, just before he ran. Anybody who heard that speech should
have been able to know that that man is a campaigner. And they
should never have written that man off." I heard him speak at
Philadelphia. I saw him go into a crowd that was all against him.
They were sure that the Democratic party was dead and that Truman
didn't have a chance. Then early next morning I called him up,
right over there. We had served together in the Senate and I had
spoken for him as a Senator. I said: "I want to congratulate you
on your meeting last night. A lot of people don't think you could
be elected now and I'm one of them but I think you can be elected

if you'll make exactly that same kind of appeal to the people all over the United States." He said: "I agree with everything you've said. Of course I couldn't get elected now. But I'm going to make that same kind of speech and I'm going to be elected."

Sevareid: Who would you say were the ablest lawyers to plead before you in your long term on the court?

Black: You're kind of putting me on the spot. I would say, just off-hand, that two come right straight to my mind — John W. Davis, a great speaker, a great man, a great advocate; and Bob Jackson, who argued cases before us as Solicitor General. Bob was always magnificent. His language was fluent. His knowledge of the law was good and he never objected to a question which most people would think was too hard to answer. I do not recall that he ever declined when some judge would say: "Do you mean to say this?" I don't recall an instance when Bob didn't say, "That's exactly what I mean."

Sevareid: Right now, much of the public clamor about the court is based on the notion that it has somehow restricted police and aided criminals because of various decisions about a man's rights. How do you look at that argument?

Black: The Constitution-makers said that no man should be compelled to convict himself. I don't see how anybody could deny that the Constitution says, absolutely, in the Fifth Amendment, that "no person shall be compelled in a criminal case to be a witness against himself." People who complain about the Constitution don't know it or its interpretation.

Agronsky: Do you think that recent decisions have made it more difficult for the police to combat crime?

Black: Certainly. Why shouldn't they? What were they written for? Why did they write the Bill of Rights? Many of the Supreme Court's decisions relate to the way cases shall be tried.

Practically all of the decisions make it more difficult to convict people of crimes. What about guaranteeing a man a right to a lawyer? Of course that makes it more difficult to convict him. What about saying he shall not be compelled to be a witness against himself? That also makes it more difficult to convict him. What about no "unreasonable search or seizure shall be made?" That makes it more difficult. It was written to make it more difficult. What the court does is try to follow the Constitution by saying you've got to try people in this and that way. Why did they want a jury?

Because they didn't want people being subject to a judge who might hang them or convict them for a political crime or something of that kind. And they said the same thing about an indictment. That's why they put it in the laws. They intended to make it more difficult for the doors of a prison to close on a man because of his trial.

I'm all for this. I'm for the Bill of Rights. I'm not saying I'd write every one of its ten amendments in the language they used. But I'll try to enforce them in the exact language they were written.

Sevareid: As a man who has read a lot of history, lived a long time, watched this country closely, why do you think we have the great rise in crime, general irresponsibility, and public disorder?

Black: Well, that assumes a premise that I'm not sure is correct. This country has always been called a country of violence.

Almost right after the Constitution went into effect there was a "Whiskey Rebellion" in Pennsylvania. George Washington had to send the army up there to stop it. There's nothing new about crime. Now it's true different types of crime increase or decrease from time to time. I think the expectations of an organized government with a Constitution is that the people would do just what they said they would in the Constitution. Let's see what it says:

"We the people of the United States, in order to form a more perfect Union, establish justice, insure domestic tranquility, provide for the common defense, promote the general welfare, and secure the blessing of liberty, to ourselves and our posterity, do ordain and establish this Constitution for the United States of America."

That's the purpose of our government. It's to have tranquility and order. I think the greatest thing our people accomplished was to discover for the first time that you would come nearer having marked boundaries if they had a Constitution. It's for this reason that I can't join those who want to make the boundaries more flexible — and more vulnerable.

Sevareid: If one assumed that there may be a really serious threat to American society from within, would it be in the direction of greater oppression by authority or a kind of spread of anarchy and disbelief? What is the progression of dissolution of a society if that sort of thing happens?

Black: Well, no two people probably could agree on that. A study of history convinces me that nations have risen, their stars have gone up, and then they gradually begin to decline, particularly if they get too big and try to run the world. That's what's happened. I don't know what will happen. I hope this nation will have a longer life. Nobody knows. Nobody can say with any degree of certainty.

Sevareid: I think John Adams said that "Power always thinks it has a great soul." Has that kind of vanity crept into our life?

Black: Of course, you'll find people saying "Well, that's just a little country. We ought to be able to whip it." Whip all of Asia? A lot of people have said, "Why, certainly, we can do it." They believe it because they think this country can do anything it pleases. That's not right. All nations have had to realize this sooner or later.

Sevareid: I gather you're not enchanted with the Vietnam war.

Black: I don't believe in war. We've had only one war that I thoroughly approved — the war against Hitler.

Sevareid: I think that more of your dissents have later become majority opinions and the law of the land than is true of any other Supreme Court Justice. What's the most important of those dissents that later became law?

Black: Adamson against California. That's the case where I asserted at full length for the first time my belief that the passage of the 14th Amendment made the Bill of Rights applicable to the states. I stated there that I thought the "due process" clause meant a case should be tried according to the laws of the land — clear laws as written unambiguously before a controversy came up.

In the Chambers case I stated my concept of due process — what it actually accomplishes according to my meaning. It has been utilized a great many times. I pointed out that many people had been convicted without compliance with the law and that people know this. Some wonderful human beings were crucified on crosses. Others were hung. The purpose of due process is to see that nobody is convicted except under the law of the land as it is written. Here's what I said about due process:

"Today, as in ages past, we are not without tragic proof that the exalted power of some governments to punish manufactured crime dictatorially is the handmaid of tyranny. Under our constitutional system, courts stand . . . as havens of refuge for those who might otherwise suffer because they are helpless, weak, outnumbered, or because they are non-conforming victims of prejudice and public excitement. Due process of law, preserved for all by our Constitution, demands that no such practice, as that disclosed by this record, shall send any accused to death." (The accused were four

colored tenant farmers — young fellows who had been questioned
for three nights in a county courthouse.)

"No higher duty, no more solemn responsibility rests upon this
court than that of translating into living law, and maintaining this
constitutional shield, deliberately planned and inscribed for the benefit of every human being subject to our Constitution, of whatever race,
creed or persuasion."

Sevareid: I think there are just two written documents in history
that have really governed a great people for a long period — the
Principate of the Emperor Augustus and the American Constitution.
How does one explain the longevity of this document of ours?

Black: I think that when the founding fathers met in Philadelphia
they had behind them knowledge of a long series of oppression in
Europe. They knew about people getting their tongues torn out,
their ears clipped off. They wanted to get away from that. I think
England had gradually moved towards an aspiration for complete
equality of treatment of everybody. They had moved a long way.
At that time it was the best government in the world — before ours.
I think our Constitution is the best document that has ever been
written to control a government. It's not perfect. I think there
are parts of it that can well be changed.

But I think we should not rush to change the Constitution too
quickly. If our form of government endures it's because this remarkable document endures. It's the basis for our government of
the people, by the people, and for the people. Its ideals of liberty,
equality, and freedom have made our country great. It's failed at
various times and in various places, but it's done mighty well by us.

Conversation With
Dean Acheson

September 28, 1969

Sevareid: Dean Acheson, now 76, is one of the last of the living legends of Washington, D. C. He's a statesman of the old school who cared nothing for popularity, suffered fools ungladly, made worshipping friends and passionate enemies, and did his job. He was one of the prime architects of the Atlantic Alliance, the Marshall Plan that gave demolished Europe another chance, and the Korean intervention that rearmed America. One of the handful of men who recast the world role of the United States, President Truman regarded him as the greatest Secretary of State of this century. Congressional enemies—including the then Representative Richard Nixon—tried to force him out of office. The last three Presidents, (Mr. Nixon included), have sought and received his private advice. He has now written an immense book on his years as Secretary, a prime document in the American story. During most of the good weather weeks of the year he spends with his artist wife Alice at his 18th century Maryland farm near Washington — host, gardener, cabinet maker, writer. He writes in longhand in this small structure, once the workshop of a leading engraver in the early 19th century.

Here, at the Maryland farm, we discussed the world, his work, the future, his associations with Presidents, his impressions of Charles De Gualle and Joe McCarthy, his views about the Alger Hiss case, and other matters.

This new book of yours, Mr. Acheson, about your stewardship in the Department of State is called "Present at the Creation." I take it this means a creation of a whole new role for this country in the world through recent U. S. policies, our first peacetime military alliance, the Marshall Plan, foreign aid in general. How would you define this role?

Acheson: It was the creation of a new world after the destruction of an old world. One of the things that was so striking to us was the slowness with which we discovered that the 19th century world has disappeared. All the great empires of the world were gone — British, French, German, Russian. They were all gone and out of the chaos into which the world had fallen something new had to be created. This was what I had in mind. Our role was one of trying to help fashion what should come after the destruction of the old world. Then came the great Marshall Plan which really built up the foundation of a new world.

The title of my book comes from a very remarkable fellow, a king of Spain in the 13th century, two hundred years before Columbus discovered America. He said: "Had I been present at the creation, I would have had a few useful hints for the better ordering of the universe."

Sevareid: Well, you were not only present as a witness at this recent genesis but you had a big hand in it. You say in the book, at the end of it, that you thought the work of the State Department in that period, Mr. Truman's time, was nobly done. Do you find no serious mistakes of basic policy as you look back now?

Acheson: Oh yes, there were many mistakes. Most of the mistakes came from a lack of understanding of the facts. For instance, General Marshall's mission to China.

Sevareid: You're not subscribing, I take it, to the "we lost China" thesis, an accusation that was once fairly popular.

Acheson: No, I'm not. Of course you can't lose something if you didn't have it and we never had it. China lost itself. We hoped that the agreement between Mao Tse-tung and Chiang Kai-shek would recreate a Chinese state and bring the two together. They had attempted to do that, I think insincerely, but they went through the forms and General Marshall went out to try and help in that effort and this just didn't come off. We should have known that this wouldn't work. But it seemed possible. It seemed to be the only choice that there was and we went ahead with it and it failed. That was one thing you have to mark down as a failure. Our attempts to draw the Russians into cooperation during the postwar period also failed. I think the attempts had to be made but they failed.

Sevareid: Mr. Nixon talked last fall about going from a period of confrontation to negotiation. He hasn't said so much about that recently but we are trying to get disarmament talks going. Isn't it possible that the Russians want a leveling off at least nuclear arms? They can't go on forever, no more than we can.

Acheson: I think you'll have to take a look at what the Russians mean by negotiation. Our concepts of negotiation come from a New England horse trade. Two people want to bring about a result. You have a horse. I want to buy a horse. I want to buy your horse. You want as much money as you can get. I want to pay as little as possible. We dicker back and forth and we make a deal. I come up in my offer, you come down in the asking price, and I get the horse. We're both trying to do the same — reach the same end. This is not the Russian idea of negotiation. The Communist idea of negotiation is carrying on war by other means. And they use negotiation in order to get the other side at a disadvantage, to gain something themselves without giving anything and not reaching a common result but continuing the same purpose with an advantage.

Sevareid: Do you extend the same general view of the Communist view on negotiations to Hanoi right now for example? Two years ago I think you said that the war in Vietnam could never be settled by negotiation and you hoped the Communists didn't even try to negotiate with us, that this would be some sort of a by-pass or trap for us. How do you feel about that now?

Acheson: I would hate to say anything that makes the President's course harder for him. I think perhaps the best way to answer your question is to compare the situation with something which has happened and which I know a lot about. Take what happened in Korea. Next June it will have been twenty years since the Korean war started. We have no agreement between North and South Korea. If in twenty years we can't do it between North and South Korea then it seems to me not in the cards that we're going to do it very quickly between North and South Vietnam.

Sevareid: We still have about fifty thousand troops on that line in Korea. Do you foresee any such bleak picture for Vietnam, even when the war is over?

Acheson: I should think that would be a bright picture.

Sevareid: Fifty thousand men for twenty years?

Acheson: I think that would probably be a pretty good settlement.

Sevareid: But they're hostages to fortune in a sense. They're a trip-wire in a sense. Can't they by their very presence involve us again?

Acheson: It might. It could involve us again and I would hope and suppose that they can be withdrawn. But if you look at the situation in Europe, you have the same thing there. We have 225,000 troops in Europe. I think it would be disastrous to withdraw them. In a way our presence is the greatest guarantee of peace there can be. We don't like it. We wish we didn't have to do it. But there are responsibilities of power and I'm not at all sure that it would be wise for us to try and avoid them.

Sevareid: Do you think the fighting, as Henry Cabot Lodge used to say out in Saigon, is just going to peter out?

Acheson: Yes, there's a remarkable little book by Clarence Day, called "This Simian World." He draws distinctions between various civilizations — ours, which is the simian world, and then he pictures a cat world from which other people evolved. He says that after a war among people we have what the monkeys have—chattering in the treetops. This is the peace conference. But, he says, cats just walk off. I think the Communists are going to walk off.

Sevareid: A friend of mine said, "Why shouldn't the war peter out? It petered in."

Acheson: I think that's a fair comment.

Sevareid: You think things will hold together domestically enough to allow a slow staging withdrawal?

Acheson: Yes, I think once people are convinced, as I am convinced, that the President wants to bring the Vietnam war to a close as much as anybody in the country does and that he is doing his very best to that end, they will support him as they should support him and not criticize every step as not being enough.

Sevareid: Two years ago you said that President Johnson should simply forget his critics on Vietnam and see the thing through. Now I take it you've changed your mind about that, along with some other people, haven't you?

Acheson: I could fall back on the rather glib interpretation of what I meant by "see the thing through." That is, if I was in the presence of a hostile audience. If, however, I was being more frank, I would say I have changed my opinion. In 1965 I was, I think, misled by optimistic views from the Pentagon.

Sevareid: You are quoted, in at least one place as having said to President Johnson that the Joint Chiefs of Staff don't know what they're talking about in regard to the military prospects in Vietnam.

Acheson: You're making me seem a little blunter than I usually am.

Sevareid: The quote appears in a magazine coming out very shortly.

Acheson: Dear me, I'm always in trouble. Perhaps I can get my story across first. It is not basically untrue. A group of us had had several briefings, from 1965 on, from the Pentagon. Spokesmen for the Defense Department led us to believe that the military situation was more favorable than I later thought it was.

President Johnson asked me, in the end of February of 1968, if I would look into the matter and get together with the rest of these elder statesmen that he had with him before. I said that I would be glad to look into it but that I would prefer to talk with people who were lower down the line than Joint Chiefs—people who had more immediate contact with both the military and the civil front in Vietnam. In going through all their reports it seemed to me that the situation was quite different from the way it appeared when the reports got sifted and came out through the Ambassador, the Chairman of the Joint Chiefs, and the head of the CIA.

I went to the President, had lunch with him at his invitation, and told him that I thought we were in a very, very difficult situation. I remember using a simile, saying what we were doing then was like expecting the Redskins to win the championship without defensive ends. We could score anytime we wanted to; there wasn't any trouble about our scoring. At the very time we would be scoring, the enemy would be going around our ends and raising havoc with the population and the government we were trying to protect.

This discussion led to calling everybody together. While there was considerable division in the group, when we got through with the discussion with the President, a large part of the group took the view which I had taken. This was in mid-March of 1968. Later on I think Secretary McNamara came to this view and, as you know, Secretary Clifford also did.

Sevareid: Well, maybe there was something to Governor Romney's remark about being brainwashed by the military.

Acheson: Perhaps, perhaps.

Sevareid: But the upshot of your advice then, to President Johnson, was that we cannot win in a military sense, on this basis, this kind of war. Did you have a specific recommendation to him?

Acheson: Not a specific recommendation. I think our general recommendation was that we were trying to perform the wrong role.

That we were taking on so much of the conduct of the war that it was becoming an American enterprise in South Vietnam, and that the thing to be done was to return it where it should be. It was basically a South Vietnamese enterprise in which we were auxiliaries and not principals.

Sevareid: Well, when President Johnson made the decision he made in March of 1968 it meant, in effect, that he had to assume you and these other gentlemen were right, that his military advisers had been wrong. Isn't this what it amounts to?

Acheson: We're rather at a psychological field. I'm not at all sure that President Johnson was quite clear in his mind what he had decided. I think he decided that the situation was very painful and that he wanted to ameliorate it. But I'm not at all sure he came to any definite conclusions as to how he was going to go about it.

Sevareid: Now we're getting an argument — a rationale, if you will — from some of the military or ex-military connected with Vietnam and some politicians, that if we had just let the military go ahead, if we had mined Haiphong and all the rest of it, or even invaded North Vietnam, they'd have the war wrapped up. Do you see much point in this kind of argument?

Acheson: Mr. Sevareid, you've come to the right person to ask that question. This is what was said to me when General MacArthur was marching bravely to the Yalu River. I was told that he was our most brilliant general, that he had won the war in the Pacific, and he was going to win it here. It seemed to me madness, utter madness, what he was doing and it turned out to be the worst defeat we've had since the battle of Bull Run. No, I do not think that you should leave war to the soldiers. Wasn't it Clemenceau who said war is too serious to leave to generals?

Sevareid: With regard to this whole matter of negotiating with the Russians about which you've expressed some views, I understand that President Nixon and Henry Kissinger and some others think that disarmament ought to be linked with other outstanding political issues — with the Middle East or Berlin or Vietnam or what not. Is this a change of strategy? I had always thought we went at disarmament quite separately.

Acheson: We have always gone at it separately. My own view is that this would still be the best way to go at it. I was not aware that the President wished to link this with other issues. If I may quote myself, I once made the wise observation that the way to solve a difficult question is not add to it insoluble ones. I think this is true.

Some of the questions you just mentioned are more difficult than disarmament. The Middle East would be one of them. I cannot think of any solution that powers not involved directly in the Middle East could agree upon, any that would ever be accepted by the two sides or that anybody would ever try to impose. You can't impose a solution in the Middle East on the Arabs and the Jews. Anyone who went through the period before the creation of the State of Israel and immediately after, as I did with Mr. Truman, must be perfectly clear that you can't impose anything on those people. They won't accept an imposition.

Sevareid: How do you account for Mr. Truman's very strong pro-Israeli stand in those days when we first recognized Israel, when they became a state. Just internal politics, votes?

Acheson: I don't think Mr. Truman was moved at all by that consideration. I think he was moved by two considerations — one which he avowed very clearly and the other which he did not avow very clearly. The first one was that we had over a hundred thousand displaced persons, mostly Jewish, in our military refugee camps at the end of the war. Here they were. They couldn't go back to Russia or Poland. They couldn't go back to Germany where so many had been murdered. Wherever they had fled from they had left forever. Now what to do with them? It was our responsibility.

Our military commanders were pressing the President. Various suggestions were made. Brazil at one time offered to take a good many. The President tried to get our immigration laws made more lax. In this he failed. And then he turned to Palestine. At that time the British quota was 1,200 immigrants a month. Well, you got nowhere at 1,200 a month. A hundred thousand and more were coming all the time. So the President, with various commissions, pressed the British to admit a hundred thousand. The Arabs said if you do this we have war. Finally, we pressed the British so hard that they threw up the mandate and chaos reigned for a time. Civil war did break out. Finally, the State of Israel was created. We recognized it and a hundred thousand went in, more than a million went in. This, I think, was the major pressure that moved Truman. The President also, I think, was morally and emotionally moved to accept the Zionist position. This came from his partner in the haberdashery business, Eddie Jacobson. Eddie was a convinced

Zionist. He talked to the President a good deal about it. Truman was very fond of him. The idea appealed to him very much. I think emotionally he was in favor of it.

Sevareid: That's an explanation I've never heard before.

Acheson: Well, it's one of the most extraordinary . . . history is made up of unexplained and rather secret pressures.

Sevareid: You know, could professional psychologists or anthropologists be of any help in this whole business of foreign and military policy? General MacArthur misjudged what the Chinese would do. When we had the Bay of Pigs we had people who thought the people of Cuba would rise up to overthrow Castro even though he was at the height of his popularity then. We bomb North Vietnam, thinking destruction of material things will break their will and we're wrong about these things. Aren't there ways to know or get advice from different kinds of people who deal in human nature all the time?

Acheson: I think one of the great problems everybody faces in dealing with foreign affairs is that not only is the future clouded but the present is clouded. What are the facts? Nobody knows what the facts are. The facts are really a matter of interpretation of a very limited segment of data that one gets. If you add more data the interpretation would be different. But what the true data are nobody knows. The poet says things are not what they seem. The great trouble is sometimes they are what they seem. The question is are they or aren't they what they seem? This is inherent in the problem. That is what makes government, particularly foreign affairs, an art and not a science.

Sevareid: I'm always meeting people who say, "Well, why don't we just do what is right in terms of foreign policy?" I suppose that what a person may do on a moral basis cannot necessarily be done by a government.

Acheson: This is very true. I think perhaps the great illustration was given by Lincoln when he was asked his views about slavery at the beginning of the Civil War. He said that his purpose was to preserve the Union. If he could preserve the Union by freeing all the slaves, he'd do that. Or if he could preserve it by freeing none of the slaves, he would do that. Or if he could preserve it by freeing some and leaving others in bondage, he would do that. Now, the question is, what is right? It depends on what right you are talking about. To Lincoln the supreme right was to save the Union. To the

Abolitionists the supreme right was to free the slaves. Therefore, it all depends on what morality you are talking about.

Sevareid: If I may switch from morality to loyalty, you and Harry Truman were utterly different in background and general style and manner. It was always a source of wonderment to many of us in Washington how this affectionate trust and intimacy between two such disparate men really developed. What was the basis for your extreme loyalty to him?

Acheson: It's a complicated matter. Part of it was that he had a tender nature, a deeply loving and tender nature. This isn't the general impression of him at all. Two things will illustrate it. During one period, when I was Secretary, my younger daughter was very ill indeed and had a most serious operation, and it was not clear whether she would pull through. The President telephoned the hospital, where my wife was, got a report on my daughter's condition and telephoned me, when I was abroad, every day as to how that girl was. Well, this is the kind of person that one can adore. You have an affection for that man that nothing can touch.

I remember making a social faux pas by inviting to a White House diplomatic dinner the Russian Ambassador Novikoff and an Ambassador from a Baltic country Russia had absorbed. Novikoff telephoned to say he was ill and couldn't come. And it turned out that his wife was ill, that the second-in-command and his wife were ill, and that all the Russians were ill. The next day the President sent for me and said: "What do you say of a fellow you don't want around any more?" I said "Persona non grata, that's what we call it." "That's what he is," he said. "Get Novikoff out of the country." "Well," I said, "why?" And he said, "He was rude to Mrs. Truman." And I said, "Now, boss, let's take this a little bit easy. This was my fault and Stanley's fault. (Stanley Woodward was Chief of Protocol). We did not really use our heads on this. We shouldn't have asked these two ambassadors to the same dinner. Novikoff's government told him he couldn't go. He wasn't being rude to Mrs. Truman. He just couldn't go to dinner with an ambassador of a state that was part of Russia so far as he was concerned."

The President argued with me for a while. Finally Mrs. Truman called him on the phone and I heard him say, "I'm talking to him now." She told him to let me talk with her. So he handed me the phone. Mrs. Truman told me: "You can't let Harry do this." I said: "That's all very well, only if I can't let him do it, how does one not let him do it?' She said: "Well, just think of what people will say." This gave me an idea. So I began pretending to repeat what she said. I said to her: "Oh, you mean too big for his breeches?" After this went on for a while he said: "Oh, give me that phone." He took it away from me: "All right, Bess, when you two line up against me, I know when I'm licked." So he said to me: "Forget about it."

Then the President added: "I want to show you something." He picked up a little framed photograph, took some pegs out of it, and gave me the photograph inside. It was a picture of a young girl of 17 or 18. On the back was written: "To Harry. This will take him safely to France and home again." And he said: "Any so-and-so who is rude to that girl is in trouble with me." It was that kind of nature that got loyalty.

And, then, he was so fair. He didn't make different decisions with different people. He called everyone in together. You were all heard and you all got the answer together. He was a square dealer all the way through. This is the best way to run a government.

Sevareid: Truman went at the running of the government, his relationship with foreign policy and with the Secretary of State very differently from President Eisenhower, for example. You make a lot of this in your book, pointing out Eisenhower's desire to have agreed-upon recommendations come to him for decision. Mr. Truman did it the opposite way. What was the consequence of doing it the Eisenhower way?

Acheson: I think the President didn't function as President the Eisenhower way. All he did was put a stamp of approval on agreement reached by his subordinates. Now, you can always reach agreement on any subject if you make it general enough. The only time you get into disagreement is when you are very specific, when an issue is brought out perfectly clearly and argued in an adversary way. Then you know the problem. This is what one side says, this is what the other side says. Now your job, as President, is to decide. Mr. Truman decided. He didn't want the problems swept under the rug. He didn't want people to say, "It's perfectly easy, boss, we're all agreed on it, and this is what you ought to do." He said, "I'm not earning my money. I'm not President; somebody else is!"

Sevareid: Well, since Mr. Kennedy, we've had a kind of second State Department in the basement of the White House, with Bundy, Rostow, Kissinger. If you were Secretary of State under those circumstances, what would you do?

Acheson: I'd cease being Secretary of State. I couldn't function that way.

Sevareid: But somehow things have functioned, badly or well, with this kind of a set-up. What's the point of it?

Acheson: It began, chiefly, under John Kennedy to be sure that the State Department wasn't putting something over on him. The State Department has always been regarded with suspicion by Presidents — all Presidents, from the beginning on. I think one of the reasons Mr. Truman made me Secretary of State was that he knew he could trust me. He knew I was as loyal to him as anybody he could find in the United States, whether he was in the White House or not. And he could count 100 per cent on my doing nothing which would be contrary to his interests or his policies. This is not always so. Presidents haven't known their Secretaries of State as well as he knew me.

Sevareid: When President Kennedy took office he was not well acquainted with Dean Rusk, whom he made Secretary of State. And there is a considerable body of evidence that you had a lot to do with that appointment or with persuading the President to consider him. Can you tell us anything about that?

Acheson: Well, the President-elect came over to my house in December of 1960 and consulted me on this appointment, saying to me that he would start off by saying that he was not considering me and that he was not considering Adlai Stevenson. I said, "I think those are two wise decisions." And then he went on and discussed various people and asked me for ideas. I gave him several. And I mentioned Dean Rusk's name. I said that Dean had worked with me, that he had been loyal above the call of duty. I thought he had been extremely competent. How any man would act when he was chief you couldn't tell until he was chief. After thinking about it — he didn't decide at this point what he was going to do — Kennedy apparently liked what I said about Dean Rusk and chose him.

Sevareid: What do you think now about Mr. Rusk's conduct of the Department and his role in the last few years?

Acheson: I think Mr. Rusk has suffered so much that I would not want to add any criticism. He had an extremely difficult time. I think he did the best he could. And it was a situation where it was hard to do what one would like to have done. Mr. Truman once said that he would like to have on his tombstone what was on that tombstone in Arizona: "Here Lies Bill Jones — He Done His Damndest." I think Dean Rusk done his damndest.

Sevareid: Since you were Secretary of State at least three Presidents have had you in, often on a private basis. But President Eisenhower never invited you to the White House, never consulted you. To what did you attribute this? Some personal animosity?

Acheson: The curious thing is that Eisenhower did the same to Mr. Truman. Mr. Truman was never invited to the White House. When Mr. Truman called on President Eisenhower when President Eisenhower was in Kansas City, Eisenhower wouldn't see him. Now why? The only explanation I could think of is that people dislike people whom they have unjustly injured. I think Eisenhower had the feeling that he had unjustly said things about Mr. Truman and unjustly said things about me. That made it embarrassing for him to have a pleasant social relation. I thought it was bad manners.

Sevareid: In the 1952 campaign Ike said your National Press Club speech supposedly excluding Korea from our defense perimeter had set off that war. He also said we should not have withdrawn our troops from Korea in the first place. Later, I think, you produced a memorandum he had signed recommending that we do this.

Acheson: I think he did.

Sevareid: Mr. Acheson, if I can go back a little further, Washington was a pretty neurotic place at the time of Joe McCarthy when you were practically the number one sitting duck for that whole business. I've often wondered why you never directly, publicly, hit back at Joe McCarthy in those days.

Acheson: This is really what Joe wanted me to do. He would have loved to have me pick him out as an equal enemy. And the war would then be "McCarthy and the Secretary of State." I chose to have other people reply to him.

Sevareid: Did he ever find a bona fide Communist in the State Department? Through his own efforts or his people?

Acheson: I doubt it very much.

Sevareid: Don't remember any?

Acheson: I don't. I'm certain there was no one that came up and said, "Here's my card. I'm a member of the party." There were people who had done things that we thought were undesirable and were asked to leave. I think I was mistaken about some of those.

Sevareid: Is there anything you have to add at all about the Alger

Hiss relationship and your statement, when he was convicted, that you would not turn your back on him?

Acheson: I got a terrible clobbering on that. It may have been I was a little grandiloquent. Perhaps it would have been better if I had said, "I haven't anything to say about it." I suppose in a way an element of pride entered into this. I knew the question was going to be asked. And I knew the press was going to believe I'd run. I just said, I'm not going to run. I'm going to let you have it right on the jaw. Perhaps I knocked myself out.

At any rate, I put on my hat and went over to the White House and said, "Mr. President, you've already heard the commotion that's started up. It's quite possible that I've become an embarrassment to you. My resignation is at your disposal whenever you'd like it." And he said, "If you think that a person who walked behind the casket of an old friend who was a convicted criminal would have had you do anything else, you're mistaken in me. Go on back and get to work."

Sevareid: Who was Truman referring to?

Acheson: Pendergast, whose funeral he had attended two months before.

Sevareid: At the time of your statement about Hiss, when you said you wouldn't turn your back on him for Christian, moral reasons, young Representative Richard Nixon said this was a disgusting statement. Has this affected your feeling toward the incumbent President at all, those hard words of those long-ago days?

Acheson: No. I feel about political battles the way Mr. Truman did, that "If you can't stand the heat you'd better stay out of the kitchen." People say pretty harsh things. I said some harsh things about Mr. Nixon. I think it's a mistake to allow that to interfere with relations. I don't think either one of us are now affected by what happened twenty years ago.

Sevareid: How about things of just a couple of years ago? I think you said publicly that you would not like to see Nixon elected President, that you'd be sad if he became President. Not a high opinion of him. What goes on between two men in public life after such statements have been made? He is President. You're still a reservoir of advice and counsel if he chooses to use you. I believe he does. Is that not right?

Acheson: Yes. That's right. After the Gridiron Club Dinner this year I met the President in one of the suites. I went up to him and introduced myself and said that I would do my best to be of whatever service I could be to him. He took that proposal very kindly and has done me the great honor of talking with me since.

Sevareid: What were your relations with Congress like when you were Secretary of State?

Acheson: A good many members of Congress didn't like me. This didn't bother me at all. I didn't care whether they liked me or didn't like me. The point is they usually did what they were asked to do. And if they did that they could have any views they liked about me.

Sevareid: You've been part of a big slice of our history. You've known some of the great figures of the last generation. How would you rate people like Churchill and de Gaulle and Roosevelt?

Acheson: I think that, looking at them as individuals, I would say that Mr. Churchill was the most outstanding man I have ever met. Almost equal with him, I would place General Marshall. The General had such a commanding nature. He was a person of much moral grandeur and tremendous self-control.

I thought Mr. Truman was a great President. In that role he was superb. He had many qualities of greatness but I don't think he had quite the scope of the two that I have mentioned.

De Gaulle was a fascinating person. I met him several times during official missions for Presidents. I always had the feeling that I was a Papal Legate going to see Louis XIV. There was an elevated position he assumed which made me take on almost the same degree of pompousness that he was putting on. All in all, he was a great actor but not a particularly great man and he had very poor judgment.

Adenauer was a remarkable person, a remarkable old man. He belongs in a high rank.

Sevareid: You say in your book that your feeling toward President Roosevelt, with whom you had a famous row at one point when you were in the Treasury, was one of admiration but not affection.

Acheson: Oh, he had a conception of continental royalty. Not British royalty, which is a kind of cozy bourgeois royalty — but Queen Marie of Roumania, for instance. European royalty regarded themselves as apart from the rest of mankind. They were in one sphere; the most distinguished other people were in another sphere. Roosevelt treated everybody like he was the Squire of Hyde Park. It didn't flatter me to have the Squire come by and speak to me familiarly, as though I were a stable boy, and I was supposed to pull my lock and say, "Aye, aye, sir." That I did not find flattering.

Sevareid: Taking this whole cast of terrific characters that you have known, you look around now, around the world, do you see anybody of corresponding stature and greatness?

Acheson: I don't. Part of this may be age. I remember old Justice Holmes saying to me, "Sonny, when policemen look like boys to you then you're getting on." I think this is probably true today. One expects, particularly in high office, to find one's grandfather.

I think in the world at the present time it would not be unfair to say that the century of the common man has come into its own. Wherever you look you'll find governments which are not outstanding in nature. They're not outstanding in strength. It doesn't make any difference whether they're Communist or democratic or European or Latin American or black or white or yellow or whatever they are. They seem to be more of an average type. I see grave problems coming from this.

Sevareid: You said "Never again" about writing books.

Acheson: It's a terrible job. I wouldn't do it again for anything. for anything.

Sevareid: What are you going to do the rest of your life?

Acheson: I'm probably going to write another book.

Conversation With George Kennan

September 7, 1975

Sevareid: Some serious students of foreign affairs have called George Kennan America's most professional diplomat and our foremost scholar of Russia. Others have called him the "Architect of the Cold War." For more than thirty years he has ranked high among the best of American diplomats. He specialized in Soviet affairs. In 1952 he received the appointment to which all his training had led—Ambassadorship to Moscow. But his expertise was troublesome to Stalin: Kennan knew too much. Within six months the Soviet leader found a pretext to kick him out.

Back in Washington a new Republican administration looked without favor on Kennan's service under the Democrats. Secretary of State John Foster Dulles, a colder warrior by many years, refused to reassign Kennan, who then resigned from the Foreign Service. Since then Kennan has devoted himself to scholarship. Though respected by diplomats and scholars, he remains a controversial figure among politicians. A short time ago he and I spent some hours talking at the Institute for Advanced Study in Princeton.

George Kennan is a diplomat whose public career was abruptly ended by warriors much more bellicose than he. But for anyone who has read the books he has written he can be called a prophet with less honor than he should have received. For many years he saw American foreign policy ahead of its formulation and execution. He still does.

A high point of American relations with the Soviet Union was reached in 1945, when the First United States Army and the First Ukranian Army met at the River Elbe. It seemed as if the two greatest nations on earth were locked forever in mutual friendship. Yet two years later friendship had turned to irritation and shapeless, undefined hostility began to appear.

The favorite magazine for diplomats is *Foreign Affairs*. In July 1947 an unsigned article appeared in its pages. Its title was "The Sources of Soviet Conduct". Its author was "X" — really George Kennan. And this is what he had to say: "Any United States policy toward the Soviet Union must be that of firm and vigilant containment of Russian expansive tendencies. It is clear that the United States cannot expect in the foreseeable future to enjoy political intimacy with the Soviet Regime." American policy, Kennan continued, should be designed "to confront the Russians with unalterable counter-force at every point . . ." Thus the ideology of the Cold War was anticipated by this scholar-diplomat.

But we must begin back in the days just after he invented the term "containment." The containment that came was not the containment he wanted. We asked him, "What were you getting at when you wrote that famous article in *Foreign Affairs?*"

Kennan: What I thought was essential in 1945, in 1946, and in 1947 was to prevent the political influence and predominant authority of the Soviet Government from spreading any further in the world, because we had had it demonstrated in the period of World War II that you didn't always have to occupy another country in order to dominate its life. You could threaten it, or you could subvert its government by various ways, including the time-honored phenomenon of puppet government. I was afraid, I must say, at that time (and I think with some reason) of what is today called the "domino theory." Western Europe, as the war ended, was in a sorry state. People were disoriented, discouraged, apprehensive, frightened by the experiences of the war, and it would not have been too difficult for Italy or for France, if they had lost their confidence in us then, to turn to the Soviet Union and let their Communist parties take over. It seemed to me that it was important for Europe, for us, and, in the long run, even for the Russians — that this should not happen. It just wasn't desirable.

When I talked about containment, what I had in mind was an effort on our part to stiffen the hope, the confidence, of European Nations in themselves, and to persuade them that they didn't need to yield to one great power or another, that they could resume life. We would help them to do it. That was all that was involved. I didn't think the Russians wanted to attack anyone. I didn't think they wanted to expand any further by force of arms. I'm sure I was absolutely right about this. In 1948, when the talk of the formation of the NATO pact began (it was actually the Europeans — the French and the British and the Benelux people — who came to us and wanted it) I was quite surprised. I said, "Why are you giving your attention to this? We're just getting the Marshall Plan through. For goodness sake, concentrate on your economic recovery. Nobody's going to attack you." But I found that all of Western Europe had what the French call "la manie d'invasion" — the mania of invasion.

Severeid: That's what revisionists forget. It was the Europeans who were terrified to death at this period.

Kennan: That's correct.

Severeid: They're less terrified than we are today, but at that time it was quite the reverse. But are you saying, in effect, that you didn't think NATO (the North Atlantic Treaty Organization) was really necessary then? The other theory was that unless you had a military shield this economic development wouldn't go forward in peace.

Kennan: Within the course of time the military shield probably would have had to be built, although it never had to assume the dimensions that it has today. I think one could have dealt with the Russians about these things. At any rate, it should never have been given the emphasis it was given. We should never have allowed the thesis to become established that, if it were not for the so-called deterrent quality of our nuclear weapons, the Russians would immediately have attacked Western Europe and overrun it. I never thought this was true.

Severeid: But wasn't it true that at this period you really did not want to see Germany armed? You wanted, I thought, a neutralized and possibly unified Germany. That was the seat of the whole argument, wasn't it?

Kennan: That's correct. The reason that this was so ill received in the Western countries (above all in Western Germany itself, in England, even in the neutral countries of Switzerland and Sweden) was that people in Europe were still more afraid of the Germans than they were . . . Put it this way: they put a higher value on American defense against the Germans than they did on the retirement of the Soviet forces from Eastern Europe. And they really didn't want the removal of the split of the continent. You must realize that this divided continent suited — and still suits — many people in Western Europe very well because, as they see it, the present arrangement means that we defend them both against the Russians and the Germans. It leaves the whole onus on this country.

Sevareid: You're really talking about the French here?

Kennan: Yes, and the English, the Dutch. They don't want to make the sacrifices that are necessary to defend themselves in Western Europe. They have the population. They have the industrial strength to keep forces fully adequate to the defense of Western Europe. They're not deficient in either of these.

Sevareid: But as long as we're there with an atomic shield and trip wire, they're not going to do it.

Kennan: That's right. It gives them an excuse for not maintaining conventional forces at the requisite level.

Sevareid: But our official line now in the Pentagon (and I suppose the State Department) is that were we not there with these troops, they wouldn't pull together and contribute more; they would just go apart.

Kennan: Well, a great deal of water has flown over the dam since the days when we argued about these things. But I will tell you two reasons why I was reluctant to see us perpetuate the division of Germany and of Europe. One was the Berlin situation, which didn't fit in with a divided Europe. I regarded Berlin as the greatest single danger spot in Europe and I thought we were going to have trouble with this if we tried to divide the continent on the present line. But the other reason is today an even more serious reason — our willingness to see the division of the continent perpetuated really consigned all the Eastern European countries by implication to the Russian sphere. Now that was, of course, rough on them, but it's also questionable how long it will last, how long it will stick. If any of these countries ever does succeed in liberating itself from the Soviet sphere of influence then our scheme of things is going to have no place for it.

Sevareid: They have no place to go.

Kennan: We have a Western European alliance. If we try to take an Eastern European country into it that's going to be a real military provocation for the Russians. They could not stand it.

Sevareid: I thought you really never believed that they could or would liberate themselves.

Kennan: I never believed that it was our duty to liberate them but

I cannot guarantee to the Russians that they will be able to bear this burden successfully forever. This is a very unnatural thing. They're sitting on ninety million people with a higher standard of living and a more Western cultural tradition than their own and there is restlessness. There's no doubt about it. A lot of people in these countries don't like it. There is practically no real communist enthusiasm in Eastern Europe from the Baltic Sea to the Black Sea.

Sevareid: What about the other side of the line? What happens if Portugal comes under Communist domination? Italy?

Kennan: That's a good question. I am sure that what is happening in Portugal presents very considerable problems for people in Moscow. In some ways I can see that they might like the Communist Party there to take charge of things but in other respects the situation in the world is such today that I'm not sure they really want this to happen. Instability in Western Europe could mean instability in Eastern Europe today and instability in Portugal could mean instability all along the northern littoral of the Mediterranean. After all, Spain next door is very closely connected with Portugal, Spain is now entering a period of great uncertainty. Obviously, the period that has existed there since the termination of the civil war is coming to an end and nobody knows what is going to happen in Spain in the coming period. What happens in Portugal certainly is going to influence it. Then you have Italy almost effectively without a government today. And you have the Greeks and the Turks at each other's throats and the Cyprus situation.

Sevareid: Everybody in Washington sees it as a great setback for us, destabilizing our whole arrangement for Europe. But you're saying this is also very destabilizing for the Russians?

Kennan: Yes, the Soviet leadership is an old leadership. The average age of the top five people is well over 70. They have many problems at home, they have problems with their zone of influence in Eastern Europe, and I think they want things kept quiet.

Sevareid: Partly because of China, I suppose?

Kennan: Because of China, too. Very important. I'm glad you mentioned that. I think that a stable Western Europe has certain virtues in the Soviet eyes in view of their relations with China. I don't mean to oversimplify this. I think it pulls both ways. One of the great dangers that we are up against now is that if the situation deteriorates further in Portugal and along the northern shores of the Mediterranean there will be voices—there probably are already voices—being raised in the Communist part of the world which say,

"What are we waiting for? What's the matter with us? Why don't we let this balloon go up? We have the best situation for revolutionary activity in Western Europe that we've had since 1945 or 1946. Are we not missing a great chance if we don't inspire the Italian Communist Party now to use its great popular strength and to seize power? Perhaps the French as well?" This is a very delicate situation.

Sevareid: But you don't mean that this necessarily makes an addition to Soviet power in the world?

Kennan: What is happening in Portugal does make a difference for Soviet power because it raises a very serious question for NATO. And I am rather surprised that the NATO countries have not already taken more account of this than they have. I think what's happening in Portugal is absolutely tragic. I don't think this is by nature a country destined or suited for a Communist dictatorship. But it may fall to its Communist party.

Sevareid: You said back in 1968 that you didn't understand talk about detente. Now, that's all we hear about.

Kennan: This whole question of detente is being rapidly undermined and made out of date by the developments that are now occurring in the world — by the energy crisis, by what's happening in Portugal, by what's happening in Indochina. We're entering a new era. I don't think the Russians are going to have the same interest in having detente with us as distinct with having it with the Western Europeans. I think we'll see them shift the burden of their talk about detente from the United States to Western Europe. In other words, they will say, "Well, what we want is detente with the West generally" but actually they will apply it to West Germany and France.

Sevareid: You see signs of that now?

Kennan: Yes, one sees already signs of it.

Sevareid: We now have a whole spate of so-called revisionist historians in this country. The premise of many of them is that the United States was really responsible for the Cold War. We started it and we perpetuated it. The Russians would have behaved very, very differently and things would be different today if it weren't for the Cold War. What do you think about this? What do you think the Russian aims were at the end of the war?

Kennan: I think they hoped, and very much wanted, to get us out of the Eurasian continent entirely so that they would have no Great Power opponent to themselves. This I felt we had to resist. It was a hope which they expected to implement, as I said before, through the Communist parties, not through further military attacks.

Sevareid: Of course, Western Europe was pretty flat, and we did take our troops back; it was a long time before we returned them to Europe. The Russians were reaching into the German Ruhr, in North Africa, and many other places.

Kennan: Yes, they were, and much of their behavior indicated to me a desire, first of all, to get us out; secondly, to get control of the German industrial district of the Ruhr; thirdly, to prevent the revival of a vigorous economic life and political confidence in Western Europe. It seemed to me that we had to combat all these things. We had at that time — and these young people who write the revisionist books forget about this — some terrible examples of what Communist rule could mean to a foreign people over which it was extended. Some of us had never forgotten what was done to the Poles in the fall of 1939 and 1940. Some 800 or 900 thousand people were evidently deported from eastern Poland after the Soviet troops came in under the most abominably cruel circumstances. I don't think half of these Poles were ever heard from again. These were not people who had taken any military action against Russia. They were eliminated solely on the basis of what was believed to be their social coloration. So I must say that some of us had a lively horror of what was going to happen in other areas of Europe if the Russians took them under their control.

Sevareid: Is there a vast difference between Stalin and his people and the present crowd in Moscow?

Kennan: I think there is a very great difference. What happened in Stalin's time was absolutely nightmarish. It was totalitarianism at its most hideous and horrible. After all, somewhere in the neighborhood of nine to eleven million people were probably executed or caused to die in one way or another, unnaturally, by this regime in the course of a few years. That is a terrible indictment of any regime.

Sevareid: You mean before World War II?

Kennan: Before, during, and after. Even during World War II the repression of the population was terrible.

Sevareid: That was one reason, wasn't it, for the apparent great bravery of Russian soldiers in the war? They didn't retreat.

Kennan: Yes. People have never understood the causes of the behavior of the Red Army. I don't say that they didn't fight for patriotism in many instances. Indeed, they did. But they were also under the most terrible sort of discipline. They were often put in impossible military situations where to remain and fight it out was almost surely to get killed. Yet to retreat was to be shot by their own people. To get taken prisoner was to be punished when they were finally repatriated. Their choices were almost impossible.

Sevareid: I think Stalin said to Harriman once that it took more courage for a Russian soldier to retreat than to advance.

Kennan: There's something to that.

Sevareid: We've had, I guess, two great movements in modern life — Christianity and Communism. I can't see that Christianity spread a lot of peace and love over the human race or that Communism has spread a lot of fraternity and equality. What is the grip of this notion? Even in prosperous Western free lands there are quite a number of youngsters who are utterly gripped by Marxist socialism in spite of all that Solzhenitsyn has written, in spite of the total obliteration of the human individual in China. How do you explain this?

Kennan: I can only explain it as a sublimated form of an aversion to modern Western society, to its materialism, to its lack of ideals, to its continued appeal to the acquisitive and selfish aims of people rather than to their capacity for self-sacrifice and devotion to public aims. I think all of us have let the youth down to some extent. This, really, rather than any understanding of Marxian doctrine, is what causes them to mouth Communist slogans.

Sevareid: How much hope should we put on the present dissident movements in the Soviet Union?

Kennan: I don't think much short-term hope, but I would put very serious long-term hope in them because they are filling a vacuum which the Soviet Government has never contrived to fill. A moment ago you mentioned Communism as one of the great movements which has moved mankind and Christianity as the other. Well, it's quite true that Christianity had its aggressive phases, the Church did, and created trouble as well as other things. But I remember Chip Bohlen saying to me, back in the 1930's, that in the end Communism is bound to fail as an ideological appeal to people because it has no answer to the phenomenon of death, and Christianity does. I think this is true. I think there is something in Marxism that causes a certain lack of appeal in the long run, that has to be filled with something else, and that is beginning to be filled with the strong, stern, moral sense of obligation that fills many of the dissidents and, outstandingly, Solzhenitsyn.

Sevareid: Well, the Bible said this long ago: You can't live by bread alone.

Kennan: Exactly. And the Marxist doctrine is a materialist doctrine. Now you may say, yes, but we just referred to the great popularity of this doctrine throughout large parts of the world. But such popularity doesn't exist among the people who have been subjected to it as a political regime. You'll find more Communists among American liberal youth or Norwegian liberal youth than you will, proportionately, among Communists in Eastern Europe and Russia.

Sevareid: You've had two famous careers — one as a diplomat and one as a scholar and writer of diplomacy and history. You're buried away now in the Smithsonian Institution writing about pre-World War I. I wonder why this period.

Kennan: Some years ago I wrote two volumes on the early period of Soviet-American relations. These first months of Soviet-American relations were also the last year of World War I. It was borne in on me, through writing those books, that World War I really caused a great many of the troubles of the remainder of the century. For one thing, it produced the Russian Revolution. The more I thought about this, the more I came to view World War I as the fundamental catastrophe of this century.

In England, in France and in Germany, during the twenty years that followed World War I, you saw the absence of the mature father's generation. Politics divided oldsters like Hindenburg and Petain and the young Nazis in the street. What was lacking was the mature generation of men who should have been in the prime of their life and in the fullness of their strength. They simply were not there.

Sevareid: You're saying that there was a kind of a break in continuity between generations which made Hitler more possible?

Kennan: Yes, indeed. Had those men — the two million men who were killed on the German side in World War I — had they been around as mature men during the thirties, I'm convinced the Nazis would never have been able to take over as they did.

Sevareid: They wouldn't have been so anxious to goosestep again.

Kennan: That's right. Europe did profound violence and damage to the fabric of its own life, even genetically and in the balance of generations, by the bloodshed of World War I. No issue which was at stake in that war could possibly have justified the hounding of eight million young men into rat-ridden, muddy trenches to be slaughtered off there by artillery fire. This was madness. There was nothing at stake in the war which could have justified their deaths in this way.

Sevareid: Mr. Kennan, you've had an immense amount of psychic remuneration in your life, a great deal of admiration and praise and awards of every kind, both for your diplomacy and your writing. There's also been a running criticism of your general stance about diplomacy in this century. You've been described as someone who really thinks diplomacy should be left to a kind of priestly cult, people think you're much too much of a perfectionist and a moralist. How do you see yourself in relation to those complaints?

Kennan: Well, there are a lot of different things embraced in what you've just said. As far as diplomacy being a priestly cult is concerned, I, in my turn, wonder about the evident conviction of political Washington that, although almost every other responsible profession requires professional training and experience, diplomacy should not. I don't know why it's necessary to have professional training and experience to be an attorney or a doctor or a number of other things, but it should not be required for diplomacy. I think there is great room for the professionals in diplomacy. I think they should have the overwhelming bulk of the jobs in this field. I do not feel that they should have exclusive control over it. I can see room for the talented nonprofessional. I can see why Presidents might want to be represented abroad at times by people who are close friends of theirs, provided that these people have the necessary educational and cultural level to represent the country credibly. But I hold a strong brief for professionalism in foreign affairs. And I think one of the troubles today with the State Department and the Foreign Service is that they have been administered for decades by people who had no knowledge or experience of the substance of their work.

Sevareid: But I think you once said that you feel most at home in the 18th century, an era of order and reason, a period of a hard-headedness in foreign policy.

Kennan: Well, that is true, but I am anything but an egalitarian. I am very much opposed to egalitarian tendencies of all sorts in governmental life and in other walks of life. Sometimes I've been charged with being an elitist. Well, of course, I am. What do people expect? God forbid that we should be without an elite. Is everything to be done by gray mediocrity? After all, our whole system is based on the selection of people for different functions in our life. When you talk about selection, you're talking about an elite.

Sevareid: There's another approach that lots of people want to take — you still hear about it — and that's the so-called "people to people" idea. President Eisenhower tried to organize this sort of thing with the notion that if all kinds of ordinary people crossed lots of borders and mixed with foreigners somehow we'd come to know each other better, somehow you'd have more peace and get along better.

Kennan: This is a very attractive and almost moving but naive idea. I don't think that this necessarily contributes to better understanding. I think that, ideally, it would be better if these contacts could be maintained by people who had some preparation for it.

Sevareid: What do you think of one-man diplomacy? It really began with Dulles. He was travelling everywhere. And then Rusk came in and said privately he was not going to do that, he was going to run things from Washington — and he travelled even more than Dulles. Now Kissinger's broken all records.

Kennan: Well, that's a very hard question. There are both pros and cons in the case of Henry Kissinger. He had two situations so unusual and so terrible that it really did require, I think, the personal self-insertion of a very high figure in our government to get anywhere. One of them was the liquidation, as we thought, of our involvement in Southeast Asia, and the other was the dangerous situation in the Middle East. I cannot bring myself to blame Kissinger seriously for involving himself in these two situations. I think he did it with extraordinary skill, fortitude, tact, and dedication; he deserves a lot of credit for this. But on principle, and except for very rare situations of this sort, I think the best thing the Secretary of State can do is sit right there in his chair and survey and direct the whole great spectrum of our foreign relations day by day, and let somebody else do the travelling. I don't think he should even go to all the NATO meetings and things like this that he's asked to go to.

Sevareid: What about the summit meetings? Apparently one is coming up before too long.

Kennan: I'm sorry if it goes against the grain of people in Washington but I do not approve of summit meetings, except for purposes of courtesy and to ratify agreements arrived at, and, even then, I think they have certain adverse effects which I don't like. The Pres-

ident is a man who sits in the thick of a welter of duties and responsibilities. He has to be at one and the same time a protocol head of
state, a prime minister, and a party leader. I don't think these three
offices should be combined in one man, but if they're going to be
then the man should not absent himself for days on end, occupying
himself with only one single question.

Sevareid: I'm thinking of something Adlai Stevenson said when
he was at the UN as Ambassador. He said that international diplomacy was one-third alcohol, one-third protocol and one-third Geritol.
He was exhausted with it.

You've been criticized occasionally as one who just cannot accept
the effect of domestic politics on foreign policy. I don't know any
way that you can completely separate these things.

Kennan: I don't so much criticize the effect in itself. But if a government (in this case our government) cannot refrain from conducting foreign policy for domestic political reasons, instead of with a
view to the general interests of the country at large, then it should
restrain itself in the ambitiousness of the policies it tries to implement.

Sevareid: Here we are a big power but acting on impulses that
are essentially parochial in many cases.

Kennan: Exactly. The impulses represent the interests only of
one portion of our population which can speak loudest or bring the
heaviest pressures to bear on Congress.

Sevareid: Are you thinking of things like Senator Jackson's amendment on the immigration of Jews from Russia as one of those things?

Kennan: I certainly do. I don't think there was any general American interest involved here at all and yet, we were asked to sacrifice,
and did sacrifice, a good deal to these impulses of Senator Jackson's.
We sacrificed the trade bill to them.

Sevareid: One of the handicaps we have, of course — at least
vis-a-vis the Russians — is that we can't do things secretly.

Kennan: Well, this too, is a very important subject. I'm very unhappy about the way the CIA has been treated in the press. Obviously,
mistakes were made, serious mistakes, but they were the affair of
a tiny proportion of the whole great apparatus of CIA. It seems to
me absolutely tragic. I have known many people in the agency. I
had to work with them when I was in government. The CIA has a
host of talented, well-informed and highly devoted government ser-
vants who have never done anything but the most legitimate sort of

work. For all of them to be tagged with the tag of sinisterism is senseless. It seems to me to be a little short of tragic.

Sevareid: How would you define the role of the CIA as you think it really ought to be?

Kennan: I think it should be primarily the scholarly study of the rest of the world and of what's happening in the world generally on the basis of legitimate sources. We discovered many years ago, those of us in the Russian field, that when we made a careful study of conditions in Russia in the way any other scholar would — on the basis of material that was available to us in legitimate ways, either in the press or through legitimate sources of observation — as a rule we knew much more than did the gumshoe agents who tried to find out things by secret operations. I think that remains true today.

But the fact of the matter is that all this can't stop just at our borders. We have, I believe, about a million, if not more, people in this country who are not even American citizens. A great many of them are here illegally. They entered clandestinely. Foreign governments operate among these people. We have every right to keep an eye on what foreign governments are doing in this country.

Sevareid: As to CIA operations abroad, do you really think we ought to be in the business of trying to knock over other governments?

Kennan: No. I must say that I favor the termination of secret political operations, as distinct from secret intelligence gathering abroad. I say this not because I think that there's never a place for it. I think there have been cases where we had a legitimate reason to want to do this, where it should have been done quietly and secretly. But I am against it because if you can't keep things like this secret you shouldn't do them at all. And if our system, as is evidently the case, is incapable of keeping these things secret over the long run then it better not get into this game at all.

Sevareid: Well, now we come back to the thing that has haunted this country for the last dozen years and torn us up badly — morally, economically, politically — and that's Vietnam. Since about the fall of 1965 I've been sure that Vietnam was a mistake. I think you were on record in the State Department pretty early as saying, "Don't get involved in it." Is that correct?

Kennan: That is correct. Of course, I was on record mostly through a whole day spent on television before the Senate Foreign Relations Committee.

Sevareid: What was your argument then?

Kennan: Well, I liked to quote the marvelous statement of John Quincy Adams given in an obscure Fourth of July speech. I fished it out, and it has since been used by many people: "America is the friend of the liberties of all the world. She is the guardian only of her own."

Severeid: What was the real reasoning — if there was coherent reasoning behind it — that this would be an extension of Chinese power and that they were expansionist and aggressive and a danger to us?

Kennan: I can only go back to the hypnotic power of the Cold War syndrome as it was — as it imposed itself on American political life at the time of the McCarthyism, at the time of the row over our policy toward China. Since that time, it seems to me, every American administration has been afraid of being accused of not having stood up to something which is described as "Communism." Well, in 1945, we knew what that was.

Today when someone says "Communism," I have to say, "What Communism?" because a host of things go under this name — Tito, the Chinese Communists, Castro, and all sorts of cliques and groups of people in other parts of the world. But people here are still hypnotized by this word, apparently hypnotized by the rather silly statement that America never lost a war and that it would be somehow intolerable. That's not really true. Who won and who lost in the War of 1812 or the Korean War? It's useless to put questions in such terms. Yet this can be done; it's a sort of a challenge in Washington. If you fling it at someone he reacts automatically.

Severeid: Suppose all of Indochina really is going to be in Communist hands. What's the danger to us there?

Kennan: Well, I can't see that there is any. This is a feeling I've had ever since the late forties and have stated since the late forties. For the time being, we won't have the same opportunities of sending businessmen and missionaries and all sorts of busybodies to this area. I don't think we're going to suffer very greatly from that. They're going to need trade, just as all other Communist countries do. We'll trade with them, eventually, to the extent that we want to. I think that we're greatly exaggerating the ills that would befall us.

Severeid: It never seemed to me that, whatever the ills might turn out to be, they had any relationship to the price we were paying for intervention.

Kennan: The price was appalling. It's rather like the retirement of the European colonial powers from their colonial possessions. They thought there was going to be a terrible loss of prestige but there wasn't.

It's my view that if today we were to take all our cards back into our hand and reduce our commitments to something resembling our ability to make good on those commitments, that our prestige in the world would only be heightened, rather than weakened. I think we couldn't lose anything at all by cutting a whole series of unsound commitments.

Sevareid: I heard Mr. Kissinger not long ago say in his anguish about Vietnam that peace is indivisible. This is a phrase the Russians began to use, as I remember, back in the Popular Front days or about the time they were getting scared of Hitler.

Kennan: It was Litvinov who used to say this.

Sevareid: I suppose it was true, more or less —

Kennan: No, I don't think it was true at all.

Sevareid: In Hitler's time?

Kennan: I don't think it's ever been true. It's a very terrible doctrine because it means that no conflicts can be isolated. Since human nature has been cantankerous and unreasonable from the beginning, there are always going to be conflicts between groups of people in this world. The only safety for humanity lies in the possibility of isolating the conflicts and preventing them from getting to be bigger ones. Therefore, anyone who says that peace is indivisible puts upon the international community the onus of solving every last minor scrap.

Sevareid: That's like saying freedom is indivisible. It always seemed to me that the two — peace and freedom — are very divisible. They will co-exist with war and tyranny, which they have during most of history.

Kennan: Of course.

Sevareid: Another thing about our policy since World War II, it seems to have been based on the premise that peace, material prosperity, and democracy were all not just good, each in itself, but interdependent, interlinked. But you have a totalitarian dictatorship like East Germany that's very prosperous. I don't see the connection, but that seems to be the theme.

Kennan: There is none. There is no connection at all. I am constantly amazed at the persistence of the view in this country that democracy is the natural state of mankind, and that there is something wrong, that we have been in some way remiss, if other countries don't have it.

I don't think this is true. I think that democracy is a form of government which has found its seat, you might say in a broad sense, among the countries or people who had their origins on the shores of the North Sea, and that it has never been very common elsewhere.

Sevareid: I know the Mideast has not been your specialty in your career but Russia has been. The two impinge very much. A lot of people now think we've been over our heads in the Mideast, that we cannot settle things without the Russians at some ultimate stage of the matter. Is there any chance of bringing the Russians in or do they just want the exacerbation of tensions?

Kennan: I think there would be a very good chance of talking with the Russians, and, at least, of preventing the Mideastern situation from developing into a world war. I think the Russians are very anxious to see something like that happen. But I must say that I find myself somewhat inhibited in speaking about our policy toward the Middle East. This is obviously a field of American policy in which we are not completely masters of ourselves. I think we have to first recover the full independence of our own policy. We have to make a certain declaration of independence from at least the lobbyists, the Zionist lobbyists, in this country before we can treat this question as it should be treated. Once we have declared that independence and once we act on behalf of the country as a whole and its interests, then I would like to see us show the greatest deference to the need for preserving the existence of the state of Israel and for preventing a second massacre of Jews in our own time.

Sevareid: Very recently, Daniel Patrick Moynihan wrote a rather electric article in *Commentary* about the so-called Third World countries, all the small countries but including the raw-material countries, saying, "Stop taking their abuse. Stop feeling guilty toward them. We really don't owe them very much, if anything. Stand up for America in these debates in the UN, UNESCO and the population and food conferences and so on." I think you said this a good twenty years ago.

Kennan: For some reason or other we have tried for twenty years to ingratiate ourselves with these people and to please them as though we were the supplicant party, as though we depended on them and not they on us. I think we really have to stop this now and let them come to their own assessment of how much we mean to them.

Sevareid: Sometimes I despair of ever pleasing any of them. We've been trying to please them for years and years, in Latin America or wherever. They accuse us of extracting their wealth, their raw materials, getting rich off them, impoverishing them in effect. And then, when we go back — as we're now doing through the multi-national corporations — and put our factories right in those countries and use their materials there and create employment and help educate and start small business and all the rest, then we're equally denounced for putting some kind of octopus over them and running their lives.

Kennan: Yes, there's a certain hysteria abroad among them today, a certain anti-American hysteria. In my opinion this won't be cured until we call their bluff and leave them alone.

Sevareid: You mean even foreign economic aid? Stop it?

Kennan: I certainly do. Most of it, I think, could be terminated, especially the arms aid. You know, what I would really like to see — it sounds extreme — but I would like to see a statement on the part of this government that, within a reasonable period (let's say five years), it would become our policy not to export any arms to anyone under any circumstances.

Sevareid: Whether the Soviets do it or not?

Kennan: Yes.

Sevareid: That doesn't add to their power particularly.

Kennan: These people are going to get the arms anyway, whether we send them or not.

Sevareid: You've been saying many things that add up to the notion that we mustn't let our reach exceed our grasp and we musn't be defensive toward everybody in the world. Is that what you mean by neo-isolationism?

Kennan: Yes, it is. I'm under no illusions that we could completely wall ourselves off from the rest of the world but I would like to see us make ourselves a great deal more independent when it comes to energy and other commodities vital to the success of our national life. I think we ought to have a period of withdrawal from a great many of our involvements if only to prove to other people that we're not trying to do something terrible to them. I don't think they'll believe it, I don't think they'll get over this complex of American imperialism, until we say to them: "Very well, we're willing to leave you entirely alone. We'll go home. You take your time. If you ever feel the time has come when you need the United States again, come and tell us. We'll think about it."

Conversation With
John McCloy

July 13, 1975

Sevareid: In 1962, at a post-and-rail fence in rural Connecticut, a Russian and an American quietly negotiated the operational finish of the Cuban missile crisis. They worked things out at the fence because the Soviet representative was afraid that the American's house was bugged. They devised a blueprint for winding down a dangerous nuclear confrontation of the atomic age. The Soviet agent was Kuznetsov. The American negotiator was John McCloy.

This man McCloy has played a key role in an astonishing number of the most important events of our time. The public knows little about him but when the history of this century is written he'll be singled out as one of its notable figures.

He has been an advisor to four Presidents—Franklin D. Roosevelt, Harry Truman, Dwight Eisenhower, and John F. Kennedy—and his friends have included men like Winston Churchill, Secretary of War Henry L. Stimson, and General George Patton.

In 1916 German agents in the U. S. blew up a New Jersey munitions factory in what became known as the "Black Tom" case. As a result of a complex lawsuit surrounding that explosion John McCloy entered the government service.

During World War II McCloy was involved in almost every major Washington decision. After serving as a top counterespionage consultant when it looked as if war with Germany was inevitable, Secretary of War Henry Stimson appointed him Assistant Secretary of the War Department. Getting the huge Pentagon building constructed was one of his many responsibilities. Like Secretary Stimson, he demurred at dropping the atomic bomb on Japan, but he participated in the agonizing decision that was reached.

In 1949 McCloy became the U. S. High Commissioner of Germany. The Germans give him much of the credit for the roots of democracy that have grown so well in that country in recent years. In 1962 he was the man who told the Russians exactly how to get their missiles out of Cuba.

John McCloy helped set up the Atlantic Alliance and he still pays a great deal of attention to world affairs. His principal concern has been the relationship between America and Europe. A colleague claims that he understands the power relationships between the two continents better than the leaders of government.

In private life McCloy is, above all, a lawyer. For a long time he has practiced law, and still does, as a partner in the Wall Street firm of Milbank, Tweed, Hadley and McCloy. He has been chairman of the Chase Manhattan Bank and he has headed up the World Bank. Currently he is chairman of the executive committee of the Squibb Corporation and a director of the Dreyfus Corporation, Mercedes Benz of North America, and the Stott Capital Development Corporation. He is a retired director of Allied Chemical, American Telephone and Telegraph, the Metropolitan Life Insurance Company, and the Westinghouse Electric Corporation.

McCloy has received honorary degrees from Amherst, Brown, Columbia, Dartmouth, Harvard, Princeton, Yale, Williams, and a dozen other universities.

In short, John McCloy is a breed that perhaps no longer exists in a world made up of specialists. At 80 he is a legendary figure who has refused to write his memoirs but he agreed to a long conversation we had a short time ago.

Sevareid: Why was the Pentagon nicknamed "McCloy's Folly?"

McCloy: Before it was constructed the War Department was scattered in about 19 or 20 different buildings. Obviously we had to bring them together. So General Somerville got hold of an architect who came up with the Pentagon idea. Like other big construction projects, it kept escalating and getting out of hand. Finally, Somerville asked me to get things under control and from then on it became known as "McCloy's Folly."

One of the problems I had at the beginning was getting the plans for the Pentagon off President Roosevelt's desk. Roosevelt, you know, fancied himself an architect. When we put the blueprints in front of him he loved playing with them and it became difficult to get them away from him. When I tried to remove them from his desk he'd rap me over the fingers and say "I have some other ideas."

At one point a Secret Service man told me the President wanted to get rid of his old classmate, Putzi Haefstengel. Putzi, you know, was the German court jester who became an English prisoner. Mr. Roosevelt got him brought over to the U. S. with the thought that he would get a lot of German secrets out of him but Roosevelt didn't do too well and soon tired of him. The Secret Service sensed this and wanted to get Haefstengel off the President's hands as well as off the White House budget. I sent back word I'd take care of Mr. Haefstengel if I could get those Pentagon blueprints okayed by FDR. And that's how we finally were able to get moving on construction. The next time I saw Roosevelt he muttered, "McCloy, you're a blackmailer."

Sevareid: There were amusing stories about the Pentagon. I like the one about the Western Union boy who got lost in the building and came out six months later a colonel in the Air Force. Incidentally, gossip has it that you really ran the place, the War Department, when you were Assistant Secretary under Stimson.

McCloy: That's not true. I was the leg man. I ran around town doing the errands. Some were pretty important errands, to be sure, but Stimson was the Secretary of War and I did things for him.

Sevareid: Was Stimson more the key to wartime operations than General George Marshall?

McCloy: I'd say that Marshall was more the key person on that. As soon as we got out of the purely procurement stage and into tactical and strategic matters, Marshall took over. He was a man of tremendous ability and character. He came closer to touching the mantle of greatness than anybody I've ever known.

Sevareid: I've heard that you were the man Stimson sent out to see General George Patton when it was necessary to get him out of trouble or, let's say, improve his character. Is that true?

McCloy: Well, I never tried to improve Patton's character. He was rather a favorite of Stimson's because he had been an aide when Stimson was Secretary of War back in 1911. When Patton got into difficulties Stimson said to me, "See if you can get things straightened out." During some Army maneuvers just before Pearl Harbor Patton created trouble by disregarding strict rules about the amount of gas his tanks could use. Patton was a man of some means and he wasn't going to be bothered with anything like that. He simply bought gas from gas stations. This enabled him to outflank and capture General Drum. There was a terrific roar about that. You weren't supposed to capture Drum. He was a genius on General Pershing's staff during World War I and had to be treated with lots of deference. Calming down General Drum wasn't easy. He insisted on all sorts of punishment for Patton but I managed to patch up things fairly well.

I think I was one of the few people who could address Patton by his first name. You know he was a pretty flashy and flamboyant fellow. "Why," I asked him once, "do you carry around pearl-handled pistols all the time?" He winced and responded, "Don't you know that only pimps and prostitutes have pearl-handled pistols? I'll have you know mine are ivory-handled!"

During the European wartime operations Patton had an elaborately equipped trailer that he used as an office. On his desk were all the great military classics—including Caesar's "Commentaries," Joplin's "Napoleon," some books by Clausewitz, and a Bible. I asked him why he kept so many books with him. "That's to impress the correspondents," he explained with a wink.

Sevareid: Was Patton slightly wacky or just impulsive?

McCloy: He was quite impulsive. He was very nervous, very explosive, very exacting — but he could also be very kindly and generous.

Sevareid: How did he manage to get his troops to the Rhine toward the end of the war?

McCloy: He was determined to reach the Rhine before General Montgomery and he did. He sent out word that officers of any of his tank columns that got to the Rhine should report to him immediately. A classmate of his who led one of the columns that managed to reach the Rhine early called out over a walkie-talkie: "General I want you to know that I've reached the Rhine." For a moment there was silence. "Which bank, you son of a bitch?" Patton shot back. I was with him then.

Sevareid: Weren't you with the troops who entered Germany when our men crossed the Rhine? How did you come to save the beautiful medieval city of Rothenburg from being blown up?

McCloy: That's a fairly interesting story. While I was with General Jacob Devers toward the end of the war, he told me he was going to put a barrage right through Rothenburg. I had never been there but I had heard a lot about it as a wonderful walled city. My mother was there some years ago and our Philadelphia home had an old etching of the Rothenburg gateway. I said, "Jake, do you have to destroy this town?" After I told him what I knew about Rothenburg, Jake said, "Well, I don't think we need to destroy it." Then he sat down and sent the commanding officer on the other side of town a message about its historical significance and told him to hold his fire. That's how Rothenburg came to be saved—by sheer chance.

Sevareid: You must be persona very grata to its people.

McCloy: Well, I was made an Ehrenburger of Rothenburg after the war was over.

Sevareid: It is true that you tried to persuade President Roosevelt to get off his anti-de Gaulle kick?

McCloy: My experience in this regard involved a very awkward episode. Mr. Roosevelt wasn't particularly partial to de Gaulle. We were about to attach ourselves to General Giraud. I told Stimson I thought this was a mistake. I said we ought to get behind de Gaulle in spite of the fact that he might be difficult. Stimson agreed with me and tried to convince the President, but Roosevelt wasn't very keen about the idea and that was that.

Several days later, when I was at a Cabinet meeting, Roosevelt said, "How fortunate we are to have Mr. McCloy here. He has some very definite ideas about the French situation and about getting ready for the invasion of North Africa. Let's hear from him." In the course of my comments I said pretty much what I had told Stimson in regard to de Gaulle. I thought I did fairly well but years later, when I was back practicing law in New York, Robert Sherwood called me up one day and said, "Jack, I have something here that I don't quite understand. It's a sheet which has at the top of it 'Cabinet Room' and it has Harry Hopkins' doodles all over it. Down at the bottom, just as clear as can be in Harry's handwriting, are these words: 'One more crack from McCloy to the boss about de Gaulle and McCloy leaves town.'" Apparently I didn't make a favorable impression.

Sevareid: There's been a lot of denigration of President Eisenhower by writers and historians who feel he really wasn't very bright. What's your estimation of him?

McCloy: I think history will upgrade Eisenhower's reputation. I've recently been reading his papers and I'm very much impressed by them. Some people haven't a high opinion of him because he wasn't a good extemporaneous speaker; his syntax wasn't the best and all that. Unfortunately it isn't generally known that he was eloquent on a yellow pad.

Sevareid: Are you sure of this?

McCloy: Oh, yes. I'll tell you why. When he became the Chief of War Plans after Pearl Harbor I was told to look over his shoulder so to speak. At about that time I had a little conspiracy with General Marshall to get into the field. He told me to get in touch with the War Plans Division and brush up on the logistics and all the stuff you have to know to be able to write suitable Army orders. "If you do that," he said, "I'll see that you get off. Besides, there's a new man coming into that setup that I'd like you to look over and tell me what you think of him. His name is Eisenhower." I did what Marshall told me to do and I became familiar with Eisenhower's abilities. He had a very real capacity for putting out clear-cut, definitive orders. He was no procrastinator. He was a man who drove himself to do his job well. Incidentally, that Guild Hall speech of his was a truly great address.

Sevareid: I remember that speech, I was very excited about it. John Gunther wrote glowingly about it. He said Ike wrote that speech himself and I believed it. But Ike's syntax at Presidential press conferences was awful. His words got all scrambled up. At one point Dean Acheson thought the New York Times should stop printing verbatim accounts of Eisenhower's news conferences because they made the President look silly. If you read the transcripts you can't figure out what he's talking about. But if you were at his sessions with the press, if you were in his presence and watched his face, you did know what he meant. Why couldn't he talk with greater lucidity?

McCloy: He had an incapacity in that regard but he could write and express himself very well on paper. Bear in mind the jobs he had, the strains he was under, the extraordinary exactions of our alliance ties. I don't know anyone else who could do what he did.

Sevareid: At least he kept us out of some foolish foreign adventures when he was President.

McCloy: He had a very firm feeling that we must not get involved on the Asian continent.

Sevareid: When Ike was MacArthur's aide in the Philippines before the war MacArthur didn't think much of him and was rather appalled when he realized Ike would be President. But the idea of MacArthur as President might have appalled a lot of people. Did you have to deal with him very much during World War II?

McCloy: I had a great deal to do with MacArthur on the surrender terms and the setting up of the situation in Japan after the war, but I didn't have anything like the contacts with him that I had with Marshall. MacArthur was an extraordinary figure and a romantic. He benefitted a lot by the experiences of his father, a great Civil War hero who won the Medal of Honor. MacArthur ran the occupation of Japan very well. I went out to see him several times in this connection. He was the new Mikado and the Japanese respected him. He ran his headquarters very strictly.

Sevareid: I remember an interesting remark General Marshall is said to have made. On one occasion MacArthur is supposed to have said to Marshall, "I want you to meet some of my staff." Marshall reportedly said, "General, you don't have a staff, you have a court."

McCloy: That's not altogether surprising. MacArthur felt his authority and position. He was like that all during his career. He was arrogant but he was a man of great ability and insight. Once he gave me a personal lecture on the future of the Far East that turned out to be prophetic.

Sevareid: I understand that he didn't really want to be on the mainland of Asia, as in the Korean war.

McCloy: I think he felt we shouldn't get involved there.

Sevareid: Was President Truman right in firing him?

McCloy: He probably was. MacArthur wasn't following Truman's policy closely enough. It took courage to fire him as Truman did.

Sevareid: What was your role in the decision to drop the atom bomb on Hiroshima? There's now all kinds of revisionist history about the matter. A new book by a young scholar says the chief aim was a Cold War purpose intended to impress the Russians. I didn't have that impression at all.

McCloy: That's nonsense, nonsense.

Sevareid: We couldn't think beyond the end of the war when the bomb was dropped. What was the primary factor in the Hiroshima decision?

McCloy: We had been working on the atomic bomb a long time. Everybody who knew anything about it wondered what it could do and what it couldn't do. Then there was the feeling that there was going to be a terrific casualty list before the war came to an end. This feeling had a lot to do with the tenacity with which the Japanese fought on the ground and the sacrifice made by the kamikaze pilots. A hecatomb of slaughter was a real possibility. Our hope was that the atomic bomb would bring the war to an end.

I regret the dropping of the bomb. I wasn't one of the determining figures but I knew all about the bomb and what its potentialities were. I had some views on it which I expressed very strongly to Mr. Stimson—not that we shouldn't use the bomb but about the conditions under which we should drop it.

There was a meeting of the Joint Chiefs of Staff in President Truman's office at which the key decisions were made. The big question was: Should our troops go ashore and attack Kiushu? That was preliminary to getting a landing on the main island, Honshu, and going across to Tokyo. Mr. Truman was very reluctant to go ashore and meet heavy casualties. He called on everyone present to speak up. "Can you," he said, "tell me whether I have any other alternative but to order this attack?" Except for one person, everyone pretty much agreed there was no alternative but to use the bomb.

When we started to pack up our papers to go out, Truman turned to me and said, "Nobody gets out of this room without committing himself. McCloy, you didn't commit yourself. What do you think?" Mr. Stimson told me to go ahead and tell the President what I thought. I said, "Now is the time to try to seek a political settlement. I would first disclose the bomb." Saying that was like mentioning "Skull and Bones" at Yale. Everybody was shook up. I said, "Well, I think it's best to let Japan know about the bomb before it is dropped." After fighting all the way across the Pacific we couldn't find another battleship to sink, we could hardly find another Japanese town for routine bombing. In view of the enormous military prestige we had built up we were in a position to tell the Japanese we wanted them to surrender. If they didn't surrender we'd use this terrible weapon. We should let the Japanese know what would happen if the bomb was dropped.

Sevareid: Do you think the Japanese would have believed us?

McCloy: Well, they might not have but in my judgment it was worth trying to talk to them. I didn't believe in dropping the bomb to convince them.

Sevareid: Don't you think it would have been fruitless to drop the bomb on an empty place—on an island or in the ocean—for demonstration purposes?

McCloy: Perhaps. I suppose the feeling was maybe the bomb wouldn't go off. After all, we had only two of them at that time and we couldn't very well waste them. It didn't seem advisable to do this. At any rate, one reason or another was adduced as an objection to the course of action I recommended. Besides it seemed a little gimmicky. I was strongly in favor of telling the Japanese just what we thought the bomb would do and that we had no alternative to using it if they didn't agree to our surrender terms. This is all sheer speculation but I believe we would have been better off if we had given them an opportunity to give up before the bomb went off. This might have won the day. I think, from the information we got after the war, that some of the Japanese militarists were at the end of their rope.

Sevareid: Unfortunately history doesn't disclose its alternatives. Weren't you at the Potsdam Conference at the time Truman told Stalin that we had the atomic bomb?

McCloy: Yes, I was. We were all exceedingly disappointed—confounded, in fact—because Stalin didn't show any reaction. "Well," he said, "isn't that interesting? That's fine. What's the next question?"

Sevareid: But surely the Russians were pretty well informed. Their spies were feeding them lots of information.

McCloy: Maybe that should have tipped us off but it didn't.

Sevareid: Didn't you have some dealings with Winston Churchill?

McCloy: I saw him on a number of occasions. The most interesting association I had with him was when I went to England in 1943 to see how our Army training was getting along. I had an appointment with P. J. Grigg, Secretary of State for War, late in the afternoon but on the way to his office I was waylaid and told fhe Prime Minister wanted to see me at 10 Downing Street. Churchill discussed many things with me. After I had gone through a great deal of questioning and started to leave, Churchill said, "I want to show you wartime London. I'll take care of Grigg. He'll wait for you."

First Churchill took me to a big bomb crater right near 10 Downing Street. Later we stopped at Green Park, where his daughter Mary was in charge of an anti-aircraft battery. As he walked about, attracting considerable attention as he did this, he told me, rather loudly, of the German buzz bomb attacks on London. Mary didn't want him coming around bothering her people and she was so mad at him she could have cut his throat. She practically chewed him up as she kept saying, "Get out of here! You're not doing us any good at all."

Late at night Churchill took me to Parliament. As we stood amid the rubble of the House of Commons he assured me that it would be rebuilt as it was before it was destroyed by Nazi bombs. He wanted it kept small because that would hold the rhetoric down and permit Members to confront their opponents. "I'm going to see to it," he said, "that there aren't enough seats for everybody. A crowded House has a dramatic effect during important debates."

When we went over to the House of Lords he sat in the Prime Minister's seat and I sat alongside him as he reminisced about his experiences in Parliament. As he talked I kept wondering: Why is he doing all this? Why is he keeping Grigg waiting? I think I understood when he added: "When I look about here I'm reminded that practically all of my contemporaries are dead. My generation was wiped out at Paaschendael and the Somme. Britain can't stand another such slaughter. I have to be very cautious about the invasion across the English Channel."

It finally dawned on me why he had spent so much time with me. You see, he had been urged to cross the Channel earlier but he kept putting it off because of his fear of the loss of another British generation. He was trying to get me to understand his motivation. "No one," he said, "can accuse me of not being a combative person. I'm as combative as anybody else but I've seen one British generation disappear and I want to be sure we don't lose another one."

Sevareid: Was it your aim to try to update the Channel crossing?

McCloy: That was what Roosevelt, Marshall, Eisenhower, and Stimson wanted above all else. But I wasn't there for that purpose. My job was to check up on the efficiency of the Army's training and see what was needed in the way of equipment. Churchill evidently worked on me because he had heard that I was pretty close to Secretary Stimson, the great proponent of early invasion.

Sevareid: Perhaps Churchill was also thinking about Soviet Russia and the post-war period. In any case, by the fall of 1944 we had practically a hundred divisions from the North Sea to Switzerland. I didn't understand why Eisenhower kept them there so long. The Germans were very badly weakened by then. I think the map of

Europe would probably be different today if the invasion had been launched earlier. Who was responsible for holding it up?

McCloy: I suppose it was Eisenhower as much as anybody. He was very much afraid of getting into some sort of confrontation with the Soviet forces. He kept Patton and Montgomery back. He didn't want to rush to Berlin. Anyhow it may not have been practical but he was terribly sensitive about what would happen when we met up with the Russians. I think Roosevelt was rather tentative about the invasion. He was also worried about confrontation with Russia.

Sevareid: There's one other controversial wartime matter that I wanted to ask you about—the evacuation of the Japanese-Americans from the West Coast into inland camps. Almost everybody has come to regret this being done. I think Earl Warren, who was Governor of California at the time, has regretted it. Some people known as liberals had something to do with it. Weren't you involved in this evacuation? Why did we treat the Japanese-American this way?

McCloy: Let me try to give you a picture of the situation. In the first place, the Japanese had just attacked Pearl Harbor. The shock that created was a shock very few people now realize. The Yellow Menace concept pretty well pervaded thinking on the West Coast in 1941. After Pearl Harbor there were immediate appeals from the commanding general in California, General DeWitt, as well as from Governor Warren. We didn't know, of course, whether the Japanese were or weren't going to attack the West Coast.. There was an hysterical situation. Barn burnings were taking place in the valley where the Japanese lived. Things were getting out of hand and we had to protect a lot of Japanese people. At any rate, President Roosevelt was in favor of their evacuation.

Sevareid: Couldn't normal police methods be used?

McCloy: I suppose they could but we didn't know if we could control the situation in California if matters got much worse. The evacuation decision was a civilian decision. It wasn't an Army decision. But only the Army knew how to move large numbers of people. As Assistant Secretary of War I spent a lot of time on this problem. I think that what we did was rather benign in the way we carried out our responsibilities.

It's true that the Japanese-Americans were kicked out overnight. They weren't adequately compensated for all the property they had to abandon. The passion of the moment after Pearl Harbor produced the exodus from California.

Sevareid: Wasn't there a move to take all the Japanese out of Hawaii and ship them off?

McCloy: I objected to that. I didn't think it was necessary. You know, many Japanese-Americans constituted the 442nd Combat Team that fought valorously in Italy. The Nisei of that unit won a great many Medals of Honor and sustained heavy casualties. It was a great unit. I helped set it up although there was a good deal of opposition to getting it authorized. The record of that fighting unit resulted in a much better attitude towards Japanese-Americans.

Sevareid: After Germany lay in ruins at the end of World War II the wreckage of the nation was ruled by the military men of its four conquerors. Within the United States a great debate took place. There were some in high places who felt that Germany should not be allowed heavy industry, that it should be kept a minor agricultural nation. But as the West and the East got into the Cold War each side began to build up its power in its part of Germany. President Truman and Secretary of State Dean Acheson sent McCloy to West Germany as High Commissioner. His mission was to plant the seeds of a democratic Germany in a land that had been ruled by Nazis and was threatened by Communism. He did his job well. He helped bring about the rebirth of German industry and the awakening of German democracy. This may have been his greatest success.

Mr. McCloy you've been called the "Godfather of German democracy" because of your efforts as the U. S. High Commissioner during the difficult postwar reconstruction years.

McCloy: I got to know a good bit about Germany during the First World War. Subsequently I became deeply involved in litigation with the German government over the Black Tom case. Indeed, that's how I got into government service. Because of my role in that litigation I learned a great deal about German espionage and that sort of thing and Secretary of War Stimson asked me to appraise the intelligence operations of his department.

I think the "Godfather of Germany" description you've used belongs to General Lucius Clay. He preceded me as military Governor and he did a superb job in shaping our German policy. He was responsible for a great many things, including the Berlin air lift. I can claim some credit for his appointment.

One day I got a call to come to the White House. As I entered the room in which President Roosevelt was sitting he held up his hand in a Hitler salute and said, "Heil, Commisar for Deutschland."

He explained that he was going to make me the first High Commissioner in Germany. I told him that I didn't think it was wise to have a civilian at that early stage of occupation, that it would be better to have a military governor, and that General Clay would be suitable for the job. "Who is Clay?" he asked somewhat testily. I reminded him that Clay was General Somerville's right-hand man. Since Roosevelt ought to have known this I had a feeling he didn't quite have full possession of his faculties. He sort of sank down and said, "Oh, I'm too tired to argue with you. Go down and talk to Jimmy Burns." Roosevelt had already had one of his strokes but I didn't know this at the time.

Several years later President Truman made me the High Commissioner for Germany. He didn't know that Roosevelt had wanted me to be the governor.

Sevareid: President Ford is sometimes compared with Harry Truman, at least in regard to some secondary characteristics. What do you think was Truman's prime virtue?

McCloy: His forthrightness. He was never deceptive. You always knew where you stood with him. You could readily understand his thinking. He was always clear-cut. And there was a certain pragmatic approach he took toward problems.

While I was serving as High Commissioner I came back to Washington to discuss some important questions with the State Department. I knew Secretary Acheson pretty well. Several times he said to me, "I'll tell you what my views are but you've got to talk to the President. He's very much interested in these matters." When I saw Truman and told him what I had in mind, I could see he was a little impatient. Once he said to me, "McCloy, I sent you over to Germany to run that country. As long as I think you're doing all right you've got my full support. If I think you're doing wrong you'll hear from me. Now go ahead and do your business and don't bother me with details."

Sevareid: Truman didn't have much formal education but he read a lot of history. So did Roosevelt. Justice Oliver Wendell Holmes said about him that he had a second-rate intellect but a first-rate temperament and what the country needed was that first-rate temperament. Do you think Roosevelt had a second-rate mind?

McCloy: I don't. He had a very agile, very quick mind. He was sometimes less than completely consistent, sometimes a little superficial and not as penetrating as you expected a President to be but he had a first-rate mind.

Sevareid: I remember those great speeches Roosevelt made. They electrified us. Is it true that he couldn't write a speech himself?

McCloy: It's interesting to contrast him with Churchill. There's no question that Rosevelt will go down as a great orator but he could no more compose a speech from beginning to end than someone utterly ill-equipped. "I'm going to write this speech myself," he would say but what he wrote didn't hang together. And so Sam Rosenman had to take over, sometimes with Robert Sherwood's help. Sam had a good mind and he knew where the facts stopped and imagination began. He could make a speech march. When an important Roosevelt speech was being planned I participated in some White House meetings, offering input about how the war was going. Sam would say to us, "Well, there comes a time when some s.o.b. has to write the speech. Now, get out!"

Churchill once told me how he composed his speeches, what effort this involved, how he stood in front of mirrors trying out little tricks of the trade. If he began to have a lapse while delivering a speech he would hold his notes up in the air and wave as if he was making a gesture. Actually he was reading his notes. He told me he could never make a good speech when he was over-confident. "Unless," he said, "I'm nervous about it, unless I go through painful effort, the result is always pedestrian."

Oratory and eloquence play a tremendous role in leadership.

July 20, 1975

Sevareid: What has happened to American leadership?

McCloy: I'll tell you an interesting story in this connection. Once I asked Henry Stimson, "Who's the greatest President you ever served under?" After hesitating a while he said:

"I can tell you who was by all odds the most efficient President I've ever known—William Howard Taft. He knew a great deal about the business of government and he was most exacting as chief executive. His cabinet meetings were models compared to some Donnybrook affairs I've seen. But I wouldn't call him the greatest President.

"If I were pressed to say who was the greatest President I would say his name was Roosevelt but I'd have to give some thought as to whether it was FDR or TR.

"After serving as President, Theodore Roosevelt came to the conclusion that his hand-picked successor, Taft, wasn't doing too well and TR evidently wanted the job back. Roosevelt proceeded to tear into Taft in an almost vicious manner. "During a visit to Sagamore Hill, Stimson recalls, he felt impelled to state, 'Theodore, you can't do that to Bill. He's a good friend and a good man.' After hearing me out, TR shook his fist under my nose and said. 'The trouble with Will, and you know it as well as I do, is that he doesn't enjoy power' " Then Stimson in his quiet way said to me, 'This isn't an attribute either of the Roosevelts lacked."

There is something in that point about the enjoyment of power. Caesar, Louis XIV, and some others had it. Lincoln had it to some degree. Churchill certainly had it. But it takes more than that for the leadership the world needs today.

Sevareid: Did you have some dealings with Khrushchev when he was the boss in Russia and you were the American High Commissioner in Germany?

McCloy: My dealings with Khrushchev took place in connection with disarmament and arms control when I served as chairman of an advisory commission to which President Kennedy appointed me.

Khrushchev was a pretty rugged and lusty type. He was an extrovert. He was very courteous as a host but he was threatening. He was always telling us about his missiles and what he could do to us. Sometimes he'd move from threats to a friendly manner but not often.

Sevareid: What were you trying to do when you saw Khrushchev?

McCloy: We were working on an agreement for the restriction of arms and limitations on nuclear weapons. That was the main objective but we talked a lot about other things.

Sevareid: I think you dealt with Kuznetsov in your living room at the time of the Cuban missile crisis.

McCloy: Kuznetsov was my opposite number in connection with that crisis. I had some sessions with him after President Kennedy decided to embargo the Russian ships headed for Cuba. I was in Europe when President Kennedy asked me to come back to see him about the situation. During our talk he asked me to go up to the United Nations and show the evidence proving that Russian missile bases were in Cuba.

Sevareid: Did you feel we were close to nuclear war?

McCloy: Oh, yes. Secretary of State Rusk said we were "eyeball to eyeball." I sensed the danger of the situation. Anything could have happened. It was amazing how threatening things looked.

Sevareid: Is it true that you favored invasion of Cuba? Dean Acheson apparently did.

McCloy: I don't think I was for an invasion. I can't recall that. I was very, very clear in my own mind that we had to do something about those Russian missiles, because otherwise our whole nuclear deterrent was gone and our commitment to protect Europe wouldn't mean a thing. We had to move decisively in some way. How to get the missiles taken out was, of course, the main problem.

Mr. Khrushchev sent over Mr. Kuznetsov, who spoke English very well. He was educated in the United States and had graduated from Lehigh. We jointly decided what was needed. In effect he said: "Exactly, what do you want?" I told him. Our destroyers were to be permitted to come alongside the Russian ships close enough to see and demand removal of the tarpaulins covering the missiles so that we could see that they were genuine missiles. The boats were to go back to Russia with those weapons.

Kuznetsov sat in my home for a while and we talked about the situation. He was a little nervous, I think, because he asked me to walk outside. I think he thought the house was bugged. At any rate, we went out and sat on the fence and we worked things out. I must say his word was as good as his bond.

Our demands were humiliating for the Russians but we had such tremendous strength, conventional and nuclear, that they really had no choice. They took the missiles away in meticulous compliance with the deal I made with Kuznetsov. When we got off the fence and shook hands on the deal, he said, "Mr. McCloy, we'll never be in this situation again."

Sevareid: You've been called the most influential private citizen in America, the chairman of the Establishment. What do you think of such identification?

McCloy: When someone calls me the chairman of the Establishment I feel like climbing the wall. I was born in very modest circumstances and had to be very competitive. I think of Establishment as something like being born into a peerage or into a high place in government. I got into government by sheer accident. Nothing was ordained about it.

Sevareid: I think the special use of "establishment" was coined by Henry Fairlie, a British journalist. He didn't necessarily mean people in the British government, in universities, in finance, etc. That's what's meant here in the U. S.

McCloy: I always thought of the British establishment as quite different from the American. In Britain the second son went into the Navy, the first son went into the Army. That sort of thing is rather stratified in England; there's nothing like that here. If there is an American establishment maybe it's establishment in business, more so than in government.

Now, of course, I did have some important jobs in the legal profession, in business, in banking. I suppose somebody thought that because I was chairman of this or chairman of that I could be called chairman of the Establishment but it always drives me mad when I hear this sort of thing.

Sevareid: For many years your law firm and the banks you were associated with were active in the field of oil petrochemicals. As you know, the oil companies—American, English, Dutch—have had an extraordinary role in the Middle East. Ought we have some centralized purchasing or bargaining government agency on oil?

McCloy: I don't think I should be discussing that. There was a long period when the oil companies were responsible for the flow of oil from the Middle East. They found the oil, made a big investment in it. The U. S., the European countries, the South American nations, and others have been enjoying this flow of so-called cheap oil. Kissinger said it was "too cheap." While the oil companies were in control of the situation we had no problems of shortage, no problems of price. Now, all of a sudden, due to a very large degree to new developments in the Middle East, oil has become a political weapon and we're paying far more for it now than we should.

Sevareid: Oil companies are not generally popular with some people, the press, or many Congressmen. A feeling exists that out of the crisis that's made everybody else suffer they have profited in an unnatural way and that this is inequitable.

McCloy: The big earnings came as a result of the quadruplication or quintupling of profits. I think you'll begin to see the profits coming down soon.

Inventory earnings are going to be much reduced. I may be wrong but I'm inclined to think that there's going to be much more moderate profits. The thought that there was a great conspiracy on the part of the oil companies and the Arabs to attain high profits is just so much nonsense in my judgment. When the companies had control of the situation they supplied oil to a large portion of the West. The world was largely rehabilitated by that cheap oil and that cheap energy we've enjoyed for such a long time.

Faisal said: "If you don't change your policy, I'm going to put an embargo on."—and he did. That wasn't because he was in a conspiracy with oil companies dealing with him on friendly terms.

I'll say this about the energy problem I don't think we're over it. We're now in another sort of euphoric period. There's no more shortage of oil than there is a so-called glut of oil. In the long run we do have a serious energy problem. We've got to cope with it. If we're going to be independent we've got to get moving. We haven't done much so far.

Sevareid: Are you thinking about sources other than oil?

McCloy: Yes. Alternate sources of development of our own oil resources with stimulus.

Sevareid: I keep reading about the necessity for higher profits to stimulate more oil exploration. I know that offshore drilling is exceedingly expensive but thousands of new wells have been drilled all over the South and Southwest of this country. Apparently not very much new oil has been found. Are prices going to go up?

McCloy: I'd much prefer not to be discussing this. Why control gas and oil prices at all? Why don't we let the companies find their price level with other products? We have been subsidizing them in the sense that we subsidize through depletion allowances and other benefits. But they have to take a great risk when they explore. I'd rather have an oil economist go into this. I'm just a lawyer. I don't know about such things.

Sevareid: I'm certainly not an oil economist but I've heard all the talk about why big profits are needed to plow back into new drilling. How do you explain a company like Mobil spending $800 million for a totally unrelated business like MARCOR?

McCloy: I can only refer to Mobil's explanation. They say that because of the regulations now being imposed so broadly against them they ought to get into some unregulated industry in order to diversify for the benefit of their shareholders.

Sevareid: That's not getting new energy for people.

McCloy: Maybe you had better ask the Mobil people about this.

Sevareid: Well, I know you represent a lot of big oil companies.

McCloy: You need money to take big risks. The chances are

that when you drill a well you're going to get a dry hole. Taking all the stimulus away while keeping controls is shortsighted.

Sevareid: Were you responsible for the law that allows American oil companies in the Middle East to charge off against U. S. taxes the royalties they pay foreign governments?

McCloy: I don't know that I ought to discuss this. The so-called foreign tax credit is a tax credit enjoyed by all companies dealing abroad. It's a matter of semantics whether you're referring to a tax or a royalty. Our government was probably a little involved in suggesting that the companies call it a tax rather than a royalty. If this is suddenly changed a very important obstacle will be placed in the path of the companies now earning smaller profits.

I guess I sound like an apologist for the oil companies and that's the last thing I want to be. I want to keep out of the oil economy. But when you look at the overall return the oil companies get on their investment, it's somewhere around the middle of what most industrial firms get on their normal investments. The huge profits are something of a myth.

Sevareid: I can't get over certain things. We're thinking in terms of democratic equity and the people's sense of justice, about who pays what, and so forth. Some oil companies, you know, pay virtually no corporate income tax and there are extremely rich oil executives who pay almost no personal income tax. This riles the American people. Aren't depletion and the other tax gimmicks wrong?

McCloy: I don't know about the taxes oil company executives pay. Do you?

Sevareid: I know of some who pay very little.

McCloy: I don't know how they get away with it, they don't tell me. They have to pay their taxes the same as I do. They go into oil ventures where, until now, they have the advantage of depletion allowances. That's something you and I don't have. Generally speaking, I think that if you added up the total of their taxes you'd find it was much greater than you imagine.

Sevareid: I would be pleased to find it but I don't believe it.

McCloy: Get an expert to talk about that. It's not for me to discuss.

Sevareid: Do you think the Atlantic Alliance is still the keystone to the whole approach to Russia? I have the feeling Europeans worry less about the Soviet threat in Europe than we do.

McCloy: The Atlantic Alliance probably isn't now what it was when, so to speak, the hordes were at the gates, when there were

real dangers, when they were pressing us on Berlin. I don't know
that the Russians have become entirely benign. I don't see that
they've changed a great deal. This doesn't mean that we're on the
verge of a war or that we have to be threatening them all the time
but I'm inclined to think that the Atlantic Alliance gives us stability
which we otherwise wouldn't have. There's some looseness, of
course, with the French moving out of military aspects of NATO.

The British are equivocating on their commitment somewhat.
Besides, we have constant demands for the withdrawal of our troops
from Germany.

Sevareid: Much of the breaking away seems to be due to internal
political and social reasons at least in regard to Portugal, Greece,
and Turkey. Italy's economic situation is almost a basket case.
So what good is the strength of an alliance? We have more power
in the Mediterranean world than the Russians and yet things are
going wrong. We can't land troops. We can't fight. What can we do?

McCloy: We can deter anyone from breaking out or breaking in.
In my judgment the Russians aren't going to start anything that's
aggressive even though they may be tempted to do so. They realize
that from the minute they start something they'll have the United
States to contend with. Our European commitment is still pretty
clear. Without it I don't know what would occur.

Sevareid: What's your feeling about the contention of some
scholars that the Cold War was American in origin, that the Russians were very peaceful-minded, that we've kept hostility going? At
the end of the war you said, I think, that the Russians undoubtedly
wanted to take over Western Europe.

McCloy: Khrushchev told me that in just so many words when I
visited him at Putzinde. Our distress, he said, doesn't come from
Middle Europe. It comes from Western Europe. We can't be happy,
we can't be content, as long as we don't have as much political
influence over the Western Europe as we have over the Balkan area.

Sevareid: What's the nature of the threat from Russia? What do
you think its maximum aim is? Dominance in the Mediterranean
world? Dominance in the Mideast?

McCloy: I don't know what the Russian intent is. I don't see any
substantial change. I see no abandonment of the Brezhnev doctrine.
I'm not intransigent about this but I have a feeling that we have to
keep our strength up. As time goes on and as people change, I believe we'll be able to work things out.

Sevareid: I think you once said that the satellite countries of East Europe would be free one day.

McCloy: I was very hopeful about this. It's less and less likely now because the Brezhnev doctrine is locked in with interests that have become crystallized and stabilized over the years. What we now have is a sort of a ratchet kind of process—what's mine is mine and what's yours is negotiable. We must not let any back-sliding take place in our relations with Russia.

Sevareid: In recent years you've been chairman of the U. S. Advisory Commission on Disarmament. You were in it pretty deep. Today the world is spending more money, five times as much, for arms in constant dollars than before World War II. The Vladivostok agreement with the Russians on nuclear weapons seems to seek an upward balance. Why can't there be parity or downward balance?

McCloy: That's a desideratum. That's what we've been trying to shoot for. We haven't accomplished much so far because the Soviets have had the feeling that they were militarily inferior and that they had to build up their strength. I can see nothing now but an accentuation of the armament business. We're selling and the Russians are selling arms of the most sophisticated type all over the world. They seem to be concentrating, to a very large degree, in the dangerous Middle East area. To deal with that is one of the great imperatives of statesmanship today. It's not only nuclear weapons that we've got to do something about. The conventional weaponry situation is out of balance in my judgment. The mass of conventional armament is now preponderantly on the Russian side. This isn't conducive to the stability that's needed.

Sevareid: We can't very well arm the European nations any further than they want to be armed.

McCloy: That's perfectly true.

Sevareid: We're now the greatest arms salesmen in the world. We're in that role everywhere—particularly in the Persian Gulf area and over in the Middle East. What's the end result going to be? Certainly not security and peace.

McCloy: I don't believe anyone can say that the outlook is re-assuring. We simply have to try to bring about a balance in a situation as tense as that in the Middle East.

Sevareid: Do you think it's really possible to get anywhere if we and Russia don't act together to impose a peace in the Middle East?

McCloy: I don't care for that use of the word "impose." It sounds pretty rough. We can't disregard Russia's ambitions in the Middle East and the Mediterranean or the strength they have there. If there's any major strategic area in the world it's the Middle East. It's the axis between the North and the South, the East and the West.

Sevareid: Whenever we Americans get away from the Western world and the Western tradition and Europe and get into totally alien parts of the world, into alien cultures like those of Asia and the Arab world, we seem to get in over our heads.

McCloy: Asia is a great amorphous mass. Maybe some experts know all the forces that play around Asia; I don't. I've always felt (and I've agreed with Eisenhower in this regard) that we musn't get involved on the Asian continent. We don't know enough about it. It's an absorbent area, we're completely unacquainted with it.

Sevareid: Well, we have a so-called detente with Russia and we're opening up relations with China. Why can't we live with a Communist Indochina? I never could see how our security was vitally involved there.

McCloy: My premise is that our security isn't involved in the Asiatic continent. That's why I've said, "Let's keep out!"

Sevareid: Didn't President Johnson once want you to be ambassador to South Vietnam?

McCloy: He wanted me to go out there after the first Lodge period and he put a great deal of pressure on me to do so. But I told him that I don't know the area and that I've spent enough time in government service. At any rate, I didn't go.

Sevareid: There's something else in your past that's pretty important—the Kennedy assassination investigation. You and President Ford are the only two members of the Warren Commission still alive. A new book says electronic scanning of Oswald's words proves that he didn't shoot Kennedy. What do you make of this? I used to talk to Justice Earl Warren a good deal during the Commission's hearings. He had me quite convinced that the Commission did everything reasonably possible to come to its verdict. Do you think anything important was left out of the Warren report?

McCloy: I don't know about the propriety of my commenting on something that was before me as a sort of a judge. I think that Justice Warren would say this is something I ought not to discuss.

Sevareid: Why not? It's been over a long time.

McCloy: I never saw a case that I thought was more completely proven than the assassination. I don't have any doubts about it.

There was a tremendous amount of charlatanry afterward. A lot of nonsense was written about the report. We worked hard on it, very hard. I joined the Commission as a Doubting Thomas but by the time the investigation was over I felt we had an open-and-shut case. Now, how do you prove a negative if somebody brings another piece of evidence to me? How can I prove that Oswald never had any contact with anybody?

Sevareid: The critics seem to be saying that there are things you might have looked into, people you should have interviewed but no positive evidence is brought forward.

McCloy: I have never heard of any.

Sevareid: President Johnson said that he was inclined to believe there was some conspiracy involved in the assassination.

McCloy: When I joined the Warren Commission I thought there must have been a conspiracy because the fellow who killed Kennedy was shot a couple of days later. It was a strange thing but I couldn't find any connection and I don't think anybody else could. The direct evidence as to who carried the rifle that killed Kennedy, where the bullet came from, and all that was so overpowering that I didn't have any doubts when the investigation was completed.

Sevareid: You write extremely well. How did you come to acquire this skill?

McCloy: Being a lawyer trains you to write. A lawyer has to put down on a piece of paper things that other people can understand. I'm a laborious writer. I never can get a good draft until the twelfth or the thirteenth version.

Sevareid: You're a much better writer than most lawyers and I've read a lot of their copy. You're somewhat like Dean Acheson. He was a lawyer and a government man but he wrote with a certain style and a sweep. So do you. How were you educated?

McCloy: Acheson was brought up in a very intellectual atmosphere; high quality intellects were all around him. That had a good deal to do with his way with words. My father was a rather remarkable man. He had no high education at all. He was a dropout from the Philadelphia public school system but he taught himself Latin. He helped a friend of his translate obscure Latin poetry but he always regretted that he didn't know Greek. He was practically on his death bed when he told my mother, "Have John study Greek." I studied Greek—four years in prep school, four years in college. It got so I really understood the surge and thunder of the

Odyssey. I think this had something to do with my writing ability.

Sevareid: Is it true that you still read poetry in Greek?

McCloy: No. I can recite it but I can't really read it any longer. When I go to Athens, though, I read the newspapers.

Sevareid: It's a shame, I suppose, that languages like Greek and Latin have gone out of the schools.

McCloy: It's too bad. Learning Greek was fortunate for me. I was able to win the Greek prize because I had little competition.

Sevareid: Dean Acheson didn't, of course, write true memoirs. He wrote about peripheral things in his books. For forty years you've been in on some of the highest policy problems of recent Presidents. Are you ever going to write your memoirs?

McCloy: Many people have asked me that. So far I've been too busy. Acheson warned me, "Don't ever think of writing a book unless you can take three years off." I couldn't do that. I've never had the urge to write memoirs. It doesn't mean much to me to reminisce. If I could distill out of my experience some really important principles I'd take the time out and go to work on them. But such principles are rather elusive. They're hard to identify, hard to crystallize. Another factor is that I've read many memoirs by my colleagues that aren't very objective.

Sevareid: Washington is full of lawyers, maybe too many, these days. They have a bad name because of Watergate. Lawyer after lawyer has been caught up in crimes and misdemeanors. These are men who were taught respect for the law. How do you explain this?

McCloy: I think the legal profession is a little stunned at some of the revelations that have come out involving lawyers. I think there has been a lessening of tone. I don't want to be croaking like Cato, "In my day I think there was more integrity," but I can't imagine such intrigues occurring in Washington in my time.

Sevareid: What went wrong with their education, their training?

McCloy: I think some attained power too soon. If you get down to Washington when you're young those flags they put behind your desk are apt to make you swell-headed and give you illusions or delusions. Unfortunately the public now has a sense of distrust that's quite paralyzing. People seem to be ready to believe the worst about practically everybody who comes along.

Sevareid: Someone has said that John McCloy, a man with a tremendous reputation for impartiality and fairness, probably couldn't get confirmed today for a top post because he has represented oil companies. Is that a fair statement?

McCloy: I imagine some folks would take a shot at me. What you say reminds me of a thought I had the other day. The feeling is that somehow President Ford and Vice President Rockefeller, because they weren't elected, are considered a little less meritorious than people who have been elected. The Congress in effect says: "We've been elected. We're in the saddle and can run things as we see fit." When Congress was in the saddle during the Reconstruction period after the Civil War there was lots of trouble and it was difficult to get anything done. The government was hamstrung a good deal of the time. I don't want to see that happen again. I don't think Congress should usurp the functions of the President.

Sevareid: But isn't that at least partly because executive power has been abused a good deal?

McCloy: It was for a long time and not only during the Nixon administration. It also happened during other administrations, probably as a result of the war. President Roosevelt certainly wasn't beyond using all the power he could get. But there is a nice balance which I hope we can arrive at. We musn't let things get imbalanced on the executive or legislative side.

Sevareid: Doesn't a lot depend on the particular man who happens to be in the White House?

McCloy: Of course it does. It also makes a great deal of difference who's in the Senate and who's in the House. Unfortunately, there seems to be a dearth of leadership in Washington these days.

It's extremely important that the Congress exert leadership. During the 1950's Senator Arthur Vandenberg brought a nonpartisan statesman-like approach to foreign policy problems. I don't see that kind of man around now.

Sevareid: You're thinking back to that exciting period after the war when people like you and Acheson and Lovett were part of the government. There was expansion of American power then. Now there's a contraction and people disagree because of this. It's pretty hard to do much about this when there isn't the kind of power that existed during the 1950's.

McCloy: That's true, but the demands, the exigencies, are as great in this period of retraction as they were in the years of expansion. It's just as important to develop statesmanship today as it was then. The problems are different, to be sure, but they can't be solved with the sort of cynicism that's growing. Remember the last paragraph in Henry Stimson's book "On Active Service"? He says there that he expects the younger ones to do their job better than we did but he warns against the deadly sin of cynicism.

Sevareid: I think Stimson once said that if you want to make a man trustworthy you must give him trust. He certainly trusted you a lot. I've read a great deal about your career. I've talked to many people who've worked with you at various stages of your life but I've yet to hear a derogatory opinion of you. Have you made no enemies, no mistakes?

McCloy: I've made plenty of mistakes but I don't like to dwell on them. I've been wrong often enough.

Sevareid: You don't seem to have any enemies.

McCloy: Well, I don't know of any. But I haven't been in a position of real prominence. I haven't been a President or a Vice President or a Senator.

Sevareid: You've been a Republican, a nominal one, all your life. Yet you've served chiefly under Democratic Presidents. One of your friends says you aren't boxed in by ideology, that your approach to everything is: What are the facts? What's best for the country?

McCloy: I think I have some ideology but I don't let it interfere with the facts. I like to think of myself as being constructive, being helpful to the country. I consider myself liberal-minded, objective-minded. I suppose that's my ideology.

Conversation With Robert Hutchins

August 31, 1975

Sevareid: There are two Chicagoans of the 1930's who have an undisputed place in American history. One was Al Capone the gangster and the other is Robert Maynard Hutchins, then the President of the University of Chicago.

Dr. Hutchins could have been, according to reliable sources, a Supreme Court Justice. He might have made a run for the Senate and been elected from California. President Franklin Roosevelt offered him the job of Chairman of the Securities and Exchange Commission. (He didn't consider the post for a moment.)

He was Dean of the Yale Law School at 29 and President of the University of Chicago at 30. At the present time he is President of the Center for the Study of Democratic Institutions.

Dr. Hutchins' training was as a lawyer. By natural extension, law leads to government. So he's an expert, by training and experience, on the relationship between law, government, and education. To him the basic ideas of Western justice lie not so much in Blackstone or common law as in the common elevated experience of mankind as expressed in the great books non-lawyers have written.

For years Dr. Hutchins has been accused of living in the top parapet of the highest towers of ivy. The Center for the Study of Democratic Institutions is unashamedly a tower of ivy. But if the ivy tower is high enough and the brains are wide enough you can peek at the future.

Today, at 76, Dr. Hutchins is considered a monument in the world of American education and one of its most controversial figures.

At the core of Dr. Hutchins' educational theory is the notion that no man, including a specialist, can consider himself educated unless he has made a study of the great books that contain the great thoughts of the Western world.

In addition to educating young people, Dr. Hutchins has taught classical humanism to butchers, bakers, candlestick makers, doctors and merchant chiefs. In a world that believes education is a way of getting a better job, he has maintained (too stubbornly, his critics say) the idea that only by learning the accumulated thought of the great thinkers of mankind can a man begin his education. Our conversation began when I talked with him about this central issue. We both have very definite ideas about education.

As I've gone back through your speeches and books, Dr. Hutchins, it's clearly evident that you feel people are or should be pretty well saturated in the whole Western tradition of thought going back to the Greeks.

Hutchins: If anybody were to say to me, "Mr. Hutchins, what is your message to the younger generation?" I'd say, "Get ready for anything!" — because something is going to happen, anything is going to happen, and it isn't going to be what you expect. How do you get ready for anything? There may be other and better ways but the way that has occurred to me is that if you understand the Western tradition (and if possible, the Eastern, too), if you have developed ideas and standards and methods and interests of an intellectual sort, they can be applied to any problem that arises.

Sevareid: You've always had a very deep-seated opposition to elites of any kind. You believe very much in the spread of the public school system, popular democracy. But how can any but an elite really acquire the kind of education you are talking about? I've read some (but by no means all) of the great books you've been promoting and I can't understand, for example, one paragraph of Newton's "Principia." In a way, aren't you encouraging elitism?

Hutchins: I think that's an undemocratic suggestion. I think anybody — and can almost prove it — can master the essential elements of Western tradition as disclosed in the books by the greatest writers of the past. I think anybody can do it, unless someone has some kind of functional damage to his brain, no matter how backward he may seem at the start. You may have to develop modifications. You may have to develop new ways of entry. But it can be done. I've participated in discussions of great books with all sorts of people, including factory workers, 14-year-old children, 75-year-old adults, bankers, even lawyers. Our discussions have invariably been fruitful, enriching, and stimulating. The great books mean something different to people at different ages, which is a good reason to keep reading them all your life. But I don't want to be technical about this. I don't want to insist on my list of great books or my way of teaching them.

Sevareid: Which are the eight or ten really essential great works?

Hutchins: On the American side, the basic documents are the Declaration of Independence, the Articles of Confederation, and the Federalist Papers. On the Greek side, the leading books by Plato and Aristotle.

Sevareid: You had a big quarrel with John Dewey long ago. As I remember, he thought that your approach is authoritarian because you decide which first principles people must grasp and follow.

Hutchins: I think Dewey was alienated by the fact that most great books are old books. He thought it was enough to say, "Why read Aristotle? He lived in a slave society." Well, the fact that Aristotle was part of a slave society doesn't necessarily mean everything he said is irrelevant today.

Sevareid: You sound optimistic about the capacity of almost anybody to grasp the great books. But there's a whole new wave of argument and evidence about genetic differences in intelligence—inherited differences that seem to show that differences of native intelligence are very serious and very wide. From such arguments it can almost be concluded that if we had a truly open society, with equal opportunities for everyone, socio-economic classes could be genetically determined.

Hutchins: It seems to me that statistics are one thing and what you can do with them is another. I don't underrate the studies of Jensen and Herrenstein or even Shockley. I think their ideas ought to be pursued. But I think it's far from established that genetic differences are such that the educational system can have no effect. You can argue the same way from the copious evidence we have on the effect of the early years of life and home situations.

You can say, of course, that unless people come from good homes they're not going to succeed in the educational system and that there's no way of giving someone from a poor home an equal chance in life because his fate is already committed. Now, Rene Dubois, whom I greatly admire, once went so far as to intimate the possibility that the conditions of an individual's future and his personal equipment are determined before birth. If you take this literally (which he didn't mean to do) and carry it as far as it can be carried the result is the proposition that there is nothing in education because all things are predetermined.

Sevareid: Your first love and study was the law. You were Dean of the Yale Law School at a very early age. Now look at all the lawyers involved in the Watergate scandals. These are men who've studied the law. What happened? Did they slip because they didn't know the great books, they didn't know the long history of human suffering that resulted in our Constitution, our Bill of Rights? Is this possibly why the Nixon administration lawyers subverted the law?

Hutchins: Well, most lawyers are very bright and very quick. Otherwise they couldn't attain the kind of examination results that are required by big Wall Street law firms. Many, perhaps most, lawyers are totally uneducated. When I went to law school and when I taught law, we were totally uneducated. We had no knowledge of society or social problems. We didn't know any psychology. We didn't know anything. In those days the sole object was to pass the bar examinations. If we did well on our exams we could get into any Wall Street firm. And so any effort to reform the law school curriculum, an effort that I made, was difficult (though not impossible) because of the attitude of the legal profession. All they wanted was lawyers who knew the rules. Law is a body of rules. If you can manipulate rules you're good.

Burke once said we were a litigious people. And we are. Any federal system is bound to develop litigation.

Sevareid: I notice that the new African nations are very litigious. Every other young man wants to be a lawyer. The Africans seem to go to court very quickly on anything. That tends to paralyze a lot of activity.

Hutchins: Yes, it does. Litigation, of course, is good for the lawyers in all sorts of ways.

Sevareid: Should someone going into medical school be expected to have a lot more liberal education than is the case now?

Hutchins: Yes. At the University of Chicago, for a while, a student couldn't specialize in any field until he had passed 14 liberal arts examinations. Those who passed carried through their lives at least some faint recollection of things outside the discipline in which they came to specialize.

Sevareid: I think you once said that you weren't particularly concerned about the economic conditions of the country or the material well-being of people. But aren't they pretty fundamental to the kind of education you want us to pursue?

Hutchins: At the bottom of the depression during the 1930's I tried to tell students that there are other things in life besides financial success. Most of them had a big headstart anyway. They didn't have to worry about personal economic problems. What I was concerned about was their moral sense. I didn't see anything come out of the depression, from an educational point of view, that was harmful. Incidentally the University of Chicago was, I think, a much better institution by the end of the depression than at the onset.

Sevareid: You stripped away a lot of things like football and created a national uproar.

Hutchins: Some of the faculty members I brought to the university were young men with a completely fresh outlook. We simply said: "Why don't we see what makes sense and what doesn't." Football didn't, of course, stand very high. The student body immediately improved.

Sevareid: A famous Chicagoan of the 1930's was Al Capone. Did you ever meet him?

Hutchins: No, but I tried to. When we launched a campaign to raise ten million dollars for the university, we started out by asking ten men to give us $100,000 each. We got nine. But where was the tenth? "Well," I said, "it's a cinch. I'll go over and ask Mr. Capone. I'm sure he'd give us $100,000." But Samuel Insull, the chairman of our campaign, said that this would be immoral, that we could not take Mr. Capone's money. Insull later went to jail for some distinctly immoral practices of his own. Insull was an interesting gentleman. Once, when I was having dinner with him, he mentioned that he couldn't get somewhere on time because of railroad connection problems. I suggested that he fly. "Young man," he said, " if you had the responsibility for $14 billion of other people's money you wouldn't fly." But when the sheriff came for him during his troubles he flew off to Canada.

Sevareid: Wasn't Al Capone born on the same day you were?

Hutchins: Yes. This proves there isn't much in astrology.

Sevareid: Can we take up a question relating to today's education that's troublesome to many?

What to be specific, are the rights of parents? Don't they have any rights over how their children's minds are formed? What's your feeling about a high school teacher who feeds youngsters books about sex or violence or political radicalism, particularly in a town with a homogeneous culture that doesn't care for education of this type?

Hutchins: This is a very complicated matter. In 1925 the Supreme Court ruled that a child is not the creature of the state. It held that children could attend parochial schools. On the other hand, the Supreme Court has held that parents do not have the sole right to determine what their children shall study. Boards of education have been upheld in the performance of their elected duties. The community as well as parents are responsible for public education. But to what degree each may decide is a very difficult question. It's a question I have been working on but I don't say that I see my way through it. In one sense the interest of parents is primary. In another sense the interests of the community are primary.

What is a community anyway? Under traditional American educational doctrine, as distinguished from every other kind of doctrine, the state is the community. But the Supreme Court says: "No, the state isn't the community. The district is the community."

It's as if a new federalism has developed—a federalism of school districts. I should never have started to study this problem. I don't think I'm ever going to find a solution. Somehow a balance has to be defined, either theoretically or practically, as to the role of the community versus the role of parents.

Sevareid: I always thought American education was practically a national religion. We've had federal acts for education way back to the Continental Congress.

Hutchins: We do reasonably well in getting everybody into schools and keeping them there as long as possible but the question of what happens to them in school is seldom raised. If you went around to a parent and said, "I understand you're sending your child to school or to college because of your respect for the mind" he would undoubtedly deny any such un-American accusation.

We take degrees seriously but I don't think we take education seriously. If you're a Yale man you don't talk about your education; you don't talk about what you learned. Only the other day I got a letter from the secretary of my Yale class saying that we could all be reassured that President Brewster was showing a greater interest in the recruitment of football players at Yale. That attitude has persisted for a long time.

Sevareid: I gather you feel that sports or social life in college actually interferes with education. But is this really valid? It's like saying that television keeps people from reading books, which I don't happen to believe because it's disputed by the figures on book sales. Aren't youngsters likely to do a lot of extra-curricular things no matter how you organize them?

Hutchins: It's all right if you don't organize their sports and social activities. I think the British system is splendid. England's students can organize whatever they want as long as they come in at the right hour at night and don't misconduct themselves too seriously. I'm all for spontaneous extra-curricular activities. I don't believe they are a proper concern of the university. They interfere with what I regard as the true purpose of a university.

Sevareid: When I was in college during the 1930's all we were concerned about was economic security. We were in the middle of the depression. There was no sexual freedom and that sort of thing. But during the 1960's students didn't care for economic security. They had it, they didn't need its symbol. They all went around dressed like tramps and the hippy movement started. But we're in for rough times again. Aren't students likely to go back to the same kind of concern and agitation we were up to during the 1930's?

Hutchins: I think so.

Sevareid: What's going to come out of the so-called counter-culture, the greening of America?

Hutchins: If I am to speak candidly I would say very, very little. It's a great thing for students to be allowed to participate in their campus government but they don't actually take any interest in it.

Sevareid: Very early in your life when you were Dean of Yale's Law School at 29 and President of the University of Chicago at 30 you were a sort of wonder boy. A lot of people thought you ought to get into the political mainstream or run for President. Why didn't you?

Hutchins: Nobody asked me or they asked me at the wrong time.

Sevareid: Did you wait around for an invitation?

Hutchins: Golly gracious, no! I was busy and I was paid to do other things. I've never been asked to go into politics, except at a time when I was sure to lose.

Sevareid: Which Presidents in your lifetime did you approve of?

Hutchins: Franklin D. Roosevelt came pretty close. There was a little of the mountebank in him and he was highly erratic in the policies he adopted at the outset of his Presidency. But I had the feeling he was really trying to do something for the country. Whatever Roosevelt's actual character was, whatever his actual achievements were, he symbolized the idea that America was going to get through the depression some way or other by everyone pulling together. He led us even though he sometimes didn't seem to be doing this at all.

Sevareid: Isn't it true that you wanted to go on to the Supreme Court in Roosevelt's time? There was talk of this.

Hutchins: Bill Douglas used to talk to me about it before he went on the court himself. But at that time I was in the midst of a big effort to maintain — and, to certain extent, redirect — the University of Chicago. I couldn't leave it without doing the effort considerable damage. But the Supreme Court was very attractive to me, I can tell you that.

Sevareid: Operating a university these days is just about impossible, isn't it?

Hutchins: Probably. Of course, if you don't care about education a university presidency is a great job. If you don't want to do anything except keep an institution rolling, enjoy a dignified position, access to the press, subsidized housing, automobiles, a good salary, and all that, then a university presidency is wonderful. But if, in the first place, you want to do something about education, you'll never be chosen. In the second place, you can't do it.

Sevareid: Let's go back to President Roosevelt.

Hutchins: He talked to me several times about coming to Washington in various capacities for which I was totally unqualified. When he asked me to head up the Securities and Exchange Commission I thought that was an odd idea. Let me tell you a perfectly characteristic Roosevelt story. After Richard Whitney, the president of the New York Stock Exchange, was sent to the penitentiary, the Exchange decided, I thought, to reform. So they elected three public trustees — General Robert Wood, the president of Sears, Roebuck; Carl C. Conway of the Continental Can Company; and I was the third.

One day I suggested to Roosevelt that he go after the J. P. Morgan Company. Undisputed testimony showed that two members of the firm knew about some strange practices. "I don't want to prejudge the cause," I told the President, "but I think the Morgan outfit ought to be investigated in view of the fact that you're stamping all over some minor crooks." Roosevelt turned green.

Shortly after I became one of the Stock Exchange trustees there was a meeting of the board of governors. Every one of the 36 people there was given an opportunity to speak all right but the voting came down to 35-to-1. So I resigned, saying that the pretentions of the Exchange to be a public institution were pure bunk.

A little while after, when President Roosevelt asked me to visit him at Warm Springs, I said "I'll come down, on the condition that I don't have to accept any job you offer me." He said: "All right, come ahead!" But when I got to Warm Springs he asked me to take on the SEC chairmanship. I turned down his proposal because, I explained, "I don't know anything about securities or exchanges. I'm totally ignorant about these things." Roosevelt said: "Well, I understand, but I'm sorry because it would have been such a wonderful joke on the Exchange." I said, "Well, you can play jokes on the Exchange but not at my expense."

Sevareid: Weren't you a very good friend of Adlai Stevenson? I know he disagreed with you on some important issues. I remember a radio speech of yours in about 1941. You opposed our entering the war and I think you argued that we were not intellectually prepared for the peace. Adlai, of course, disagreed with you on that. And you opposed Lend-Lease. He disagreed on that, too. Did you later have cause to regret the position you took?

Hutchins: Well, you know what a Chinese historian said about fifty years ago. He was asked what he thought of the French Revolution. He said it's too early to tell.

Sevareid: Surely you don't really think that it's too early to tell about the war, do you?

Hutchins: I think it's pretty early to tell. My theory was that if the United States got involved in the war, in the state of its morale and intelligence at the time, it was almost certain to succumb to the influences it was fighting against.

Sevareid: You think we've done that?

Hutchins: I think we're not as democratic a nation as we ought to be although we're still a democratic nation where essential constitutional lines have been maintained. Frankly, I didn't think they would be; I was certainly mistaken in that respect.

Sevareid: Hitler said the strength of totalitarian nations was that it forced its opponents to imitate them. You were worried about our becoming imperialistic or fascist or moving in their direction?

Hutchins: That's right.

Sevareid: We certainly learned the arms and intervention habits.

Hutchins: That's why it's too early to tell. If we hadn't gone into the war nobody, of course, knows what would have happened. But we would have been spared certain things. On the other hand, we might have suffered certain things.

Sevareid: After the war I thought we did pretty well in rebuilding Europe and trying to straighten things out.

Hutchins: The Marshall Plan was fine until it became an instrument of the Cold War. When Paul Hoffman and I were in the Ford Foundation we talked about this a great deal. Even in his mind the plan rapidly became a plan, not for the rehabilitation of Europe, but for the strengthening of the United States against Soviet Russia.

Sevareid: Still, the Marshall Plan did its basic job.

Hutchins: I won't deny that.

Sevareid: You were raised in a very Calvinistic household. I guess I was, too. We believed, or were taught to believe, that your personal fate depended on your character and brains and effort — not on looking to others to solve your problems. And then we fell in love with the New Deal. A force called "government" could pick us up out of the depression and solve all our problems. Since then we've been steadily piling up government at all levels. I find myself feeling very negative about this. It's something that's gone too far. It's become an immobilizing and paralyzing force.

Hutchins: I have similar feelings but I don't quite know what to do about them.

Servareid: People have the sense, these days, that everything is too big — the government, the press, the corporations. We talk about participatory democracy, about getting government back into the hands of people. But how does one go about this? How can it work in a unitary country like ours? We can't break up into different autarchies—a Western America, an eastern, a middle.

Hutchins: Regionalism has a future but it's hard to believe it's going to be realized very soon. I don't think there's any future in decentralization when it merely reflects the desires of a group — an ethnic group or any other group. What seems to be required is some adaptation of a fairly complicated idea — the principle of subsidiarity. This principle was very famous among lawyers centuries ago. It supposes that there is some central authority but that the authority above does nothing that the authority below can do. You never do anything in the community that the family ought to be doing; you never do anything in the state that the local community ought to be doing; you never do anything in the federal government that the state can do.

Sevareid: Doesn't our Constitution say something like this?

Hutchins: Yes, but it's overlooked. If the principle of subsidiarity could be developed in a way that could be understood we could perhaps have government at every level with its assigned duties and no government at any level exceeding what it can effectively do.

Sevareid: But who makes the decisions?

Hutchins: We have to have a Constitutional Convention to settle that question.

Sevareid: We're apparently no closer to an answer to a question de Tocqueville raised 140 years ago. Would equality, democracy lead to servitude or freedom, to knowledge or barbarism? Are we any closer to knowing the answer?

Hutchins: No. We are still barbarians and, in a large way, we manufacture them. Career education is an example of the latter trend. The American idea of success has its value but it's a rather inadequate statement of what life is about.

Sevareid: Maybe we need another depression.

Hutchins: A depression certainly isn't a pleasant experience. I don't recommend it. It's a dreadful thing. We really didn't, you know, get ourselves out of the last depression. The war got us out. Hitler got us out. We could never find the way out. It's like the present stagflation situation. All our expensive, highly-trained economists have been telling us for years that we could never have another depression because they knew all the answers. Now they're not so sure.

If you pick up a copy of "Fortune" or "Business Week" of a year or two ago and read about the stock market you'll find yourself in another world. The whole question of futurology bothers me a great deal. We know things are going to change but don't really know what the change is going to be. And we don't know how what we are now doing is going to affect the nature of the change that will take place.

Sevareid: I don't want to end our conversation without asking you about television. You once headed up a commission that issued a big report on the printed press. You looked at the press, particularly its monopolistic aspect, with some disfavor. What do you think television is doing to us? What should television be doing?

Hutchins: Television is making us what we are today. I watch quite a little of it. I used to tell Henry R. Luce that his magazines had more influence than the whole educational system put together. Television is infinitely more effective than any other means of communication. This bothers me. If it were ineffective I wouldn't mind.

Sevareid: I meet many people of great intellectual status who pretend they never watch television. It's quite beneath them. But they evidently watch it a great deal. I think of something Felix Frankfurter once said that perhaps explains a lot of popular culture, including television. "There's no highbrow," he said, "in any lowbrow, but there's a lot of lowbrow in every highbrow." What would you like to see on television?

Hutchins: If you accept my major premise — that television is making us what we are, that television is making our culture — then you have to consider what television could contribute to the kind of civilization we'd like to see.

I don't believe in solemnity. It has its place — usually at the graveside — but not in ordinary life. What is television trying to do? If what it's trying to do is attract forty million watchers so that you can run up the ratings and get bigger advertising contracts, well then I don't think the ultimate result is in doubt. It's going to be lousy. As a result, if you accept my major premise, American culture is going to be lousier all the time. I was the Ford Foundation officer responsible for general oversight of "Omnibus," a program that was an attempt to see how far you could go with really good stuff that would be paid for by advertisers. We found out you can't go very far, not even with a heavily subsidized program that made it possible to keep down the charges to the advertiser.

Sevareid: You've now been out in Santa Barbara on a mountaintop a long time, thinking about all sorts of things. Like most of us, you seem to have more questions than answers.

Hutchins: The older I get the more questions I have and the fewer answers I find.

Sevareid: I have a feeling that you think America is quite a country, that you haven't written it off by any means. Am I right?

Hutchins: Oh, yes. I think we have something that doesn't exist anywhere else. Perhaps I say this because I was brought up as a lawyer. I think the Constitution of the United States is just what Gladstone thought of it: the greatest single document ever struck off at one time by the hand of man. The Constitution works fairly well. It established a form of government that we don't really understand but it seems to be working fairly well. And then there is the history and the spirit of the American people.

In all this I would include the educational system I've always attacked. Back in 1935 I wrote a series of articles for the *Saturday Evening Post* saying we're getting no brighter and calling attention to the tremendous expenditures we were making on education. And there we were, just as stupid as ever. Nonetheless the idea of American education is a wonderful exhibition of faith both in democracy on the one hand and in intellectual development on the other.

Sevareid: I conclude from what you've just said that you don't feel that Columbus went too far.

Hutchins: No, I don't.

Conversation With
Leo Rosten

August 24, 1975

Sevareid: "Wisdom," according to Leo Rosten, "is only the capacity to confront intolerable ideas, with composure. Most men debase the pursuit of happiness by transforming it into a foolish pursuit of fun. But where was it promised that the purpose of life is to be happy? To me, the most important thing in life is to matter, to count, to stand for something. In short, to have it make some difference that you lived at all." Rosten says this in a book of his called "Captain Newman, M.D." He has written or edited twenty-five books on a wide variety of subjects — from "The Joys of Yiddish" and "The Education of Hyman Kaplan" to a sociological study of the Washington press corps. He is what is fast disappearing in our society of specialists. He's a generalist. He moves easily through the worlds of literature, high finance, government, and academia.

Leo Rosten has taught at Yale, Stanford, Columbia and the University of California. In addition to all else, he's an astute economist trained at the University of Chicago and the London School of Economics. He belongs to an interesting intellectual mutation. He was a New Deal liberal in Franklin Roosevelt's day; today he's a neo-conservative. From old liberal to new conservative is paradoxically a function of aging and changing society. Neo-conservatives don't believe that education or government can determine the total picture of American society.

Rosten: We didn't assume thirty years ago that the schools could solve all our problems. We never assumed that politics could solve them. In fact, this country was based on the commanding idea that what the politicians should do and what the government should do is make it possible for people to pursue happiness. Now the disenchanted say, "Make me happy!" Schools can't make anyone happy.

Sevareid: What has happened? Some of the Supreme Court decisions, some of the rules from the Department of Health, Education, and Welfare, from the federal government, are going to instruct every high school in every local community what boys and girls can do, what sports they can play at together, and what can or can't be done in the locker room. This would have made Alexander Hamilton and Ben Franklin turn in their graves. Why shouldn't local communities have something to say about how children are educated?

Rosten: I think the tide has to turn. The story of the growth of federal power is one of the most lamentable in American history. I think historians of the future will mark 1932 as one of the black years of American history — not that Roosevelt was a bad President, not that he didn't do extraordinary things. His greatest talent was that of a politician. He cemented a society that was falling to pieces in very ugly ways. But what he did was start the pattern by which instead of fixing your community's bridge you wrote to your Congressman and asked him to get Congress to appropriate $28,000 for your bridge — a pattern by which everything is taken care of by federal money. What's wrong with this is that it prevents the most powerful engine mankind has ever known, the free market, from working.

I think we are now beginning to learn that it is foolish to assume that people in Washington know better how to run Alameda County than the men who are farming in Alameda County. I think that the program of subsidies for people not to work or for some products not to be raised has become such a scandal that even workers and farmers oppose it. But you know much more about that than I do. You're in Washington.

Sevareid: Maybe we get too close to government here. I remember Justice Douglas saying to me in an interview that he told Roosevelt in the early days: put a terminal-point date on all programs; they should die after a few years unless there's some tremendous need to keep them going. But if you try to stop a government program hornets come swarming over you.

Rosten: There are all those vested interests. I've long thought that we have reached the point where the President of the United

States has to become the teacher of the people. This is the one area in which Roosevelt was absolutely supreme. When he got on the radio he was your beloved father, your beloved uncle, your beloved brother, explaining to you why the government must do things.

It's appalling that we expect people to vote on things which are far beyond the present state of their knowledge. As a result they vote according to how their parents vote, along party lines.

Sevareid: I really wonder sometimes if it is actually possible for a democratic system to act in anticipation of great problems.

Rosten: Winston Churchill once said, "Of all the forms of government ever invented, the worst may be democracy — except for one thing; there's nothing we know that's any better." We pay a price for it but it's a price we have to pay.

Sevareid: You've argued that free democracy and a free market have to go together. What's your reasoning on this?

Rosten: History has performed the experiment for us. Never has there been such an increase in the well-being of people as from the time when the creative forces of industry, or manufacturing, and farming were permitted freedom to produce and to respond to the response of the market.

Consider what's happened in Germany. After the war in which it was almost destroyed, West Germany became capitalist; East Germany became Communist. In West Germany you have freedom, a viable press, argumentation, parliamentary government. And there's an incredible increase in the standard of living. West Germans are not trying to climb over the wall to get into East Germany. It's the other way around. And look at what has happened in Japan.

People seem to forget that the human race consists of so much potential talent that if you let that talent operate to its full you can take care of the excess. You can take care of the so-called injuries. Now in some situations you can't have free enterprise. You and I can't decide we're each going to buy our own battleships or our own cannon. It just can't be done. The government has to do that. There are only two things that government does well — collect taxes and prevent society from achieving its potential.

Sevareid: In a recent book Peter Drucker says: "Government can make war and inflate the currency but can solve nothing."

Rosten: Government produces nothing! Every person in the United States today is working one day out of five for government — local, county, state, and federal government. Now, when you put matters this sharply, people who take government for granted sit up and say, "What's going on? Where's the money going?"

You know what a bureaucracy is like. I've had about a dozen jobs in government, none of them of great importance, but I was proud to have them. Once I had a secretary who was a perfectly delightful girl from the South. But her IQ was not staggering. Her typing skills were about that of my grandson's. Now, what do you do about her in government? In industry you can say, "Well, you'll have to get another job." I couldn't take the time to go before the Civil Service Commission and explain why I wanted her transferred and so we had a game. I would call a friend in another division and say, "I've got a charming, beautiful idiot. Would you like her on your payroll? Keep her six months. Then send her to Charlie. Then send her to Joe" — and so on. The evidence of incompetence is appalling. Government is a one-industry business and when you have no competition you get the worst thing you could have in a free society — monopoly.

Sevareid: Government pay scales and fringe benefits are now on the average going beyond those of private industry.

Rosten: A private industry which isn't successful goes broke. Some people say, "Oh, how terrible!" I say, "How wonderful!"

Sevareid: But, Leo, how free is the free enterprise economic system in this country? Government aside, big corporations can simply administer prices (no matter what the demand is) so that automobiles sell less and less but the price goes up. The big trade unions virtually administer wages. In short, free enterprise isn't at all very flexible, is it?

Rosten: A free competing system is as flexible as a system can be if you allow it to be. I don't believe that ever in human history will we solve all problems and make everyone happy. I believe some people are meant to be miserable and enjoy it. I think some people are meant to be drifters and enjoy it. I think some people are dictatorial and we must watch out for them.

We have shrunk the area within which it is possible for our enormous productive capacity to flower. But it is not true to think that when prices rise it is because some greedy men decided this.

One reason prices rise is that we've inflated the money supply. The Federal Reserve Board has printed money. Now, if you print enough money, the money you have becomes less valuable; therefore

the price increase is almost a fake figure. Let me put it this way —
the true value of the dollar has been diminished.

We are lucky in the United States that unions are responsible.
We have nothing to compare with the situation in England where
a 37% wage increase in a government-controlled business is rejected
out of hand because the shop stewards aren't satisfied. England's
shop stewards are dominated by a handful of Marxists.

I know of no system that's better than free enterprise to give
you freedom because power is dispersed. Look at what happens
when prices are controlled or administered. People use alternates.
They use substitutes or they stop buying.

Sevareid: With all that we've learned in the last sixty years about
totalitarian society, beginning with the Soviet Union, why is it
that democracy seems to be receding in many parts of the world
while Communism, totalitarianism of one kind or another, is ad-
vancing? Aren't you scared about this?

Rosten: I am more than scared. A dictatorship is very easy to
explain. "We'll take care of all your problems." There's no unemployment in a dictatorship. Neither is there unemployment in prison.
"We'll fix your prices. We'll give you all happiness. Everyone will
live beautifully, happily. No strikes, no crises, nothing!"

A democracy is very hard to explain to someone in a totalitarian country. I'll give you an example. When I was in the Soviet
Union someone said to me, "The American press doesn't tell the
truth the way our press does." I said, "Well, give me an example
of the truth the America press doesn't tell." He said, "Well did
you read about that riot in the South?" I said, "Where did you
read it?" He said, "In Pravda." I said "Where did Pravda get it?"
The New York Times." I said, "You haven't given me an example
of what the American press does not tell the public."

We know of no dictatorship in which people's standard of life or
the variety of their life is worth the price they pay — the fear of
the knock on the door in the middle of the night. My father came
here from Poland. He worked a hundred hours a week. And he
worked over the weekend so that he could make sweaters which we
could then sell in the front of our flat. He said one thing I'll never
forget: "You know the most wonderful thing about the United
States? It isn't that the streets are paved with gold. It's the fact that
I can walk out in the street and say, 'The mayor is a crook!' And if

that night there's a knock on the door, I don't worry." That's a wonderful thing to know.

Sevareid: Is it true that you got into movie writing by mistake? Some thirty-five years ago you wrote a sociological book about Hollywood film-makers. It's said that someone who didn't read the book heard that you knew something about the movies. So they hired you at a fabulous salary and you wrote or hacked out movies for a short period.

Rosten: I used to "commit" movies. Oh, I loved movies because they were problem-solving. Today I go to movies because I'm anxious to see what the young movie-makers are doing and I watch with great anticipation. What they have done is rebel and say, "Away with the old tradition! Away with the old form! Away with the standard plot of the happy ending and boy-wants-girl, boy-doesn't-get-girl, boy-does—" Nonsense!

Once you learn how to fake honesty you can make a fortune. There's a picture called "The Trial of Billy Jack." It preaches sweetness and pacifism and decency but the big moment comes when the hero commits such mayhem and such murder on his enemies that you begin to say, "Whatever happened to pacifism and sweet love and all that sort of thing?" Fake honesty is what this is about. "Easy Rider," a brilliantly made film, is about two guys who smuggle marijuana and go into a terrible fit of drug addiction in a graveyard. "Now what on earth," I thought to myself, "is this supposed to say? That society has driven them to drugs?"

They say society or capitalism does terrible things. It makes criminals. Simple question: Take a family of twelve children. One becomes a crook. Why don't the others? Same family, same background, same parents, same neighborhood! Why not?

Sevareid: And then we get to the whole genetic question that's stirring everybody up now. Doesn't it seem to you that when novelists, movie-makers, playwrights, come to the point of glorifying sadism they have broken the rules that make civilization possible?

Rosten: Edmund Burke once said, "To have a civilization of any kind, however primitive, men must place restraints upon their passions, their greed and their irrationality. And to the degree that these restraints are not self-imposed, external and tyrannical powers will impose them."

The current exaltation of sadism is such that you'll see people turn their heads away in a movie house because they can't stand the unnecessary glorying in savagery. Now this doesn't mean that I'm in favor of censorship. But I'm in favor of the critics not abdicating their responsibility. Why don't they say: "This is a disgusting movie. It's just obscene. It isn't talented at all. It's no more talented than a pool of garbage." Why are they afraid? Because they're afraid that their own judgments may not be correct.

The other day I went to the movies. A mother and a nine-year-old child sat in front of me. The child was in such a state of panic because he didn't know how to react, watching scenes not only of sexuality but masturbation, fetishism. He didn't know what he was supposed to react to. He was muddled. I wanted to lean forward and say to him: "Sonny, pay no attention. These fellows are nuts."

Sevareid: Well, how many people do you think are nuts?

Rosten: If you mean dangerously insane, perhaps eight percent. If you mean incapable of following a logical, sensible decent disagreement, about forty percent — people who are incapable of listening, who are threatened by an idea.

Every campus now has courses called "Communication." The fact is that many people don't want to be communicated with because it is an invasion of the self and may involve changing ideas in which they have deeply invested emotions. To change the mind is a hard but liberating thing.

Sevareid: A long time ago, during the 1930's, you wrote the first real sociological study of the Washinton press corps. A lot has changed since then. It's now a vast herd of people. The tone has changed. The press has itself become a great controversial issue. What's the big difference now?

Rosten: The decline of newspapers, the decline of local papers, the pabulumized news leads me to read weekly journals more than ever because they at least put things into perspective. The kind of person who now goes into journalism may also be different.

Sevareid: The Watergate adventures have something to do with it. Press people have been lured and forced out of their normal roles to a degree. They've become actors in the play themselves. They're writing about each other. There also is a new level of howling monkeys at news conferences. They've given the press a pretty bad image with lots of people. Some reporters seem to think they're prosecuting attorneys at every encounter with officials. They don't understand that civility is not the enemy of freedom; it's an ally.

Rosten: I have the feeling that the editorial pages of this country, with the exception of the Wall Street Journal, are repeating the cliches of the 1940's and 1950's. "If a government program fails it's because not enough money was put into it. Let's put more money into it!" And more and more money is poured down the rat hole. Now, this money comes from the men who drive the cabs and run the stores and work in the shops. The people who devise the programs have a vested interest in not saying "This was a mistake. Let's cut it out." On the contrary, they say, "We need a larger enforcement agency. We need more field inspectors" and so on.

Sevareid: I think one of the failures of the press is in what I would call not investigative reporting but "accountability" reporting. We have not tried to add up the net effect of a great many social programs. What do they cost? What do they do? Take the Peace Corps. What has it done in terms of per capita income in other countries, the extension of democracy or the reverse? Surely people are entitled to some kind of accounting in understandable terms where hundreds of billions of dollars have gone. Don't you agree?

Rosten: It mystifies me that we don't have that sort of thing as a permanent feature in the Sunday sections. That's why I read the weekly reviews and the specialized magazines. They have a sense of real perspective. This brings me back to the function of the press as educator. The press can educate as well as report. It can put the facts together, it can give them pattern and meaning—just as the President or a politician can and should.

The standard of living in the United States of even the lowest or poorest people has undergone a quiet revolution during the last thirty to forty years.

Think of this, Eric! The President of the United States of America resigns. There are no police in the streets. The National Guard is not called out. There are no riots. No one is executed. No one is tortured. No one is thrown into jail. The new President moves right into office. I said to myself, "What a system, that it can work this way!" It's really remarkable.

Sevareid: What do you think was the matter with Richard Nixon?

Rosten: I don't think anyone knows. I don't think Nixon knows. I can't pretend to say what motivated him. Whenever anyone says to me "The reason that Truman or Eisenhower did that" I say "Stop, you're wrong." They say "I haven't finished." I say "You're wrong. No one ever does anything for one reason."

The essential vulgarity of Nixon came out in a singular way.

"Vulgarity" is a curious word. It comes from the Latin which means "of the people" — and that's fine. I rather like vulgar things. I like vulgar sports. But in high office vulgarity is an offense. I've watched Mr. Nixon's career since I've lived in Southern California.

In Venice, once, I was staying at a hotel with my wife and we were on a little landing. A motor launch pulled up and out came the Vice President of the United States, Mr. Nixon, and his wife Pat. Next to us was a table of Americans. They stood up, took their chairs, and put them so that their backs would be to him. Well, this offended me. Whatever the man was, he was also the Vice President, a symbol. Two days later we were having coffee on a rainy day in the Piazza San Marco when it was almost deserted.

From under the horological tower came the epitome of the American tourist—shambling, looking. As he came closer I noticed it was Nixon. I had met him, but I didn't think he would remember that. I stood up and said, "Mr. Vice President, would you like some coffee?" "Oh, that would be fine." He sat down. We had coffee and some conversation: "Gee, isn't this an interesting city?" "Yes, it is." "It's really a very old city." "Yes, it is." "You know I've never been here before. Golly, you can get lost in this city." Well, these comments went on until I thought to myself, and I don't mean this in a nasty sense, he's a hick. Here's a small-town boy who has come into all this historical splendor. Now translate that for a moment to the White House. Remember the speech in which Nixon said, rather movingly, "When I was a little boy in Whittier and I used to hear lonely train whistles and dreamed of the places I could go to . . ." People say power corrupts. Lord Ashton said it. Power also ennobles. Think of what power did for Harry Truman and compare it to Mr. Nixon. What was it that fed his blind determination not to tell, not to yield, and, if need be, go to the very brink of impeachment? I don't know.

Sevareid: Everything in the world is grist for your mill if you're a writer. Ordinary people take the bus to go to work. Writers are already at work even on the bus, listening for lines that are better than anything they can invent.

Rosten: I love to eavesdrop. I can't make up stuff as funny as things I hear. And it's impossible to go through life for twenty-four hours without encountering some revelation of the human comedy, the human sillinesses, the human glory. One can see and hear tender, wonderful things all around.

Sevareid: Leo, I want you to recite from the Book of Laws — Rosten's Laws.

Rosten: The book isn't done because every day I find a new law. "According to statistics, if a man has his head in an oven and his feet in a deep-freeze he feels pretty good on the average."

"Those who shout 'All power to the people' are people who want power to go to those who shout 'All power to the people.'"

"Crime doesn't pay. The only crimes that don't pay are the ones that are botched."

"People in glass houses shouldn't get stoned."

"If you give a man enough rope, he'll hang you."

I've been collecting these things out of a sense of impatience. I was very lucky as a boy. I was raised in a household where my mother and father talked a great deal and where I was regarded as part of the discussion group. I wasn't treated as a child. I was treated as a person who was going to grow up and assume responsibilities. My father had a wonderful habit. Whenever the trash needed to be taken out I'd grab a book, any book. I'd open it up and start reading. My father would walk by, nod, and say: "Good, putting in inventory." And then he would take the garbage out.

As a kid I used to hear constant questioning, Socratic dialogues that went on and on. Our home was full of people who kept arguing. They were trade unionists, socialists, all sorts.

I'll never forget when the Communists tried to move into the needle trades when we lived in Chicago.

My father said: "It's a very simple problem. All Communists are liars. Don't trust a man who's a liar." Well I wasn't accustomed to generalizations. I said, "Why are they all liars?" He said, "Because they'll do anything to get into power. They think they're lying for a noble cause. But, my boy, they're liars."

Sevareid: Leo, you've written about everything, thought about everything, studied everything. You're a great generalist, which is not much in fashion any more. What's happened to the knowledge industry? Sociologists, economists, psychologists, psychiatrists, seem rather bankrupt. Have we overburdened the human mind with too many facts? Vocabulary seems to have outrun knowledge, which has outrun wisdom. Where do we turn?

Rosten: We've always gone on the assumption (a good one) that education will liberate the human mind or the human spirit. There's a second assumption that's forgotten. Some people are meant to be educated and to learn and to enjoy the uses of the mind. Some people are meant to paint. Some people are meant to draw castles in the sand and make them into sculpture. Some people love to prune trees and gardens. What we have done is assume that everyone potentially can become an intellectual. We've confused learning with schooling.

It's absolutely absurd that in this country today there should be seven million youngsters going to college. There are not seven million people who want to read Plato or Aristotle or Montesquieu. And there's no reason why they should. We have failed to see that there aren't enough jobs for those who learn esoteric things. For a while there was a big fling on learning Swahili in New York. Lots of kids were studying it because it was part of the Black movement, the idea of Black identity, Black liberation. It so happens that Swahili was the language of the Arab slave traders. In any event, what good does it do to know Swahili? I don't mean "good" simply in terms of economics. What sort of good does it do?

When you're young, when your mind and spirit are like a sponge, there is no better time to learn certain things and there is no worse time to learn certain things. I would abolish the study of some courses except for students aged thirty or above.

I was lucky as a child of the depression. I couldn't get a job for three years. I was lonely and miserable. At the end of those three years, because I was desperate, I went back to school. I was older than my classmates, I had learned something. I had learned how hard it is to walk all day long, trying to earn a dollar. I had learned how important it is to save, to appraise people, to figure out if this or that guy can be trusted or not trusted. This is what life and the world are about.

We're practically using the colleges as a dump into which to put youngsters we do not know what to do with. There are today 45 million people between the age of roughly 7 and 24. Their parents don't know what to do with them. They want them to go to college and they often think that they're being trained for jobs. But they're not getting training for useful employment.

Someone has said that education is what remains after everything you've learned is forgotten. The purpose of educating young people is not only to illuminate their spirit and enrich their memory bank but to teach them the pleasures of thinking and reading. How do you use the mind? As a teacher, I always was astonished by the number of people in the classroom who wanted to learn as against those who just wanted to pass. I took pride in my ability to communicate. Generally, "communicate" meant one thing. Now the young think "communicate" means "Agree with me!"

The student rebellions of the 1960's exposed the fact that our entire educational system has forgotten the most imporant thing it can do prior to college: indoctrinate. I believe in the indoctrination of moral values. There's a lot to be said for being good and kind and decent. You owe a duty to those who have taken care of you. You owe a duty to whatever it is that God or fate gave you — to use your brain or your heart. It's senseless to whine, to blame society for every grievance, or to assume that the presence of a hammer means you have to go out and smash things.

The young want everything. They think they can get everything swiftly and painlessly. They are far too confident. They don't know what their problems are, not really. They talk too much. They demand too much. Their ideas have not been tempered by the hard facts of reality. They're idealists but they don't sense that it's the easiest thing in the world to be an idealist. It doesn't take any brains. This was said by Aristotle 2300 years ago. Mencken once said an idealist is someone who, upon observing that a rose smells better than a cabbage, assumes it will also make better soup.

Sevareid: My grandfather came to America in the middle of the nineteenth century as a young man. He went out to the midwest, broke ground, built a farm on a homestead. Today a different kind of immigrant is coming into the big cities.

Rosten: In fact New York City says to people, "Please come to New York. If you promise you won't work we'll give you $248 a month, plus $138 rent subsidy, plus free milk." Not too long ago, when the Russians at the United Nations wanted to see the slums of New York, they were taken by a friend of mine into the worst part of East Harlem. The Russians said: "Oh, no, no! We want to see the real slums." My friend said: "There aren't any. This is real." The Russians said, "Look at the television aerials. Who are you trying to fool?"

As for the new type of immigrant, New York now has a million and a half Hispanics. Many of them are American citizens. They're

The glory of this country is that it has proved what men thought very bright. They're very good. They work very hard. They're having a very hard time.

wasn't possible. It has also proved something alarming — the depth, the power, the awfulness of prejudice. You cannot legislate it away. We've assumed that it's enough to pass laws saying that all men are born equal or created equal when what we mean is that they're born or created with a right to equal treatment. But the young say we ought to have a law about this and about that on the assumption that legislation can perform miracles. I say to them: "Okay! Many people suffer because of nature. Nature made some people weak, some people stupid, some people small. Let's correct the injustice. Let's start by getting Congress to pass a law stipulating that from now on everyone shall be six feet tall."

Severaid: In view of all the training, the burst of so-called education — the immense finding of facts, all the think-tanks, etc., why is it we can't solve social problems any better than we do? Are solutions the cause of problems? I sometimes think so.

Rosten: Nobody quite understands how a society works. Reformers never realize how much worse things can be made by reforms that are palliatives.

Severaid: Solzhenitsyn is now saying in effect that all violent revolutions are bad.

Rosten: I don't think that was true in medieval Europe. I don't think it applies to the United States, where we had a very civilized revolution led by the greatest collection of brains ever assembled anywhere, not excluding Athens.

Severaid: I think of this when people use the old cliche about getting the kind of government we deserve. I don't know if all those yeomen and farmers of 1776 deserved all the great men they had. Do you?

Rosten: There are not many people who have first-rate brains, who are geniuses, or who are very creative. There's nothing wrong with that. It's just the way life is. Of those who have first-rate brains, fewer have imagination. Of those who have imagination, much fewer have something called judgment. The "ability to judge," you know, saved this country because of one man — George Washington.

Severaid: Justice Hugo Black said about Washington that he wasn't the greatest intellectual, the greatest speaker, or the greatest strategist. He was just the greatest man.

Rosten: Winston Churchill said this about Washington: "He was not a great general. He was not a great strategist. He was not a great tactician. But nowhere in history is there an example of a man who could hold an army together under such adversity." Churchill was very perceptive about the rebellions that broke out in England. "I cannot," he said, "be impartial as between the fire and the fire brigade."

Sevareid: Winston had a great line about youth. He said, "I admire a manly man and I rejoice in a womanly woman, but I cannot abide a boyly boy."

Rosten: Youth is an enormous advantage — in music, in physics, in science, in painting — unlike other fields which require discipline and accumulated knowledge.

Sevareid: You haven't given up on what we used to call the American Dream or the American Ideal?

Rosten: Oh, I think we have a moral obligation to be optimistic. We've had plenty of adversities. Think of the Civil War. Think of what Abraham Lincoln said: "I am going to save this Union. If I have to abolish slavery, I will do it to save the Union. If I have to preserve slavery I will do it in order to preserve this Union. Because, if and when we preserve this Union, we can solve these problems by peaceful, humane means."

The greatest thing we've got going for us is our knack for change, enormous change, without throwing people into concentration camps, without torturing them, without beating their brains in — change through discussion, without violence.

Look at what's happened lately. We've exposed the invasion of personal liberties. The people who tap wires are now on the defensive. Can you imagine a Russian or a Chinese agent being on the defensive about tapping wires?

I must be an optimist. I'm proud of the fact that our values go on, that we've resisted the barbarians. There are always barbarians. They will kill you because of your opinion. And we don't. Nevertheless, there are moments in the deep dark of the night when I recall the bitter but wonderful line of a very great man, Lorenz, the ethnologist, who said, "I do believe that Man is the missing link between Apes and Human Beings."

Sevareid: Man is not a fallen angel; he's a risen ape trapped between earth and a glimpse of heaven. There he stays.

Conversation With Eric Hoffer

September 19, 1967

Sevareid: Between the ages of seven and fifteen Eric Hoffer was totally blind. He never went to school. He has worked at manual labor all his life, the last 25 years as a longshoreman on the San Francisco docks. The University of California tried to hire him as a full professor. Publishers compete for his books, which are translated and read over half the world. His big body feels the twilight now, but his mind remains young as sunrise.

Great intellects have come from the working class and then have written about the so-called "masses." Hoffer is working class. He's a phenomenon. He is a stroke of national good luck — the most authentic voice of the poor about whom even the rich are now writing. He does not judge America by today's headlines and news-film. He sees this country in its place on the wheel of time. "America," says Eric Hoffer, "is the only new thing in history."

Mr. Hoffer lives in one room in the Chinese section of San Francisco. No telephone. No radio or TV. No easy chair. His own files and a few books. A folding bed.

Retired now as a longshoreman, he walks almost every day through Golden Gate Park, about two and a half miles. He sees or hears some little thing. An idea begins to be born. He may jot down a short note about it. A special set of muscles in his brain holds the idea, refines it, maybe for a week, a month, a year, before he writes it out in a paragraph. Then one day, people here and abroad read it with the startled sense of recognition that this is original, profound, and simple. Some people call it genius.

Mr. Hoffer, I've always wondered why you kept on as a laborer after you became a very successful and established writer.

Hoffer: Well, I never became a successful writer. I could never earn my living writing and I'm not a writer. I'm never sure I can write anything. Look, if you think a thing through to the bitter end there isn't much to say as far as human affairs are concerned. There isn't a thought that I couldn't express in 200 words and you can't earn a living writing 200 words.

Severeid: Everybody has a sort of mechanical process at which one arrives at ideas. Does manual labor start something going in your mind, leave your mind free to think abstractly? How does it work with you?

Hoffer: I think some of the most original ideas I've had came to me while I was working. You know, what a glorious feeling it is! Here you work, you talk with your partner, and in the back of your head you compose sentences. That's when life is glorious. You have two sides of your head, you know. Oh, it's a feeling that nothing could surpass this — this glory of being able all day long to compose sentence by sentence. And then you come home in the evening and, before you even wash your hands, you sit down and it's all there. It's a glorious feeling.

I got the longshoremen mad when I told them: "You know, I can't think of anything more exciting than going to bed with a half-finished paragraph." You take this unfinished paragraph to bed with you and in the morning can you think of anything more salubrious, more healthful, more glorious than to sit up in your bed and the first thing you think about is the other half of the paragraph. Your day is made! It's a good life.

Severeid: Words are pretty powerful things, aren't they?

Hoffer: Oh, yes. They destroy but they also revive. You know I'm practically illiterate. The only way I learned to write is by seeing how other people write. I still ask, whenever I read (my chief preoccupation): How did he do it? How did he do it? I'm still learning. I'm never sure that I know how to write.

When I finished this little book, "The Temper of Our Time," I sent it to my new editor, a very fine person, a very bright person, but young, you know. He mixed up quality with quantity. He sent me a letter: "Mr. Hoffer, couldn't we thicken it a little bit, I mean, add something, make it a little bigger?" I didn't get mad. I wrote him a letter, "Dear Mr. McRae," I said, "The book has six chapters. Each chapter has at least one original idea so you have six original ideas. Each chapter has at least two good sentences. Add it up. You have six original ideas, twelve good sentences. Now when I find a book, even a thousand pages thick, that has six original ideas, twelve good sentences, I celebrate for a month!"

Right now, as I'm getting older, how hard it is to find anything that will touch me. If I get just one little sentence in my little book I will remember the book to the end of my life.

Sevareid: How do your friends on the waterfront treat you, knowing that you write books?

Hoffer: Oh, every longshoreman knows that if he tried hard enough he could write like Shakespeare. I have often been told by longshoremen that if they did what I do, which is to bury myself in printed matter when there is no work, they could write, too.

Sevareid: Well, when I was young and worked in gangs and teams and one thing and another, the idea that I was a kind of kid-writer, a newspaperman, a pseudo-intellectual or something, created a certain alienation with the fellows.

Hoffer: Yes, but I am one of them. They know I am one of them. I am really average. If you want to know how the average longshoreman's going to vote on anything, you ask me. They're going to vote exactly the way I'm going to vote, not because I propagandize them but because I'm one of them. I just happen to be interested in ideas. What's wrong with that? I think you could be a Michelangelo and still be a plain working man. That is what I am. They know that no matter how many books I write, I'm still one of them. There's never been a feeling of separation. They know that if I had the choice of all the tea in China I would never change.

Sevareid: I can't understand how you make the two sides of your nature, your life, operate. You work with these people. You can sit down and drink a beer with them. You're just like them. They take you as one of them. On the other hand, you're seeing them in a different way.

Hoffer: Well, you assume that these people are not intelligent or, let's say, intellectual. Let me tell you, those people are tremendously intelligent and there isn't an idea in the world that I couldn't discuss with them. I remember the night I wrote the only political section in "The True Believer." It was the chapter on "Things Which Are Not." From the beginning of time men fought most desperately "for cities yet to be built and gardens yet to be planted." In the morning I was full of it and I had to talk to somebody. I went to work with a Negro in a ship's hold. I talked to him; he caught on. It turned out that he was a preacher and on the following Sunday he preached on "Things Which Are Not."

Take another instance: In January I received a "help, help" telegram from Harvey Shapiro of the New York Times saying they needed an article for Brotherhood Day, February 14th. Would I write an article on the brotherhood of men? Well, I never had thought about that. But I happen to like Harvey Shapiro and if I can do anything for him I'll do it. So I started to think and write about brotherhood of men. My first sentence read, " It's much easier to love humanity as a whole than to love one's neighbor."

My article was not going to be about the brotherhood of men, but about the love of neighbor. Every longshoreman is a neighbor so I had to find out what it takes to love your neighbor. That whole article was discussed on the company's time right under the hook, on the stringer, see! And *they* wrote it!

Sevareid: You know, you write a kind of icy objectivity, but you talk with quite a different tone. How do you explain this?

Hoffer: Well, I don't know about the icy objectivity. You try to write the best way you know how. I don't feel I'm full of ice or anything like it. I'm full of passion, actually. If I wasn't a passionate person, if I didn't have a passionate state of mind, how the heck would I write about mass movement? How could I write the book, "The Passionate State of Mind"? How do I know? Does anybody know about this unless he has it in him?

This is the fantastic thing. I have Hitler in me. I have Stalin in me. I have all the murderers in me. Nothing that man has ever done or thought is foreign to me. Goethe said he never heard of a crime that he couldn't commit. There are crumbs of everything inside us. If you know yourself you know the whole world.

Sevareid: You've written a great deal about leisure. Isn't free time now the privilege of everybody?

Hoffer: Of course. America is for the poor — but we have a good time in this country. The rich have it much better elsewhere — better service, more deference. Even in Russia the rich are better off than they are here. And certainly the intellectuals are better off everywhere else. You know, the only people who really feel at home in this country are the common people. America is God's

gift to the poor. For the first time in history, the common people can
do things on their own.

Oh, nobody mentions this. Our civilization is a business civilization. It's the only mass civilization there ever was. The masses eloped'
with history to America and we have been living in common-law
marriage with it, without the incantations of the intellectuals.

Sevareid: I wanted to get into the business of intellectuals in this
country you've written about so much. I think in one of your books
you say that a mass society like ours is not conducive to producing
an effective or powerful intellectual group. But in your last book
you say the intellectual is really coming into his own in this country.
Aren't you contradicting yourself here?

Hoffer: No, I'm not contradicting myself. Since Sputnik this is
how history is made. What is Sputnik? A little gimmick. The
nature of a society is determined by the direction into which
energies and ambitions flow — in other words, by the tilt of the
social landscape.

Until recently in this country the tilt was toward business. No
matter where you started you wound up as a businessman. Many
potential poets and philosophers became businessmen.

I happen to think the Promethean nature of American business
is due to the fact that it was built not by conventional businessmen
but by potential philosophers and poets. If you take a potential
philosopher and make him a businessman he acts in a beautiful
way. To him, all action is the same. He can be a prize fighter
or prize promoter today. He's going to be a manufacturer tomorrow.
Business is business.

Sevareid: He puts some kind of soul into it, doesn't he?

Hoffer: Not only this — he will combine factories, mines, railroads, the way a philosopher generalizes ideas. You know, I think
the intellectual is becoming a more important person now, more
than ever before. Henry James tells us that he and his brother
William in their childhood were ashamed to admit that their father
was a philosopher and an author rather than a businessman. Right
now the kids on the campus at Berkeley would be ashamed to admit
that their father was a businessman, just a grubbing businessman.
They wouldn't be proud.

Take it the other way. Suppose twenty years ago you lined up a
businessman, a painter, a poet, a sculptor, a professor and asked
a beautiful girl to pick a husband. The chances are she would have

picked the businessman. Right now, you can't be sure. She might even pick the poet, especially if he has a Guggenheim fellowship.

Sevareid: You seem to have a fear about the rise of intellectuals in political life and power. Why are you so frightened of them?

Hoffer: First of all, I ought to tell you that I have no grievance against intellectuals. All that I know about them is what I read in history books and what I've observed in our time. I'm convinced that the intellectuals as a type, as a group, are more corrupted by power than any other human type. It's disconcerting to realize that businessmen, generals, soldiers, men of action are less corrupted by power than intellectuals.

In my new book I elaborate on this and I offer an explanation why. You take a conventional man of action, he's satisfied if you obey, eh? But not the intellectual. He doesn't want you just to obey. He wants you to get down on your knees and praise the one who makes you love what you hate and hate what you love. In other words, whenever the intellectuals are in power there's soul-raping going on.

Sevareid: I think it's true in Russia but is it true here?

Hoffer: In this country the intellectuals aren't in power. Mass movements haven't a chance for the simple reason that they aren't started by the masses. They're started by intellectuals.

In America the intellectual has neither status, nor prestige, nor influence. We, the common people, are not impressed by intellectuals. We have a disdain for pencil-pushers. We actually define efficiency by the small number of pencil-pushers. If you asked me what I consider an efficient society I'd say the ratio between the office personnel and the producing personal.

The smaller the amount of supervision the better, the healthier, the more vigorous a society. The highest supervisory personnel is where the intellectuals are in power — in the Communist countries. There half of the population is supervising the other half. The intellectuals have a tremendous contempt for the masses. Intellectuals can't operate unless they're convinced that the masses are lazy, incompetent, dishonest, you have to breathe down their necks, and you have to watch them all the time. We in America are sitting pretty because the masses perform only if we leave them alone. That's where we are at our best.

Sevareid: In Britain, however, much of the pencil-pushing bureaucracy grew right out of the labor movement, people who were laborers. They became worse than the intellectuals.

Hoffer: Do you know why? Because they have aristocratic ideas. The moment anyone in Britain gets anywhere, he wants to be an aristocrat although he says that he's contemptuous of aristocrats. England has lots of class worship. Even Communists behave like aristocrats. They're aristocrats from the word "go." Our strength is in the ability to work without supervision — our tremendous, widely-diffuse competence.

Let me tell you a story. During the depression a construction company had to build a road in the San Bernardino Mountains and the man who was in charge, instead of calling up an employment agency and asking for so many men, sent two empty trucks out to skid row. Anybody who could climb up on that truck was hired even if he had only one leg. Once the trucks were full they drove us out to the mountains and dumped us on the side of a hill. The company had only one man on the job and he didn't even open his mouth. We found bundles of equipment and supplies and then we started to sort ourselves out.

It was the most glorious experience I ever had. We had so many carpenters, so many blacksmiths, so many cooks, so many foremen, so many men who could drive a bulldozer, handle a jackhammer. We put up the tents, put up the cook's shack, the toilet, the shower bath and cooked supper.

The next day we went out and started to build a road. If we had to write the Constitution there would have been somebody who knew all the "whereases" and "wherefores." We were just a shovelful of slime scooped off the pavement of skid row but we could have built America on the side of the hill in the San Bernardino Mountains. Now you show me anywhere in the world such diffuse competence. It's fantastic. When I talk about Americans being a skilled people I don't mean only technical skills. I also mean social and political skills.

The vigor of a society should be gauged by its ability to get along without outstanding leaders. When I said this at a lecture all the young intellectuals were up in arms. They ran after me when I finished and said, "Mr. Hoffer, the vigor of a society should be gauged by its ability to produce great leaders." I stood there and I said, "Brother, a society that can get along without leaders is the one that's producing leaders."

Look at the case of Harry Truman. You remember the picture when he was sworn in — all the brainy ones were standing around and wondering "Look who is being sworn in as President." Now Trumans are a dime a dozen in this country. You can almost close your eyes, reach over the sidewalk, make a man President, and he'll turn out to be a Truman. Show me any other society that could do a thing like that. It's breathtaking.

Sevareid: Now, Mr. Hoffer, in Washington where I work, there's a lot of talk and controversy about intellectuals in the federal government—the writers that have been in and out of government. Do you think they contribute anything to governing this country?

Hoffer: Well, I don't know. But I know they haven't got the power. The power is in the hand of President Johnson and he's not an intellectual, although he has been a school teacher. Johnson is one of us, yes. And this is why I have faith in him.

The intellectuals are, I suppose, important people. After all, they produce our books, paint our paintings and all that sort of thing. As for science, where would we be without intellectuals? I say, pamper them, pet them, give them everything they want but not power! Not power!

You see, the problem that faces a modern society is how to use the energies of the intellectual and yet not give him power. Get it? That's what we have to do.

Sevareid: Why do intellectuals hate President Johnson?

....*Hoffer:* Oh, well, it's just that they can't stand the common American . . . Look at our American intellectuals—real intellectuals and two-bit intellectuals. Look everywhere in the world — Africa, Asia, Europe. Intellectuals are making history. Intellectuals are even generals. Intellectuals are many things. Here in America the intellectuals have no power, and they are mad.

Now I told you that there has been a change in the tilt of the social landscape right now. People who should be wheeling and dealing on Wall Street or should be building industrial empires are now throwing their weight around on the campus. They are pulling their way up the academic ladder. They are throwing their weight around in artistic and literary cliques. You won't believe it but making history is a substitute for making a million dollars.

At 65 I know the whole cycle. You try to make history at 20 and then when you are 40 you are actually trying to make a million dollars on Wall Sreet. I could give you instances. On the water-front the richest longshoremen are all ex-Communists.

Actually, from my own experience, I would say that the Communist Party in the United States is a vehicle for transforming true believers into successful real estate dealers. And there is a certain regularity: If you were a Stalinist at 20 the chances are you're going to be a real estate dealer at 40. If you are a Trotskyite at 20 you'll probably be a successful professor of sociology at 40 and you'll be sneering at the young, two-bit intellectuals. Recently a few Maoists came to see me and I had fun with them.

Sevareid: Now, wait a minute. Maoists?

Hoffer: Yeah. They worship Mao. I had real fun with them. I told them what I just told you. I said, "I know what the Stalinists are going to be. I know what the Trotskyites are going to be. But what are the Maoists going to be? Let me predict your future. You are going to be laundrymen. You know, there's only one step from brainwashing to laundry washing."

Sevareid: Something has bothered me a lot, particularly in traveling around Latin America. I think you've written about it — the special talent for maintenance. In Brazil, for example, they've built a big city, Brazilia, that's gorgeous to look at. Six months later the washbowls are coming out of the plaster and the whole place is going down. Does this have something to do with the stamina quality you were talking about?

Hoffer: Of course. You know, after the last war when Western Europe was in ruins, I thought to myself: If the President should send me to Europe to predict which country is going to recover first, I would get the answer in five minutes. I would say, "Bring me the records of maintenance. The nation with the best maintenance will recover first." If I should go to Africa to tell you which of its 30-some nations is going to be here 50 years from now, I would look around for rudiments of maintenance.

If I got into a warehouse, let's say, and I saw that the broom had a special nail, I would say, "This is the nail of immortality!" That's it. Maintenance is something very specifically western. It doesn't exist anywhere else. I don't think a nation becomes modernized, really becomes renovated, unless it has the capacity for maintenance. They haven't got it in Russia. They haven't it anywhere outside narrow Western Europe.

Sevareid: Tell me something. You're living here in San Francisco where are all the hippies, beatniks, whatever they call them now, these kids who seem to want to retire from the normal life that most of us live. Do you think that there's any chance they've really got something, that they are a prophetic minority?

Hoffer: If it wasn't for the question of drugs I would be all for the hippy movement because it's a healthy reaction against the rat race. Now with automation coming on strong, we have to know how to enjoy leisure.

We don't know what the drugs are going to do to many of the hippies — how many of them are going to be flawed, how many are going to be destroyed, how many are going to be wasted.

Sevareid: But the fact that the hippies need these drugs must tell something about their strength or weakness, doesn't it?

Hoffer: It doesn't tell anything. History is made by example. Somebody starts it. You can't explain something that happens by saying there was a real need for it. History is made by third-rate or even fourth-rate people who are anonymous, who are buried in unmarked and unvisited graves. To me, whenever I see something new coming up in history, I'm always certain that somebody was there, somebody we don't know anything about.

You know there's a whole string of towns in San Joaquin Valley — Turlock, Modesto, Madera, Merced. I want to show you how I generalize about history from an experience that happened there. Now all these towns have the same climate, the same economic conditions. They raise the same crops. But only Modesto has the most beautiful lawns in Christendom. Nowhere in the world will you find such beautiful lawns. The people here don't seem to do anything but mow their lawns.

How come the lawns of Modesto? Turlock hasn't them. Merced hasn't them. Madera hasn't them. If I were a sociologist I probably could figure it out. What the scientist does is count so I counted the churches. Plenty of churches. Plenty of chiropractors. But what the hell connection could there be between churches and chiropractors and lawns? And then I had a hunch. I went to Modesto's cemetery and I looked up the oldest graves. The people came from Essex, Wessex, just where the lawns were first cultivated. This is the way things get started. So when we talk about the hippies, don't

Sevareid: Why is it that they so detest the middle class? Is that always true of young people?

attribute the drug habit out of any need. Somebody started it.

Hoffer: Well, perhaps no country is good for its juveniles. They have to adjust themselves to situations. One of the chief characteristics of human uniqueness is that instead of changing ourselves we try to change what we are supposed to adjust to. I'd say that the young are against their middle class parents.

Young people are assuming the intellectual attitude. The intellecual, you know, was against the middle class all through the nineteenth century. The intellectuals entered that century convinced they were going to make history. Hadn't they made the French Revolution?

Sevareid: But then the industrial revolution produced the middle class that intellectuals resent so much.

Hoffer: Yeah, but they didn't know that it was an industrial revolution. The intellectuals of the first decades of the nineteenth century thought they were going to make history. And then one morning they woke up and found out that their low-brow relatives—their uncles, their fathers and brothers, their low-brow brothers—had grabbed possession of everything in sight and they were the ruling class. The intellectuals were enraged.

This, to me, is the only explanation of what was going on during the nineteenth and twentieth centuries. The cold war started somewhere in the middle of the last century. The intellectuals are now winning the cold war against the middle class. The middle class isn't being destroyed by the aristocrats. Napoleon put it this way: "Cannon destroyed the feudal society. Ink will destroy the middle class society."

Sevareid: It seems to me that American middle class society keeps growing bigger and bigger.

Hoffer: In this country, and probably everywhere, this is the effect of Americanization. I've been watching it closely. When American interests started to penetrate Britain and Germany I wanted to see what happened first. You would think that if a business civilization like America — supposedly a business civilization — penetrates a country the first people to be influenced would be the businessmen. But that's not true. The first people to be influenced are the common people. Something happens to their backbone. Straighten up!

In other words, the first effect of Americanization is the deproletarianization of the working man. He ceases to be a proletarian. He thinks he's as good as everybody else. He wants to look like everybody else. He wants to live like everybody else. You know, the first effect of Americanization on a country is that the working man insists on having lockers and shower baths in the factories. He wants to change into street clothes when he leaves the factory so that you can't recognize he's a worker unless you look at his hands.

Sevareid: This is something new in history, isn't it?

Hoffer: The only new thing in history is America. It's blasphemous to say that but it's true. Do you know what I feel when I talk about the common people of America to the professors? I feel like I'm talking about mysterious people living on a mysterious continent. The professors don't know anything about them. Nothing! We're supposed to be just a bunch of saps who are told to vote. But we elected Roosevelt four times in the teeth of all the newspapers, in the teeth of Wall Street. And we elected Truman when all the newspapers said that Dewey was elected.

You know, when the young, two-bit intellectuals at the University of California talk about the masses they call them the Pavlovian dogs. They call them the mindless masses. It makes me furious. What the hell do these intellectuals know about us? How dare they write books about us! Who among these so-called intellectuals could have predicted that an Oakland machine politician would become Chief Justice Earl Warren? When Warren was picked all the intellectuals had a nervous breakdown: "Look who is becoming Chief Justice!"

What do they know about what's inside us? Who could have predicted that a hack politician endorsed by the Ku Klux Klan would become Justice Hugo Black?

Sevareid: But you Californians also elected Ronald Reagan. Does this change anything?

Hoffer: We make mistakes and we can unmake them. Ronald Reagan is a "B" picture hero. He has a mortal hatred of "A" pictures. He wants to turn California into a "B" picture to be run on a "B" picture budget, if he can. But California is not a "B" picture. California is an "A" picture, whether Reagan wants it or not. And we're going to shake him off.

Sevareid: Would you say that President Kennedy is about as close to a charismatic leader as we've had?

Hoffer: He was to me. You know, I had no feel for Kennedy at all. He was a European. All you have to do is tabulate how many times he crossed the Atlantic and how many times he crossed the Appalachian Mountains and you know where he belonged. Then tabulate the same thing for Johnson — how many times he crossed the Atlantic and how many times he crossed the Appalachians.

Sevareid: When you talk to Johnson privately you realize that the core of his memory and thought is all with domestic American things. Foreign policy seems a great effort for him.

Hoffer: When you're in the Middle West there is no other world but America.

We are so big that foreign affairs don't seem to count. Really, the only reason we are interested in foreign affairs is that we have to prevent a third world war. This, to me, has been our foreign policy since the end of the last war — how to prevent a third world war.

We are a learning people. You know, when the immigrants came to this country they had to learn a new language. They had to watch the game. We are a learning people, perhaps we're the only nation that learns from experience.

We learned our lesson during the 1930's. We know how third world wars start and how to prevent them. The way to prevent a third war is to pick the potential bully and get as close to him as possible and breathe down his neck until he settles down. Everyone of us knows that if France and Britain had turned Spain and Ethiopia into Vietnam in the 1930's, if they had committed there all the atrocities we supposedly commit in Vietnam, if they made all the mistakes we supposedly are making in Vietnam, there wouldn't have been a Second World War. There wouldn't have been a Hitler. There wouldn't have been gas chambers. You do not start a world war when a democracy throws its weight around facing a bully. World wars are started when the democracies are too unprepared, too cowardly, too reasonable, too frightened, too tired, too humanitarian. I'm not going to tell Johnson what to do because I have faith in him. Johnson will do the right thing. I've lived with Johnsons all my life. I know them. He'll do the right thing. He'll be the foremost President of the twentieth century. I'm convinced.

Sevareid: Doesn't he have to get us out of Vietnam somehow?

Hoffer: He had better. He had better. We'll find a solution to the Vietnam problem. You know, we fumbled. We've never fought a war like this before. We have to learn how to fight.

Sevareid: Do you think we can throw our weight around in the Middle East, for example, without making things worse?

Hoffer: Of course. We'll have to. We'll have to.

Sevareid: Have we not discharged our so-called moral obligation to Israel already many times over? How far does it go?

Hoffer: Well, Mr. Sevareid, no country of the Occident will ever discharge its debt to Israel. Don't forget that the whole of the Occident was involved in the persecution, the humiliation, and the final annihilation of six million Jewish men, women and children. Not one country with all their open spaces — not Brazil, not this country, not Australia — not one threw its gates open to the Jews while escape was still possible. The Jews had to crawl on their knees to beg for visas. Not one country remonstrated with Hitler. Not one country broke diplomatic relations with him. We're all involved in it.

I have a premonition. As it goes with Israel, so it will go with all of us. If Israel perishes the holocaust will be upon us and history will cease to have meaning.

I wrote my first book in 1948 when the miracle of Israel happened. Imagine, after all that unimaginable suffering and degradation came the miracle of 1948, when a few thousand fugitives from Hitler's gas chambers got up on their hind legs and defied 14 million Arabs. I remember. I'm barely literate, trying to write a book, trying to make sense of the enormities and calamities which had befallen us. That miracle of Israel put heart into me. I feel that history can have meaning. History can make sense.

Israel must not perish. If Israel perishes there will be nothing to talk about, nothing to write about. Nothing will have any meaning anymore and history has to have some meaning.

Sevareid: Why do you say our so-called Negro revolution is a fraud?

Hoffer: The Negro revolution, if you watched it from the very beginning, has been used as an instrument by the Negro middle class to fulfill its own desires. The leaders of the Negro revolution have no faith in the Negro masses, no concern for them. It was used, as I say, by a relatively prosperous Negro middle class to attain its ends. Imagine, a Negro revolution starting to move. The first thing they worry about is desegregation. Who the hell needs desegregation except the Negro middle class family with a boy they want to put in a special school.

The tragedy is that this so-called revolution not only didn't bring about any meaningful transformation of the Negro masses, but it didn't give the Negro middle class what it wanted. The Negro middle class is just finding this out. It will have to integrate itself with the Negro masses if the Negro is going to attain anything.

Ask any longshoreman what a Negro leader should do and he'll tell you. It's the most obvious thing that what a Negro leader should do is dovetail the Negro's difficulties into opportunities for growth. Let me give an example. You go to Chicago or New York. They have the Negro slums, Negro unemployed. Now what a Negro has to do is to train these unemployed into skilled carpenters, masons, plasterers, plumbers, painters.

The Negro has to master the art of slum renovation. He has to organize Negro workers into a solid black union and renovate the slums. You don't worry about who owns the slums. You just go ahead and turn a slum into a garden. After you have renovated you challenge the discriminating white unions to open up or get wiped out. This is the way you get power.

Sevareid: How do they get the resources to renovate slums?

Hoffer: You don't need much in resources and there's money floating around. I bet you, Mr. Sevareid, any time a Negro leader proposes what I propose, the money will come to him from government, from private corporations. They are just beginning to realize this. I have been saying it for years and years and years.

Sevareid: Well, what about the new young Negro leaders like Stokely Carmichael? They sound as though they're racist.

Hoffer: Oh, they just sound like it. They're all phonies.

Sevareid: But it's race hatred they're preaching.

Hoffer: Yeah, but who's going to listen to them? Maybe a few. They are not going to get anywhere because they have naive conceptions of power. They say: "Power, power. Give me power." Nobody can give you power. Power doesn't come in cans. Carmichael is always saying: "Give me the can opener. I'll open the cans of power." They're all phony, these people. They simply do not realize that it's the long-term projects, things that you go about doing patiently and quietly, that achieve results. Once you have realized this you don't waste your energies on anything except building.

I've been advocating build yourself a community for a long time. Let me tell you about something that happened to me. One day I came to Pier 35 and right there on the wall was a poem. I don't know whether it's good poetry. I don't know anything about poetry. But the darn thing sunk into me: I think it should be the anthem of the Negro. It's called "Build Yourself a City." Here's how it goes:

Build yourself a city,
Found yourself a state.
Do not cry for pity,
Grab and master fate.
Grab a swamp and drain it,
Cut the log and plane it,
Make the hill the valley field
And on the manmade plain
Breathe your last complaint.
Slay your shame, forget your name,
Build! Do not cry for pity,
Build yourself a city.

This is what I say, "Build yourself a city." Any average American sees that's what has to be done. You waste energies on demonstrations, on riots. They do not produce one atom of pride. The Negro is beginning to realize that he has to do things by himself, that anything he is given will turn into wormwood and ashes in his mouth. Pride is what the Negro needs.

You don't get pride by having other people do your work for you or by giving you things. This is why I say the only hope for the Negro now is the Negro veterans out of Vietnam. Their tremendous performance has been generating a pride that's radiating across the Pacific and reaching into many Negro households. Vietnam is going to do for the Negro what Israel has done for the Jews. They are proving themselves. If I was a Negro leader I would pitch a tent on the water's edge and grab those Negro veterans as they come back. They are the seed of the future. They are the kind of leaders the Negro needs. The moment the Negro is proud of being a Negro he'll cease worrying about being a Negro. This is a great country because you can be a human being first and only secondly something else.

Sevareid: Well, now, why is it that our mythology says we're a country of individuals, of competition, of self-seeking capitalists, et cetera? There's more capacity for human cooperation here than any place else.

Hoffer: It's fantastic, unbelievable. I don't know how we get it but you should see the readiness for mutual help that we have in this country. This connects with my idea about kindness. Anybody who writes a book about America and doesn't mention kindness doesn't know what this country is about. But it's more than that. It's not a role you play. You don't preach about it. You don't sing about it. You don't grandstand about it. Kindness is part of the mechanics of American life.

Let me tell you something. One year I was picking peas. I think they paid us 35 cents a hamper and a hamper had to be full if you wanted to get paid. If a hamper wasn't full that was just too bad. Well, my last hamper wasn't full so I went on back into the field and I find some rows that haven't been picked clean and I start to pick. I wasn't making much headway when I saw a fellow at the other end of the row picking peas right into his hat. I was furious. "Here's a son-of-a-bitch," I said to myself. "He knows that I need these few peas to get me my 35 cents and he is picking them for himself." By the time we met I was ready to jump at his throat. What did he do? He emptied his hat into my hamper. "Now," he said, "you owe a hatful of peas to somebody else." We pass on whatever good that we do. We expect somebody else to pay the debt to somebody else, not to us. We start a chain.

Sevareid: There's kindness here but there's also violence. Isn't there a contradiction here?

Hoffer: Look, Mr. Sevareid, it wasn't the cream of creation that built this country. You know, there was a time in Italy when you had a choice to go to jail or go to America. We haven't been peopled by philosophers and Milquetoasts. We have been peopled by violent people. But it's remarkable how little violence there is when you think of it.

The Orient isn't mysterious to me. What the hell is there mysterious about sloth and decay and hot air? To me the real mystery is America. What makes us run? What makes us do things? How do we do things? Nobody knows anything about us.

Haven't you noticed what tremendous trust we have here? By the way, this trust has gone against Marxist doctrine. Marxist history is heretical. If Marx was around now he'd be put in a concentration camp. He doesn't conform to the party line at all.

During my early years on the San Francisco waterfront the Communists were revolted by the fact that everybody was trusted to pay a nickel for the newspaper on the corner. They wanted to destroy such trust, so they stole the papers. It offended them that a capitalist, self-seeking society should have so much trust.

Sevareid: When you stopped working as a longshoreman a few months ago I think the union obligated you to retire, didn't it?

Hoffer: Yeah, yeah.

Sevareid: You've written a lot about the ordeal of change. You've written a lot about leisure. How does it affect you?

Hoffer: It doesn't affect me much because this is a fantastic country and it's been good to me. I'll tell you why. I think a society is good where a person can feel, first of all, a human being before he's anything else. And this is what I've felt all my life here. When I sit down to write, when I get to my room, I'm a human being first and only secondly a working man. Although I've been working all my life I've never felt like a working man. I've felt like Eric Hoffer all my life.

As far as a sense of usefulness is concerned, I put in fifty years of hard work and even a horse that works that long has earned his rest. So I don't feel any sense of guilt. I'm used to getting along without the things I like. I've trained myself to it all my life. There's nothing I have to have except three meals a day and a few books to read, and maybe a few lines to scribble. If I have these things I can go on forever.

Sevareid: How, Eric, are you going to spend the rest of your life?

Hoffer: Well, I never worry. The woman who brought me up told me that I had nothing to worry about. I was going to die at 40 and so I went through life like a tourist. When I was 40 I took my pulse and everything was functioning fine. I'm living on velvet now.

Death will come tomorrow. Death will come this evening. It matters not. I have no grievance against anybody. I always got more than I deserved. I'm not just talking. I've always felt that I got more than I deserved and that I have to treat people better than they deserve. There's no bookkeeping as far as people are concerned, see.

I've lived a long life. Sixty-five years. According to the insurance companies I ought to curl up and die right now. Let me tell you something that happened this spring. I have a room in the Chinese section of San Francisco. Looking out my window, I see the Golden Gate Bridge. It's an old house but I love that room and the hills on the other side.

The grass was just coming out and I remember how the sentences came to me:

On the grey, green hills every end has a beginning.
Kissed to life by dancing showers.
My end has no beginning,
No slumbering seed of velvet and flowers.

I'm reconciled. I'm reconciled.

January 28, 1969

Sevareid: On September 19, 1967, Eric Hoffer appeared on CBS News for an interview and people have been discussing him ever since. The longshoreman has visited the White House and become a member of a Presidential Commission appointed by Lyndon Johnson. But his theme has not changed.

Mr. Hoffer, it's now a little over a year since you became a celebrity. What has this done to your life?

Hoffer: Fame doesn't mean a thing to me. Fame means to be known by people who don't know you. Now, how the hell are you going to get excited about that?

Sevareid: Wouldn't you like your books to be around forty or fifty years from now?

Hoffer: Well, Montaigne died four hundred years ago and every day I think of him. Do you think it makes a lot of difference to him that I read him, that I love him? When you are dead you are dead. When I go down the street and people talk to me that helps because I love the human species. I love its smell. I love its smudge. I don't want to run away from people.

Anytime somebody tells me he has to go to the top of a mountain to think I feel like telling him, brother, you'd better sit right where you are. You've got nothing to think about.

Sevareid: I know, Mr. Hoffer, that you received tons of mail after our first television. How did you handle it?

Hoffer: I don't answer the mail. How could I answer it? I don't think the people who write to me get sore about this. I glance through the mail. Every once in a while some letter will really touch me but if I answer one out of a hundred that's an awful lot.

I enjoy charming letters. If a letter is charming I cannot resist it. By charm I don't mean flattery. Charm means genuineness. You know, it's very hard to pretend. If you want to impress other people you have to be genuine. Once in a while I get a letter like that, that touches me. I don't like to write letters. I don't write much anyhow and when I see five or six letters piled up on my table I begin to feel guilty and I don't like to feel guilty. That's another reason why I'm not an intellectual. An intellectual wallows in his sense of guilt. He feels distinguished when he feels guilty. I don't want to feel guilty. I don't owe anybody anything and nobody owes me anything.

Sevareid: You mean, you've never done anything or said anything in your life that made you feel guilty?

Hoffer: Of course I know my sins, all my sins. But what I also know is that imperfection is an essential ingredient of human life. Anybody who expects any human being to be perfect doesn't love humanity. This is the great fault of the idealists, of the Messianic hounds. They really don't love humanity. If you really love humanity you have compassion for it. I can't imagine any love without compassion and compassion hasn't a good name among intellectuals. When they talk about it they think it's an inferior quality.

I don't expect too much of people. Anyone who expects too much from people wants to be disappointed. You really don't expect much of the people you love. The idealists keep saying they won't compromise, they want things perfect. I say they don't love us. That's all there is to it.

Sevareid: It seems to me you lump all intellectuals together when you condemn them so much. Surely you don't mean that.

Hoffer: I talk of a specific type of literate person when I talk about an intellectual. I have defined an intellectual a hundred times and yet, again and again, the first question they ask is, "How do you define an intellectual?" To me an intellectual is a man of some education who considers himself a member of the educated elite, who thinks he has a God-given right to direct affairs. To me an intellectual doesn't even have to be intelligent in order to be an intellectual. He can be highly educated like Arnold Toynbee, like Arthur Schlesinger, or he can be illiterate like Lee Oswald.

You know, Oswald read one book, "Capital," and he became an intellectual. He looked down on the masses as if they were dirt. Hitler was an intellectual too; he considered himself a member of the educated elite. These are the intellectuals I am talking about.

I'm not talking about Alfred North Whitehead; I'm not talking about Jacques Maritain; I'm not talking about Richard Hofstadter, or Nathan Glazer or Daniel P. Moynihan or Daniel Bell. These are genuinely cultivated persons. These are my masters. These are people I read with delight, with reverence. I listen to everything they have to say, but I ignore those people who consider themselves members of an elite with a God-given right to run things.

Sevareid: It's their attitude toward ordinary people that is the dividing line in your mind?

Hoffer: That's right.

Sevareid: We had an intellectual running for President last spring and summer in Senator McCarthy, who said that he didn't think you were much of a philosopher. What do you think of him?

Hoffer: Well, I didn't read what he said. I'll tell you one thing. I've always thought that this country is lucky. Anytime you doubt it imagine what would happen if that so-and-so got elected President. You'd have a yogi sitting in that White House mumbling under his goddamned nose. He wouldn't be able to do a thing with the Congress. He wouldn't be able to think or talk to anybody. He would just go into a trance. We would have had chaos. This country wouldn't last twenty-four hours.

And how vain that man is, how un-American. A genuine American knows how to lose gracefully. Humphrey showed him up. I am sure that when Humphrey congratulated Nixon after the election he was showing up McCarthy. McCarthy treated Humphrey shabbily.

If I was Humphrey I would wipe the floor with McCarthy. I wouldn't try to court the McCarthyites. They are the most treacherous people in the world and, by the way, if McCarthy got elected, these young McCarthyites would have torn him apart. We are lucky he didn't get elected. He's going to be the great forgotten man. I guarantee you that.

Sevareid: Since I talked with you in 1967 the President of the United States has had you at the White House many times and has talked about you a great deal. Were your feelings about him any different after you knew him than they were before?

Hoffer: No, I love the President. To me Johnson means much more than just a President. To me Johnson means one of us — a longshoreman as a President. When I first saw him I said something that made people around him think that I put my foot into it or something. I said, "Mr. President, isn't it wonderful that a Johnson is the President?" And he said, "You're damn tooting!"

I didn't tell the President a joke I had on the tip of my tongue —

which shows that I sometimes don't yield to stupidity. My joke tells a lot about the President and about me. The joke goes like this: A fellow came into a saloon. He saw two men and a dog playing poker and the dog was playing a good hand of poker. So he walked over to the bar and the bartender nudges him and says, "Hey, what do you think of that?" He said, "Bah, any time the dog gets a good hand, he wiggles his tail."

Now, to find fault in me for not writing perfect prose, to find fault with Johnson for not being a perfect President, is just like finding fault with a dog playing poker. We do our best and this is why being in the White House with Johnson was for me a tremendous thing. I slept there one night and I walked around the White House and I said, "We are here — we are here!" Now, I'm not going to be there with Nixon although I think Nixon will make a good President. But Johnson to me is someone very special.

Sevareid: You said in 1967 that you thought Johnson would go down as the greatest President of the century. Do you still think so?

Hoffer: Oh yes. History will be good to Johnson. The Johnson era will loom larger than any other, including the Roosevelt era. The Johnson era for good or for evil is the watershed in our history. All the legislation that he passed, so many seeds planted, will have to germinate for decades, maybe for centuries. To me he's already a great President. He made mistakes, sure, but we don't know whether the mistakes are mistakes. Nobody knows what is going to turn up in Vietnam, what Vietnam will look like 10 or 20 years from now.

Sevareid: Do you think Johnson did the right thing last March in taking himself out?

Hoffer: Well, I don't know. You can't tell him how to do things. If a Johnson gets a job on the waterfront I would never dare to come around and tell him how to do it. The Johnsons do everything the best way they know how and sometimes it isn't good enough but what the heck!

Sevareid: You were appointed to the President's Commission on Violence and the premise of that is, I assume, that there's been a great rise in violence, that it's dangerous to this country. In 1967 you thought we weren't a violent people.

Hoffer: We aren't. Just scratch your head and try to find the last occurrence of violence that you have seen. You have been riding freights, you have been through the depression, how much violence did we have? The sociologists are brazen enough to tell us that poverty breeds violence. We have been poor, you have been poor, a 120 or 140 millions of us have had first-hand experience of poverty. We were just one step ahead of hunger. When we went to sleep in the evening we didn't know where we were going to have our breakfast. Did we become violent? Did we start mugging? Did we become criminals? For heaven's sake!

There was a convention of lawyers in Philadelphia not so long ago. You ought to read a report of what was said at that convention — sociological crap that we have to right every wrong, we have to send every soul to the cleaner, that we have to eliminate poverty, eliminate slums, before there is going to be an end to violence. The only person at that convention who spoke up against this sort of thing was an Englishman, John Widgerly, Lord Chief Justice of the Court of Appeals. He said anybody who is ignorant enough to say that if you eliminate the slums, if you eliminate poverty, you eliminate crime is as innocent as an unborn child. Look, he says, Hitler eliminated our slums in England. He bombed them out. And then came the Labor Government and eliminated poverty but crime just keeps on rising.

Sevareid: Don't you think boredom has about as much to do with violence, perhaps, as poverty and turmoil?

Hoffer: In human affairs everything is a paradox. Boredom is the seed of creativeness. Boredom creates great literature, great painting. It also creates revolution. All these things go together. I don't know whether we are really bored. I've never been bored in my life. You know, some people are afraid to admit this. I've lived all my life with people who never read a book, who wouldn't know an idea if you shoved it down their throat. I never felt cut off from intellectual intercourse. I aways felt that I had plenty of people to talk to. Why? Because I wanted to learn and when you want to learn the moment you come in contact with a person you find out what he is good at, what he knows, and then you bring him out and you're never bored.

To me the American people are full of surprises. I've been humbled by them all my life because I have a savage heart, you know, and they have tremendous forbearance. You get on a job and there's a drunk. I bristle right away. Oh, the son-of-a-bitch. I'm going to do his work for him? And then I look at the rest of the gang. They take it playfully. They take him in their stride with forbearance. This is why I say what I am saying here. The moment I open my mouth I'm shooting it off.

I'm not going to give advice. I prefer to listen to the gentle heart of the Americans, all of them. They put me to shame all the time you know. This is what I told President Johnson — I have a savage heart and I don't fit on a commission. I haven't the forbearance to deal gently and humanely with all these explosions. I warned him of this. What my savage heart tells me now everybody else tells me a year or two later. This is the terrible thing about a savage heart.

Sevareid: I don't know quite what you mean by savage. I think you're very gentle.

Hoffer: No. I really have a savage heart. Besides, I don't know how to tame the spoken word. Only when I write am I controlled.

Sevareid: I wouldn't think you ever hit anybody in your life.

Hoffer: No. Because nobody hit me.

Sevareid: Well, so you're not a savage.

Hoffer: You know, student hoodlums are educated people but they have a hoodlum society. The only civilized society I can find is on the waterfront. If on the waterfront you called anybody a mother so-and-so you'd have your teeth knocked in, you'd be thrown into the drink. The most civilized society in the world is on the waterfront.

Sevareid: Somebody said that our Victorian ancestors were embarrassed in the presence of the base. We seem to be embarrassed in the presence of the noble.

Hoffer: Well, we have a new generation, a new world. I go down to Polk Street. I feel like an immigrant who just arrived in a foreign country. It's hell to immigrate at sixty-seven. I hate the idea but I don't know anything about this new generation. I don't know anything about the new world.

But in the back of my mind, no matter how I am about this new generation, I have an inkling that maybe they're as good as they think they are. Maybe we ought to give them a chance. Now, you take, for instance, California State College. It's an awful mess. If I was Reagan I would give the college to the young ones. Nobody over twenty-five should dare step into this college. They should run everything and hire professors as they want — black ones and white ones. I wish them well but I think it's going to be an animal kingdom. They'll just eat each other up. But we have to give them a chance. I suggested not so long ago that we should give them a state. Take all the grown people out of Nevada and give it to the hippies. Let's see what happens.

Sevareid: Well, you can't expect people to be trustworthy unless you give them trust, can you?

Hoffer: Yes, yes. I'd give the new generation plenty of chances because they have shown real powers of organization. They're tremendous organizers. Maybe they are much more noble, much more proficient, much more competent than we give them credit.

Sevareid: Does idealism require any brains particularly?

Hoffer: I don't know. All I know is that ideals are a dime a dozen. What is hard to get is ideas.

Sevareid: Since you became celebrated because of the broadcast in 1967 a great many of the New Left and the Negro militants and what not have been awful hard on you, Mr. Hoffer. They say you're old hat, that you're a racist, that you don't really understand what's going on today. Does this upset you much?

Hoffer: No, no. Big Higginbottom has been calling me a racist. I happen to be less afraid of being called a racist than Higginbottom is afraid of being called an Uncle Tom. That's a fact. It's fantastic, you know, how they intimidate you. Good heavens, with all the things that are going on, if you don't speak up, if you take all this insolence lying down, do you think you're helping the Negro?

I have a higher opinion of the Negro masses than Higginbottom. You know, the distance between the average and the exception among Negroes is tremendous. Any time Negroes make good they think they are a special people. They actually separate themselves from the Negro race. I have a better opinion of the Negro masses and that's why I expect as much from Negroes as I would expect from myself. Let me put it a little different: Although it might not be legitimate to expect as much from the Negro as we expect from ourselves, the fact remains that if the Negro does not expect much from himself he will not accomplish anything.

Sevareid: Well, what you're saying, I take it, is that unless one treats a Negro exactly like any other human being, then you're not treating him as an equal.

Hoffer: You know, I've lived all my life with Negroes, worked with them, never went any place where a Negro couldn't go. I never earned more than a Negro who worked side by side with me and it never occurred to me that the Negro wouldn't be my equal. Now, if you think that the Negro is your equal then you expect something from him. On the other hand, if you think that the Negro is your inferior, that he isn't capable of doing anything, then you want to treat him with extra special care and you want to make him more equal than equal.

Sevareid: Certain ones. I suppose most are not treated that way.

Hoffer: The Kerner Report tells us that unless we eliminate poverty from the earth and cleanse ourselves of racism and selfishness there are going to be riots and crimes. This is absolute poppycock. The only way the Negro is going to achieve something is by Negroes accomplishing something together on their own. All that we outsiders can do for the Negro is wish them well and give money.

Sevareid: You keep talking about black power and separatism, the opposite of integration.

Hoffer: Let's talk about black power. How is the Negro to get power? The only way he can do this is through organization. Organization is the accumulation of power without instruments of coercion. But in order to be able to organize you have to have mutual trust. If the black man wants power he has to generate trust.

Sevareid: What do you think of present Negro leadership?

Hoffer: The only person for whom I have respect is Roy Wilkins. Have you noticed that his is the only ascetic face in the whole goddamned leadership? Almost every one of their leaders is living off the fat of the land. Roy Wilkins is the only one that's honest. He isn't afraid of being called an Uncle Tom.

I can imagine myself being a Negro. Almost every thought I have about the Negro stems from what I would do if I were a Negro. I've lived long enough with them and gotten along fine with them although I never mince words.

Sevareid: Do you see any young Negro leaders coming up that strike you as important?

Hoffer: Phony, phony. Look at that misbegotten Eldridge Cleaver. A sewer rat if ever there was one, talking about "Soul on Ice." It's soul on manure if you ask me.

Cleaver recently came over to talk to some San Francisco lawyers who call themselves the Barrister Club — gentle, civilized people. Comes Cleaver. He has an earring. I think he also has a nose ring. And he has a necklace of animal teeth. What does he say? He calls the lawyers "Mother . . .," you know the rest of it. He insulted them with crude, stupid obscenities. When he's through, what do they do? They clap. What can we do for you, Mr. Cleaver? What we have there is insolence on one side and cowardice on the other. That explains how Hitler came to power. If insolence faces cowardice, Hitler is inevitable.

Sevareid: Is this a case of "Conscience doth make cowards of us all?"

Hoffer: I don't think so. These people who listened to Cleaver haven't any conscience. Let me tell you about them. They live in exclusive neighborhoods, send their children to exclusive schools.

Sevareid: Who would you include in this group?

Hoffer: White people who are so patient, so gentle, so humanitarian when you talk to them about the Negro. They feel guilty. They love to feel guilty. And then they confess, but when they confess the breasts they beat are our breasts, not theirs. They beat our breasts into a pulp. They tell us we are supposed to cleanse ourselves of racism, that we are supposed to send our school children all across the town in buses. It's our breasts they are beating.

Sevareid: You're talking about working people now.

Hoffer: Yes, working people. I'm talking about seventy per cent of the people in the United States. You know, when the riots first started, every one of us of the seventy per cent had an alarm ringing in us — the most dangerous thing that could happen. After all, who built this country? We built this country, not the sociologists and all the others. We built this country and we know that disorder destroys a society. We know the importance of order. We established democratic practice. Intellectuals don't know a goddamn thing about democracy. When they have a chance to create a society you'll be surprised. It will be a hierarchical society. It will be like a Communist country or what Salazar created in Portugal.

What's the essence of democratic practice? First of all, it's discipline, good nature toward the opponent when he wins. It's also fierce resentment against those who break the public peace. If you ask me if a society has a choice between injustice and disorder I would take injustice any time because with injustice we can live long enough to correct it, but with disorder we can't live long enough to do justice.

Sevareid: You know, the Frenchman Maritain said, "The pure man of the left always prefers what is not to what is and the pure man of the right always prefers injustice to disorder." Would you classify him as a man of the right?

Hoffer: I don't give a damn what Maritain said. My feeling is that a just society must be a stern society, a just society must be a strong society. None of those sociologists who set themselves up as authorities warned us that when we started the avalanche of civil rights laws we should gird our loins and get ready for trouble. Nobody told us that. Nobody.

Sevareid: Aren't you a little worried about people who accuse you of giving respectability to a movement of anti-intellectualism, which has never been good really for any country, has it?

....*Hoffer:* My worry is to write a line, write a paragraph. This is my worry. There is no other worry. You cannot give me peace of mind by praising me, by people saying I'm an angel or anything like that. I don't worry about what people call me. I don't consider myself a public figure. I consider myself a retired longshoreman who has a right to shoot his mouth off and I think in this free country we should shoot our mouth off. There's no use holding back the resentment inside us and then go and vote for George Wallace because he said something we're afraid to say. When these riots first came I said to myself what's the danger? I said to myself the riots are a plowing and a harrowing of the Northern cities for the transplantation of the South to the North. This is why I say that Wallace is a portent. If we are going to have four more years of rioting we're going to have a Wallace or somebody worse than Wallace. That's what we are afraid of. It's the spread of the South to the North and riots will bring it.

Sevareid: In your diaries you express some doubt that even total integration would leave the American Negro without grievances. What do you mean?

*Hoffer:*Well, in a white society, the Negro for the foreseeable future will be a Negro first and only secondly an individual. Right now, look at him. Suppose you knew for sure that Jesus Christ was supposed to come in through the door. If Jesus Christ turns out to be a Negro you'll see the Negro first and only then Jesus.

We're not going to send 180 million souls to the cleaner, see. We can't clean them of prejudice in one night. Besides, the Kerner Report said we are racist anyhow. What I say is this: If in this siuation, where the Negro gets everything he asks for, then the blowup must come. You really have an explosive situation when you have everything but one thing. For the Negro living in a white society there is one thing he cannot be. He can't cease being black.

What the Negro needs is pride, pride of achievement. You don't acquire pride by having fuzzy wuzzy hair, by wearing a necklace of teeth, or by dressing up like Africans. You don't get pride that way. You have to earn it. Once the Negro has pride of achievement he'll be proud of being a Negro. This is all that's needed. It takes co-operative effort. This requires trust among Negroes.

Resentment is cheap. It's an onanism of the soul, a masturbation of the soul. The easiest thing in the world is to work yourself up into a rage. Patient effort, patient organization, are the seeds of achievement. Negroes should learn something from the Israelis. They should build kibbutzim. What's wrong with taking a thousand Negro juveniles out of a city and putting them to work building a kibbutz? The Negroes I know say to me we don't trust each other enough to do that. If someone calls me a racist I say go jump!

Sevareid: You don't agree with the Kerner Commission conclusion that white racism is the core of all the trouble?

Hoffer: Once they have said it, what do they do? The Commission has done untold harm. They tell us we're all racists. So we are racists, so what? What kind of solution is that? They ought to say what the Negro can do, what he should do, how we can help the Negro. The Kerner Report doesn't have a word about what the Negro should do. Every line says what we have to do, what we have to give. He has to have something that he alone can do without any whitey around. Any time the Negro tries to do something and you come around and offer to do it for him he'll hate your guts because you're taking something away from him.

Sevareid: Do you think racial tension is getting worse? Are you alarmed by the ten million votes George Wallace got? Do you think it was a race vote?

Hoffer: Well, it's resentment and I hate the idea that Americans should be intimidated, should be afraid to speak out and have to vote for Wallace because that cracker said what they were afraid to say. That's shameful.

Let's speak out. Then we don't need a Wallace to speak for us. We don't need anyone to speak for us. This insolence on one side and this cowardly silence on the other is the most explosive situation there is. You know, the radicals, the potential revolutionaries, have stood Louis XV on his head. Remember what Louis XV said? "Apres moi, le deluge." All the would-be revolutionaries say, "Apres le deluge, moi." I say, "Apres le deluge, Hitler."

We built this country — the sociologists didn't build it — and

we know that disorder is going to destroy it. We can repair injustice
if we have an orderly society but if we allow disorder to run its
course we'll have to live with violence. The hell I say. We won't
live with violence! Why should we? You can't have a democracy
with violence. You have nothing if you have violence.

Sevareid: Do you think we're a sick society?

Hoffer: When I recently said we're not a sick society Arthur
Schlesinger attacked me as if I was uttering a terrible heresy. Let
me tell you about something that happened right here on the campus
of the University of California. I delivered a lecture on man and
nature, a subject I love to talk about. Later I received a letter from
a professor of mathematics — a sensible letter. Enclosed with his
letter was a reprint of a lecture the professor gave in Kyoto while
he was there on a Fulbright Fellowship. He talked on the future
of science or something like that.

When I leafed through his pamphlet I came across a paragraph
in which he described America to the Japanese professors. It would
raise your hair on end. He said in America there are no neighbors,
there are no friends, everybody cuts your throat, everybody stabs
you in the back, you are afraid to leave your house. I said, what
the hell is he saying? The man is intelligent and honest. And then
it hit me between the eyes — the son-of-a-bitch was describing the
department of mathematics here at the University of California.
There they cut your throat. If you write a paper ahead of somebody
else they hate your guts. They have no neighbors, no friends. They
project their own society on us and then they call us sick.

The trouble with Arthur Schlesinger is that he has lived with
Schlesingers all of his life. This is a sick society if we have to live
with Schlesingers.

Sevareid: Schlesinger said, I think, that we are the most frightening
people on earth.

Hoffer: Ohhhh. I don't think we're that sort. How do we judge
a society? You can't judge it by its constitution. You can't judge
it by its literature or by its art. You have to judge it by the quality of
its people. What sort of people have we produced in this country?
My conviction — without hesitation, without qualification — is that
we have produced as fine a society as the world has ever seen on a
large scale. And we did it without the advice of the sociologists. You
know we built this country when they weren't around.

Sevareid: I don't quite grasp your attitude about nature. You sound almost as if you think it ought to be wiped out by man.

Hoffer: No, no. Sometimes people accuse me of exaggerating. Of course I exaggerate. You can't think if you don't exaggerate. and you'll never have a girl friend if you don't exaggerate.

You know, we found a savage continent here, fit only for a few thousand Indians. We tamed this continent. We turned it into a cornucopia of plenty. Now what do we find here? University students reading poetry. Whom do they read? Shelley, Wordsworth and others — poets of a manicured little island where nature is quite tame. And so they get the idea, for instance, that if you want to make love you're supposed to get up close to nature. So these boys and girls go out into the hills and get a bad case of poison oak. They come back all swollen up. They never knew that in this country you are not supposed to make love out in the woods. Utter ignorance, utter ignorance.

We have to watch nature all the time. That's why we have so much maintenance in this country. We have to or we'll get wiped off the face of the earth.

Now, I love nature as much as anybody else. I love the grass. I love the trees. I want to be in harmony with nature, but the harmony I am after is a harmony I can control. And I don't worship nature. I think man became what he is by separating himself from nature and this is a great role the Jews have played. The Jewish religion is the only religion that separates God from nature. In all other religions God and nature are identical. The Jewish God created both man and nature and he appointed men his viceroys. This is an important contribution of the Jews to our civilization. Why didn't the Chinese invent the machine age? Why didn't the Hindus? The reason is they stand in awe of nature. To them nature is God. The first chapter of Genesis says: "Be fruitful and multiply and subdue the earth!" That's the beginning of our machine age. If you didn't have a God as a Christian who made the earth, who made man, you wouldn't have had the machine age, you wouldn't have any science.

Besides, I don't think any society that stands in awe of nature can be a free society because if the ruler is identified with the force of nature you are not going to start a revolution against nature. To me separation from nature is a very precious quality. I don't hate nature. I think man and nature go well together, but the intellectuals don't think so. They think that man is a defiler.

Sevareid: You wouldn't be very happy if all the redwoods were cut down, would you?

Hoffer: Of course, I wouldn't be. The redwoods are part of us. I want to turn the whole darn world into my garden. I want the globe to be mine, I don't want to be a guest on the globe. Let me tell you a story. General Bing, a British General who served in India Gods knows how long, comes back to England and retires to write a book. He absorbs all that romanticism crap from the intellectuals and then he describes his first encounter with the Himalayas: "I stood in front of the Himalayas and I felt that I didn't exist, and that it didn't matter that I didn't exist." Imagine! A man, the greatest miracle of creation, stands in front of a pile of rock and ice and feels that he doesn't exist and that it doesn't matter that he doesn't exist. Why this is blasphemy I tell you!

The first time I had a chance to talk at an architectural school, I told the students to build a bungalow on the top of the Himalayas so that all the Himalayas will look like a background to that bungalow. That's what an architect is supposed to be. All the talk about dovetailing with nature is nonsense.

You have to arrange it so that after you've dovetailed with nature, the observer will feel that man was there before nature. That's the great architect's doing. You know, I'm a self-appointed inspector of buildings in San Francisco. I get to talk with the architects and the workers there and that's what I preach. You blend with nature when you plant trees where you want them and so on and so forth. If you build a gate, it should look as if it was there first and the trees were planted after the gate was built. In other words, man comes first. I don't think the human species is defiling this continent despite all the propaganda about our pollution tendencies. I think we have the power and the knowledge to rebuild everything, to restock everything. In fifty years we can make this continent more virgin than it ever was.

Our weakness is that we don't know how to build and operate viable cities. It's in the city that man became human and the city is where, if America is going to decay, it will decay. It won't decay because we have cut down too many redwood trees or anything like that. You don't have to be a scholar to know that no noble conception, no noble idea was ever conceived outside the cities.

All our great ideas were conceived in the crowded, stinking, twisted city streets of Jerusalem, of Athens, of Shakespeare's London and of Rembrandt's Amsterdam. Yet we don't know how to operate cities. How to make our cities viable should preoccupy us much more.

Sevareid: You're now going into your late sixties, which is a lot longer than you expected to live. Do you think about death much?

Hoffer: I think of death all the time and I'm on very friendly terms with death. The only time I'm poetic is when I think of death.

You know, the great French painter Degas once told Mallarme, "Monsieur, I have so many ideas but I cannot write poetry." And Monsieur Mallarme said, "Monsieur Degas, you don't start a poem with ideas, you start it with a word!" Once while I was sitting at my table playing whist I said to myself:

How far ahead my waiting and the road runs straight.
I see no bend, but somewhere there, I know not where,
I'll meet my end, my waiting friend.
He knows I come; I know he waits.
There is no bend; there are no gates.
The road is endless, but my end is somewhere there,
To meet a friend.

Those lines are with me all the time. When death comes I almost feel sure I'm going to shake hands with him. Death is a familiar thing for me. None of my forebears lived to be over fifty. I lived with death all my life in a lumber camp. Often I woke up in the morning to find the fellow in the next bunk dead.

I've seen more dead men than you can count. Death is always with me. I'm not afraid of it. This doesn't mean I want to die. I want to live, especially now that I know people I love. There is nothing more precious, you know, than to have friends, to have people you love and to give them pleasure. My old age is beautiful, good, real good. I've always felt everything depends on how a story ends, not how it begins.

Conversation With
Mary Peabody, Marietta Tree,
and Frances Fitzgerald

August 10, 1975

Sevareid: These three Yankee women are related but they have differing views on politics, marriage, and life in America.

Mary Peabody, the grandmother, is straight out of Mayflower Massachusetts and High Episcopalian stock. She's a conservative but some years ago she deliberately got herself arrested in the South because she felt she had to take a stand on civil rights.

Her daughter, Marietta Peabody Tree, the first American woman to hold the rank of Ambassador at the United Nations, has been called "the Golden Girl" of the Democratic Party. She has presided over one of our few genuine political salons.

Mrs. Tree's daughter, Frances Fitzgerald, recently won a Pulitzer Prize for her best-selling book on Vietnam, "Fire in the Lake."

Mary Peabody's mother was a founder of Radcliffe. Her father was a banker. Her husband was a Bishop. One of her sons was Governor of Massachusetts; the other three sons have been in public service and the public eye. Money, religion and public service surround her. In 1965 she did to the South what New Englanders have done since the American Revolution—she taught the South a lesson in civil politics. She got herself arrested by sitting in at a segregated restaurant. Southerners called it "genteel carpetbagging"; Northerners called it "civil rights." In full view of national cameras, she was taken to the lock-up and spent two nights in a Florida jail. She did it because she thought it was her obligation. Marietta has called her mother "one who answers to the stern voice of duty." If there's anything in the Puritan ethic, it answers to the name of Mary Elizabeth Parkman Peabody.

Mrs. Peabody, you have a rather special famliy heritage. Your family goes way back, practically to the beginning of this country. Do you have a sense of being sort of special or set apart? Do you feel you have special obligations?

Mary Peabody: What I've felt as a responsibility is that I've had the benefit of education and a certain amount of money and that I owed it to society to give it back. I've never thought about tradition particularly or of being part of a separate group because we had descended from people who came over, more or less, on the Mayflower.

Sevareid: But isn't it tough being a minister's wife? Don't you have to be a kind of example all the time?

Mary Peabody: No, I think it's great fun being a minister's wife.

Marietta Tree: Didn't you say that you wanted to be a minister's wife long before you were married and that you waited a long time until you found one?

Mary Peabody: I always wanted to marry a minister. At one time I wanted to be a missionary but that seemed to be too much of a good thing. So then I thought the next best thing to that would be marrying a minister. I almost gave that up as I grew up but suddenly a minister turned up, a very nice one. We managed to make it together rather well.

Sevareid: Frances, you haven't been an activist in the sense of directly taking hold of people and doing them good but writing, in the existentialist philosophy, is action, isn't it?

Frances Fitzgerald: Writing is an activity of some kind but I really have no hope for books as a means of persuading people. I don't think you can write in a way that you hope will convince a particular government official or a particular section of the population. You just write in the hope that somebody out there will listen. I think you just can't write with an absolute audience in mind.

Sevareid: What did you feel, Marietta and Mrs. Peabody, when Frances turned out to be an important writer?

Marietta Tree: She's genuinely unselfconscious. The day she learned about the Pulitzer Prize she was typing an article. A telephone rang. Somebody said: "Hello. You've won the Pulitzer Prize." She put down the phone and went on typing.

Sevareid: She must have had some thoughts, some feeling.

Marietta Tree: Well, she probably was thinking about the deadline for her article. I probably would have leaped all over the room.

Sevareid: What did you think when Marietta became Ambassador to the United Nations?

Mary Peabody: Well, we certainly were impressed.

Sevareid: How did you react when Mrs. Peabody went to jail?

Marietta Tree: My husband and I happened to be in Barbados on that day—the very same day that the present Queen Mother of England came for lunch. I was so concerned about my mother going to jail that my ear was next to a small radio all the time and I could hardly speak to our distinguished guest. Ronnie, my husband, explained: "My wife's mother is going to jail and that's why she can't really pay too much attention to what's going on here." Afterwards the Queen Mother came up to me, looked deeply into my eyes, smiled, and said: "Congratulations on your mother."

Sevareid: Mrs. Peabody, did you feel like a criminal when you went behind bars?

Mary Peabody: Oh no. But I felt embarrassed about all the publicity because it really isn't hard to go to jail when you know you are going to get out. I was there only two nights. It happened to be a nice jail. And it was clean. The room I was put in was supposed to be for eight people but there were fifteen. Three were serving out sentences. The rest of us had been arrested for demonstrating.

Marietta Tree: Mother immediately began to organize the jail, doing what she could with all her resourcefulness and leadership. Since there weren't enough knives and forks and spoons to go around, mother said to everybody in the room, "Now let's pretend we're on a picnic. We'll just eat with our fingers."

Sevareid: Did you feel you deserved to go to jail, Mrs. Peabody?

Mary Peabody: Well, I wanted to be arrested because that would bring publicity to the civil rights cause.

Sevareid: Lots of people who break ordinances feel they should not be punished. You didn't feel that?

Mary Peabody: I believe that when you break a law you've got to take the consequences. I think I would have refused to go to war but I think I would have gone to jail rather than leave the country.

Sevareid: There's about a fifty-year spread in ages from Grandmother to Frances. I know you get along with each other fairly well. Do you understand each other?

Mary Peabody: I think so, much better now than I used to because

I've seen in print what my daughter thinks of me. I didn't know it before. Now I know better.

Sevareid: Were you happily surprised or otherwise?

Mary Peabody: Unhappily surprised, I think.

Marietta Tree: Oh, Mother! How sad! What was it that upset you?

Mary Peabody: Well you accused me of not being loving and affectionate and thinking enough about my children. I'm very much aware of that now.

Marietta Peabody: I don't remember this at all.

Mary Peabody: I'll show you chapter and verse sometime.

Sevareid: Your daughter must have written that at a pretty tender age.

Mary Peabody: She wrote it just the other day. I suppose there's nothing like being on television when you discuss family affairs.

Sevareid: Are you saying that your daughter, Marietta, didn't understand you?

Mary Peabody: Oh, she understood me very well. Her criticism was very justified.

Marietta Tree: I think Mother is being much too humble. She showed her affection to us by acts—not necessarily by calling us "darling" and giving us hugs and kisses. She never seemed to buy anything for herself. When we grew up in a poor minister's home, the few extra dollars we had went to send me to a good school or to buy me an Easter hat that I fancied. For my brothers she made endless sacrifices. It seems to me that her entire life, when we were growing up, was spent doing things for us all the time. When there are five children that's a full-time pursuit, quite apart from all the other activities she was involved in because she was a real partner of my father's.

Sevareid: During the 1950's a town house on the upper East Side of Manhattan was a political salon for the Democratic Party. The woman who presided over the discussions that took place there, Marietta Tree, now works in a private office planning new cities in the Western Hemisphere. She's helping plan thirteen new towns right now. On the wall of her office are some of the plaques that tell of other work she has done. She once held the rank of Ambassador on the U. S. delegation to the United Nations. She was sworn in when Adlai Stevenson was our spokesman at the UN. At one time she worked as a researcher-reporter for Life magazine.

Marietta Tree was brought up affluent and conservative but a sense of duty brought her to the forefront of liberal causes. She traces her sense of duty back to her family. One of her grandfathers founded Groton, a boys' preparatory school, and she spent some of her formative years under her Puritan grandfather's influence in a school that taught the Protestant work ethic before anything else.

Marietta Tree: I very much gained the aspirations and idealism that my grandfather had for his boys. He helped them sense that a great deal is expected of you in later life and that you should go into public service. That's what you must do—give your life to the service of other people, for your country, for your church. That went very deep with me and I know it did with all my cousins.

Mary Peabody: There's a wonderful story about Marietta. When she was about fifteen years old she went to see Dr. Francis Peabody, who was no relation. He said to her: "What are you going to do with your life, Marietta?" She said: "I'm going to reform the Senate." He said: "Well, how are you going to do that?" And she said: "Well, I've got some boys who will help me do it." I think she's been trying to do that kind of thing ever since.

Sevareid: Your house, Marietta, has been called a political salon for years. Do you think of it that way?

Marietta Tree: Not anymore. When I was appointed to the United Nations by President Kennedy in 1961 that was the end of politics for me.

Sevareid: The salon was a great institution during the eighteenth century. Some women got very powerful that way. Did you feel you were influencing the fate of nations at your salon?

Marietta Tree: Oh, no. I just saw it as very exciting to see political friends and people I knew about. They came here from all over as a result of a convention in town, a speech somebody made, or something of that sort. It was great fun to have them come together and to see the ferment they created.

I used to conduct sociological surveys and I wondered if the politicians had anything in their background in common. I discovered that most of them grew up in big families or were children of people like doctors. Most of them saw lots of people in their homes, people asking advice of their fathers or their mothers. I think you'll find, if you look into the backgrounds of most politicians, that they're used to living with people, used to the compromises that are made when one has to live closely together.

Sevareid: What was your family tradition, politically?

Mary Peabody: We were Republicans.

Marietta Tree: I think, Mother, that you voted for Willkie. I remember imploring father, unsuccessfully to vote for Roosevelt in 1944. When I went to work on Life I changed quite a bit. I became a sort of political reporter and researcher. That was when I became a passionate convert.

Sevareid: Mrs. Tree, why didn't you ever run for public office?

Marietta Tree: I happen to have a very supportive husband. He said to me: "You must do what you think is important. Otherwise, you'll be unhappy and our marriage will be unhappy." But when it came to running for office I realized that if I were successful we'd have to move to Albany or Washington. He objected to that.

Sevareid: Today there's a lot of women's activity in party politics and many women office holders. What difference has this actually made in public policy? Do women approach public policy any differently than men?

Marietta Tree: I don't think so. In politics everything depends on what kind of a person you are, not particularly on your sex. In England, the last home of male chauvinism, Margaret Thatcher is the head of the Conservative Party, and Shirley Williams is a very articulate spokesman for certain factions of the Labor Party. I don't think anybody in India thinks of Indira Gandhi primarily as a woman. In Israel Mrs. Golda Meir has for many years been an overwhelming force. She was often at the United Nations when I was there. I was very lucky to get to know her.

Sevareid: When you talk to Golda Meir you don't think of her as a woman. Her spirit is so overpowering you forget everything else.

Marietta Tree: When then-Congressman John F. Kennedy came up to me at a party many years ago, he said to me, while talking about a woman politician we both knew quite well, "Tell me, Marietta, shall I treat her as a woman or as a politician?" I told him, of course, that he should treat her as a person. I don't think any American politician would today ask the same sort of question.

Sevareid: Not now. You know, somebody has called you "The Goddess of Liberal Causes."

Marietta Tree: That really is twash and twaddle.

Sevareid: I take it that you don't care for that description. Something very profound has been happening to traditional, conventional liberalism since Franklin Roosevelt. Whole new schools of ex-liberals and neo-conservatives are now taking a whole new look at the role of government, the handing out of largesse to every group. Has the apparent inability of public programs to solve our problems bothered you?

Marietta Tree: Of course, it's bothered me but I don't think it's entirely the fault of the programs. When I was in the government in 1965, when Lyndon Johnson was just starting with his wonderful Great Society program, I had great hopes. I remember saying at a lecture I delivered at the University of Tokyo: "The miracle is going to happen. We in America are going to stamp out poverty and we're going to do it in the next few years. And as a result of stamping out poverty, obviously, all the problems of racism will begin to disappear." I really believed that. And I still think that if Johnson hadn't got mired in the Vietnam War, if he had kept on with his central purpose, the goals of his program might very well have been realized. This is one of the reasons that terrible war was such a great tragedy.

Sevareid: You knew Adlai Stevenson as well as anybody. How would you sum up the great and weak things about him?

Marietta Tree: As a public man he was absolutely perfect on questions of foreign policy as far as I was concerned. I regret terribly that he wasn't Secretary of State, although I understand why President Kennedy wanted to be his own Secretary of State in effect. Strong Presidents are usually their own Secretaries of State. Adlai would have been the first person to stop the rot of John Foster Dulles, whose only idea of foreign policy was that it should be anticommunist and anybody who thought differently was dangerous.

Sevareid: People said Adlai was indecisive about things. I thought he was that way on personal matters. On objective policy matters it seemed to me he was a very decisive man. Certainly he was that way as a Governor. But do you thing he was equal to the Presidency?

Marietta Tree: You've got it just right. It was awful for him to decide where to go, let's say, for the weekend. He kept everybody in suspense until the last minute. But when it came to really important matters, about foreign policy or upholding the law, he was firm and very sure. Another of his great talents was the ability to pick very good men who were devoted to him. I think that's what made him an excellent executive; he knew how to pick men.

Sevareid: At least he made party politics seem fun again. There was a certain happiness about it when he was around. That was quite a contribution. I recall, incidentally, that you were with him the day he died while walking down the street in London.

Marietta Tree: And you were very close by at the time.

Sevareid: I had been with him the night before. I knew he was very tired but did you have any sense that he was that ill?

Marietta Tree: No, none at all. While I was walking with him just before he died, he talked about all kinds of things relating to the future—what he might be doing next January, for example. You know, he asked me to play tennis just as we started our walk. I told him I was too tired.

Sevareid: You were at the United Nations for quite a time. It seems to me that our new Ambassador there, Patrick Moynihan, has a little bit of Stevenson in him—especially his gift with words and the ability to stimulate people's ideas. He wants us to stop taking abuse from small countries that really haven't any moral right to criticize us in some respects. How is the United Nations changing? I can't quite make out what is happening these days.

Marietta Tree: It's hard to predict what is going to happen. If Moynihan's recent article in "Commentary" suggests his behavior at the UN I don't think he'll stop people from hitting out at the United States. That's a pretty difficult thing to do. We have sacrificed a lot of the world's good opinion in the last few years over Vietnam and the bombing of Cambodia. What I think Moynihan will do is state very positively what we stand for. He'll go into what we call honorable opposition. He'll talk about our real concern for individual rights and what we're doing to achieve them. Heaven knows, we're far from perfect, but we're working for real protection of human rights at the United Nations.

Sevareid: If there's going to be a constant, chronic anti-American majority in vote after vote in the Assembly on Israel, for example, what do you think will happen in this country about that?

Marietta Tree: I don't know, but it seems to me that the UN is either a universal organization or it isn't. This means that both Koreas should be in it. Nobody should try to push anybody else out.

Sevareid: You think the UN is still a forum, not just a colosseum or an arena?

Marietta Tree: The Assembly is, of course, just a forum. I'm afraid that's why so many of the African and Asian nations feel it's impotent. The Security Council is where the power is. And power is where the money goes—into agencies like the World Bank, which, I must say, has been using its money very wisely.

Sevareid: Frances Fitzgerald is Marietta Tree's daughter by an earlier marriage. She's affluent, she graduated magna cum laude from Radcliffe and she did the obligatory grand tour of Europe while she was in her twenties. Her mother was in the United Nations; her father in the CIA. So it's a bit surprising that she has turned out to be the left wing of a dove.

When she was only 32 she published "Fire in the Lake," a best seller that won the Pulitzer Prize. Her book has been called "a most profound examination of Vietnamese life" and "the most devastating attack ever written on the American involvement in that country." Some journalists consider it the most important book in English on that subject. Now that that war is over she has begun research in a field related to American history.

Frances, you're just about 35. Does this age seem like a watershed to you in any way?

Frances Fitzgerald: It's hard to tell about watersheds until you're on the other side of them.

Sevareid: Sure! But I assume you're going to go on writing. Have you thought about writing novels?

Frances Fitzgerald: I'd love to write a novel but I'm scared of it. It's terrifying to make something up.

Sevareid: Yes, but that's the way you can tell the real truth, all the way down the line.

Frances Fitzgerald: That's the scary part.

Marietta Tree: John Gunther, at the end of his long and distinguished career—after all those "Inside" books of his which were such a revelation to so many people—said to me: "My whole life has been a failure because I've never made it in the humanities." That meant he had never written a decent novel. He felt all his reporting, his wonderful journalism, really didn't count at all.

Sevareid: Reporting tends to fade. Frances, when you were covering the Vietnam war, wasn't it pretty tough, being a woman in the middle of a war between a lot of men?

Frances Fitzgerald: It was tough being in the war, man or woman, period. But in a way, I think, it was slightly easier for me in dealing with the Vietnamese people because I didn't seem quite as threatening as a man might have been, perhaps there's less suspicion toward a woman. Personal relations with the Vietnamese were very difficult in the South during the war. Everything was an extension of politics. Being a woman was, of course, difficult where the American military were involved. But I didn't cover combat much.

Sevareid: Frances, your book on Vietnam is probably going to be as much the Bible on this subject for future students as any other book. What motivated you to go to Indochina? At college you had studied Mideast things. You were very young when I met you in Vietnam. Did you go there out of a sense of curiosity or outrage about the war?

Frances Fitzgerald: I went to Vietnam because I was a journalist and that was the place to be at the time. When I arrived I didn't know very much about the war or even the issues involved. I tended to be a dove but that was mild compared to what I became. At first I thought that if people could be shown that the war didn't work, that it was a foolish idea, that it was wrong, that it would stop. I felt that rational argument could prevail. In the beginning I took seriously, to the extent of wanting to disprove them, the arguments that were made for purposes of winning hearts and minds or exporting democracy or our way of life—that kind of thing. And so I spent much too long a time trying to show the opposite. In a way, I think, the journalists failed completely in Vietnam. The thing that really taught us about the war was the Pentagon Papers.

Sevareid: Well, why do you think we went through the war?

Frances Fitzgerald: The Cold War was a war for control or domination of the Third World or whatever other countries could be dominated. Vietnam was simply an expression of the Cold War and this was seen as very important for foreign policy and economic reasons. Control over natural resources in the rest of the world has been very important to American foreign policy.

Sevareid: What natural resources in Vietnam did we want?

Frances Fitzgerald: Well, the war was never fought because there was anything inherently valuable in Vietnam. That's the interesting part about our involvement. No American has ever cared about the Vietnamese or indeed about the counry itself. But it's been seen as a symbol. It's perhaps the last truly symbolic war. We were fighting the war against all wars of national liberation around the world. And, in the end, we were fighting for American credibility.

Sevareid: If we were trying to exploit Indochina we certainly made a bad investment. We'll never get back one-thousandth percent of what we spent on it.

Frances Fitzgerald: True! And that is why the Vietnam war seemed to me to have a highly irrational element.

Sevareid: You say the journalists failed there. I had that feeling myself. Most reporters had to cover the battles and the cutting edge of the day's action; that was their job. But none of them spoke the Vietnamese language. I felt like an alien. I really didn't understand what was going on. Did you come to a point where you felt you had a grasp of Vietnamese culture and what resistance to the war was all about?

Frances Fitzgerald: In a way the essential points weren't too difficult to understand. Obviously, Vietnamese society is complex and interesting but that's another point. I think the essential dynamics were visible since the French war in Indochina. To me the interesting part of the war, the war that was not really covered by American reporters was in Washington.

What was it that got us into the war? We reporters were lied to for ten, fifteen years and are still being lied to. The coverage of the end of the war was very much different than that of the beginning. The end was a sort of Operation Babylift, stage-managed to show a triumph of American virtue over Vietnamese savagery.

Sevareid: The most serious criticism of press and television coverage of the war was not that we retailed what administration people said but that we didn't believe them and we were telling our own story, which was at variance with the administration's story. The result was a fair amount of anti-press feeling. I didn't think we were just puppets in the hands of the administration.

Frances Fitzgerald: I think many journalists were very courageous but they could have been braver. What bothers me especially is that administration after administration had increasing powers over foreign affairs—to the point where there's been almost a sort of dictatorship of the executive branch over foreign affairs and it became extremely difficult to get other people's voices heard.

Sevareid: The press is the reason people know that administrations lie from time to time. No one else has told them the truth.

Frances Fitzgerald: I don't mean to be too hard on the press. I'm saying that to a certain extent they were really incapable of dealing with the problem. What is required is institutional change, not in the press, but in our control over foreign affairs.

Sevareid: What line do you think the U. S. should take toward the present Vietnam government? Recognize them? Give them aid if they want it? What should we do?

Frances Fitzgerald: Recognition, first of all, is important because they're obviously an important part of Southeast Asia. Their victory has already changed the constellation of politics in Southeast Asia. They have, of course, declared that they want recognition and aid from the United States.

Sevareid: Why should they ask us for aid? I would think they'd want all vestiges of America out of Indochina.

Frances Fitzgerald: They don't want us to control aid in the way we did before. I think they're so interested in maintaining their own independence that they would like a counter-balance to the Soviet Union and China. They want a third way. The United States can be exceedingly important in creating that third way.

Sevareid: In an article you wrote after the South Vietnam collapse this spring you wrote that the "Vietnamese were now reunited with their history." What did you mean by this?

Frances Fitzgerald: A great many Vietnamese see this war as simply an interregnum of violence during which nothing of a positive nature was accomplished. Southerners who regrouped with the North in 1954 are now suddenly discovering that their villages have been liberated. They're now talking about going home. It's very odd to hear somebody fifty years old saying that he's going home to see his father. They act almost like children in their excitement about this. Life is now once again beginning for them.

Sevareid: An impression a lot of people have about the three of you is that here are women who have done exactly what they wanted to do in life and haven't been all fouled up by a lot of other problems or other desires and fantasies. Is this impression valid? Have you ever wanted to be anything else but what you are?

Mary Peabody: I'm perfectly satisfied with my life, it's been a very happy life. But I've had some fantasies. Once I thought it would be great fun to be a Rockette.

Marietta Tree: Well, mother, there's no reason why you can't try now. You haven't any responsibilities at home. And I'm sure Rockefeller Center would love to have you. You've got very good legs and you dance so beautifully.

Frances Fitzgerald: I've had rather similar fantasies. At the age of twelve I wanted to be an opera star. I still do.

Sevareid: Marietta, weren't you once in a movie with Clark Gable? Did that fulfill a fantasy?

Marietta Tree: That experience had nothing to do with fantasy. One day while I was being shown around the set of a film by a friend of mine, director John Huston, we came into a room where Clark Gable was interviewing ladies for a very small part. After he had interviewed several he wheeled around and said "I'll take that one," pointing right at me. I said, "I'm not an actress." He said, "Honey, it's the easiest thing in the world. Just stand up here with me and we'll go through the part."

At eight o'clock in the morning of the following day I found myself in front of a huge camera crew. There I was with Clark Gable, knee to knee, tummy to tummy. We were waiting for a train to come in. I was to get on the train and he was to kiss me goodbye. While we were waiting for the train to arrive we were in a very intimate position having what appeared to be intimate conversation. But instead of saying "I love you darling" he said, "I've got an 11-year-old stepson. Do you think I should send him to military school?" Our noses were touching as he said this. It was a very peculiar kind of conversation.

The scene was part of "The Misfits," a film with Marilyn Monroe. It was the last picture she and Clark Gable ever starred in.

Sevareid: Was that also your last movie?

Marietta Tree: Well, my life's not over yet.

Sevareid: Mrs. Peabody, you've lived, and very vigorously, to a great age and you've seen an awful lot of change in this country. Is it all for the good or for the bad? How do you cope with it?

Mary Peabody: I've been able to cope with it because, luckily, I haven't had many problems. But I think it's very difficult for young married people. I can't get over what young women are now doing. Sometimes they put their husbands through college and even take on bringing up of children and the drudgery that comes with looking after a family.

Sevareid: Wasn't there drudgery when you were a young woman?

Mary Peabody: When I raised my family I had a staff of three people to help me with the housework and the children. I had a very easy life.

Sevareid: How does one escape household drudgery? Somebody has to do it.

Mary Peabody: I don't know how you do it unless you go into communes or day-care centers. I think that's so dreary for you and your children. I don't see how household drudgery can be escaped. You just have to assume the woman's burden.

Sevareid: Perhaps these things just go in cycles. Marriage is now rather unpopular but don't you think it will come back?

Mary Peabody: Marriage is a very good institution. It stands up better than other arrangements.

Frances Fitzgerald: I don't think one can say marriage is good or not good. It fits or it doesn't fit with society. It's a basic economic institution. It has to do with inheritance and the care and feeding of children. If that can get done in other ways then I don't think marriage will come back.

Sevareid: You don't think marriage has much to do with love and companionship?

Frances Fitzgerald: Well, that's a whole other aspect. It doesn't necessarily demand the particular institution of marriage.

Marietta Tree: I think it does. Companionship is very much a product of a good marriage. If I were living unmarried with my husband I'd be nervous the whole time. What's he doing when he's out of the house? Et cetera. I'm fairly secure under the present arrangement. My husband is right now in London. He's seeing all kinds of people, including attractive women. I'm not worried. I think we're going to stay married, which is a very fine, secure feeling. I'd be terribly nervous if I weren't married to him.

Sevareid: Marriage has endured through all kinds of different social systems in all kinds of different countries. There must be something about it that is more than just an economic necessity or social convenience.

Frances Fitzgerald: I'm not saying that's all that goes into marriage. People obviously have very important needs for companionship and love but getting married at age twenty and remaining married until age of eighty is just becoming less and less easy. Things are not that permanent. American society is going through a series of transformations and people are experimenting in a creative way with different ways of living—communes, temporary marriage, and so on. Not all of it works terribly well, of course, it's experimental.

Marietta Tree: Few people have a sense of inner stability by themselves. I think it's probably best to stick to an institution where everybody knows where they are, more or less, even though it may not last forever. Margaret Mead says that every person should have three marriages—one for children, one for sex, and one for companionship. I've forgotten what order she had in mind.

Sevareid: Marietta, you were divorced at one point in your life. Was this the first divorce in your family?

Marietta Tree: Yes, it was. And, believe me, it was a searing experience for everybody—for me, for my family, for my father, who was then a bishop. I thought my divorce was probably destroying his entire career. I was torn as on the wheel for a long time. But I'm immensely grateful that the divorce took place. My ex-husband went on to have a much more fruitful and happy life. And so did I. And I hope Frances benefitted from it by having more of an extended family.

Sevareid: Did you have much family support when the divorce took place?

Marietta Tree: I can't say that I did. Nobody came to the wedding from my side of the family.

Mary Peabody: Father and I did!

Marietta Tree: Not to the wedding. I didn't see you there.

Mary Peabody: Why, Marietta! Your father and I were there. We didn't like the divorce but we came to your second wedding.

Marietta Tree: Well, this shows how unsupported I felt.

Sevareid: Well, Frances, for people who intend to get married, do you think there's an optimum age?

Frances Fitzgerald: I don't. The difficulty people have is with forms. My mother was the first one in the family to break with form. Her divorce was a tremendous sort of emotional trial. What was resisted and objected to was the form as opposed to the trial itself. For my generation forms are becoming less important and people are breaking away from them with much greater ease. But it's more complicated to figure out what to do under the circumstances without a program.

Marietta Tree: That's it! No program.

Frances Fitzgerald: Well, you can't impose a program. It simply won't work.

Marietta Tree: I think that's awfully hard on people. If you merely live with somebody how are you going to get a divorce? I know people who have lived together for a long time and then got married in order to get a divorce. This makes everything much easier.

Frances Fitzgerald: You see, people are still brainwashed by the marriage-divorce routine.

Sevareid: Marietta, you said that a woman's best years begin after 35. Why?

Marietta Tree: I probably meant that I felt, for myself, that my best years were after 35. I was terribly lucky to be able to choose jobs that I found interesting and important but at no time was it required of me to support Frances and/or the family. That's why I think women today who have had education are so lucky. They can choose what they want to do. Nobody much thinks about how much they bring in. I have a great deal of sympathy for men now, especially since I started a business of my own a few years ago. I have such sympathy for them because they have to support the family. They're not able to choose jobs they like; they have to choose jobs that are best for the family income.

Sevareid: That's practically a revolutionary thought you're uttering — that men have a hard time. Frances said something to that effect in an interview I read recently.

Frances Fitzgerald: Objectively, it's true that men have a difficult time. I think women will have a very hard time, sort of subjectively, because of the way they get brought up in their relationships to men. But the reverse is also true.

Sevareid: Mrs. Peabody, do you think you were happier and more effective after 35?

Mary Peabody: No, I don't feel so. I don't remember any difference. I know, though, that the women's liberation movement has meant something to me. Previously it never occurred to me that I was really a person and that I should act like one and take responsibility. I always have had to take responsibility but somehow I always thought that men were far more important than women.

Sevareid: I have the feeling that during much of your life you just didn't think about yourself very much. You were just doing, doing, doing. Evidently the women's liberation movement has made you think about yourself.

Mary Peabody: I've had more chance to think about myself. I've nobody else to think about because, I'm sorry to say, members of my family have all gone their different ways. I'm not enjoying this much but it's understandable. The end of your life can't be quite as much fun as the first part.

Sevareid: You've all been pretty lucky about being comfortable in life and not having to worry much about money. What's the connection between personal affluence and happiness? I'm not sure I ever could find it. Is it important to happiness or does it just mean you can be unhappy in comfort?

Mary Peabody: I think it's important to have enough so that you don't have to worry about where the next dollar's coming from, so that you can be interested in other things, and do what you want.

Marietta Tree: It's the freedom of it. Fanny Brice put it this way: "I've been rich and I've been poor, and rich is better."

Conversation With
Daniel Patrick Moynihan

May 30, 1976

Sevareid: Daniel Patrick Moynihan, counsellor to four Presidents, former Ambassador to India and the United Nations, is one of the most colorful and controversial men in American public life. He has been praised and attacked by blacks and whites, by the far left and the new right. America's allies and enemies publicly deplore and privately admire his scholar's mind, his political instincts. A conversation with him is like the skies of Ireland—suddenly filled with scudding dark clouds that give way to shafts of clear sunlight. An opponent once said, "the trouble with Moynihan is that he thinks too clearly, and speaks English too well."

Last year, in the magazine *Commentary,* an article appeared under the title "The United States in Opposition." What it said is that the United States, instead of suffering in silence the continuous abuse and attacks against it in the United Nations, ought to go into opposition; it ought to state its case far more bluntly than it had until now. The article got Pat Moynihan the job of Ambassador.

Moynihan, a poor Irishman from dingy Tenth Avenue, had crossed Manhattan to fashionable First Avenue. He had that Tenth Avenue style, hand in pocket, as he strutted to the UN podium. Even before he had spoken, the word was leaked that this was a declaration of war on the Third World—something that didn't turn out to be true. The British Ambassador to the United Nations called him "Wyatt Earp." It made our Ambassador a kind of folk hero to ordinary Americans. There is no doubt that even now, while he teaches at Harvard, his public career is not yet over.

Mr. Moynihan you went into the UN because you had written and said we must stand up to this assault, we can no longer go on

with a dignified, long suffering silence even though there are small
countries attacking us. And then, after just a few months, you're
out of the job. Why did you leave?

Moynihan: Well, let me first say that I had gone to the job under
real protest—I mean kicking and screaming, sending telegrams saying "No, No!" I'd done it because we were sort of on our beam
end in the spring of '75 with Southeast Asia going down and Portugal
shaky as can be and the failure of the Middle East shuttle. It looked
pretty grim and I was asked to come back from India. I said yes
I would. Then I tried to reconsider but they had my marker and I
paid up. At the first press conference I gave in the UN I quoted that
French doggerel, "cet animal est tres mechant quand on l'attaque,
il se defend"—"This animal is very wicked, when attacked it defends
itself." Temperatures rose and, among other things, our allies grew
to be uneasy. I think our allies have been less than helpful to us in
that UN setting because, very frankly, they have been quite prepared
to go along with attacks on the United States from former colonies
of theirs and whatnot, while advising us to be calm about it, saying
how calm they were when they used to get it. It's a way of currying
favor with persons who are attacking the democracies. I say it's
spinach and I say to hell with it.

Sevareid: What about the UN gang-up on Israel? This is a most
extraordinary development. As you've said, Israel is the only
democracy on the mainland of Asia. Are the Russians behind this
thing?

Moynihan: You may be sure they are behind it. For a complex of
reasons having to do with ethnic and other tensions in the Soviet
Union and maybe just a touch of anti-Semitism, maybe more than a
touch. It started in a two-part article in *Pravda,* as clear an announce-
ment of a campaign beginning as you ever get from the Russians.

They hit upon this obscene but, in a sense, brilliant Orwellian inversion. They said: The Jews, far from being victims of Hitler, are
themselves Hitlerian. And they began to put on television films in
which the head of Ben-Gurion would be superimposed on that of
Hitler. Last winter it was planned that there would be a move to
expel Israel from the UN General Assembly. We blocked that by
diplomatic action in capitals last summer. In the meantime there
arose at the Women's Year Conference in Mexico City the proposition that Zionism is a form of racism. Well, it is the most shocking
thing! But in the Orwellian sense the most shocking thing might just

be believed. They take that hideous phenomenon, racism, and they direct it against a society that is not racist. I mean Zionism, whatever it is, is a religious nationalist doctrine. It is specifically not concerned with race. It is concerned with religion. The state of Israel could be many things, including many undesirable things, but it couldn't be racist unless it ceased to be Zionist. Now those are the facts and yet, suddenly, this racist proposition comes forward. The purpose was to systematically delegitimate the state of Israel. A declaration of the Human Rights Commission in February accused Israel of war crimes, crimes against culture, crimes against religion. The whole set of indictments at Nuremburg are now being moved over to Israel. Now is that an isolated thing? Is it just Israel or is it free society that is such an affront in the midst of non-free societies?

Sevareid: How far do you think the campaign will go? Economic boycott of Israel? An attempt to throw them out of the UN entirely?

Moynihan: If they can discredit Israel they don't have to go much further. I don't think they can do that but they have got this Orwellian inversion going for them and they can take any free society and make it look like a criminal society. They also have many internal allies in free societies that will say, "Yes, that's right, we are terrible."

Sevareid: Are votes on these things bought in the UN?

Moynihan: I have never seen money change hands but I know that money does change hands. Last fall a vote changed hands at the UN for $600. That was thought very bad for the reputation of the institution. It's like when seats on the Stock Exchange got down to $2100 in 1932. I mean, votes at the UN are supposed to be worth more than that. You want to know what is said? Two thousand dollars will usually get you a vote. There are the bloc votes for which money changes hands, and it's in that $600 to $2000 range. I'm not very shocked by it. Governments maximize their interests— I don't know that charging cash or charging wheat loans is such a different thing. But I wish I thought the money for votes went into the exchequer of the nations involved. I sometimes doubt it.

Sevareid: You don't want to identify who's involved in this connection?

Moynihan: No, I do not. And let me also say that I'm telling you what we all tell one another at the UN. I certainly haven't received any envelopes and most assuredly haven't passed any. But do not have any doubt about what's been happening.

Sevareid: Is this sort of thing much different from using our economic aid abroad as a diplomatic tool or weapon?

Moynihan: Not so much different, no. I don't think that nations are any better then they ought to be. On this question of aid I think we talk a lot of silliness about this, you know. We have always attached conditions to the support we give countries. We have sort of wanted to help this country or that for one reason or another. I'm not talking about emergency aid when people are dying. That's different, that's humanitarian aid. I'm talking about what kind of countries do we want to see prosper by additional support we can provide? My judgment is that in the main the democracies ought to help those countries which are willing to help the democracies, if only to the minimum extent of not associating themselves with assaults upon us or assaults upon nations whose reputation is important to us. Our reputation is essential. In a funny way the good name of free societies is losing out everywhere but in the totalitarian societies. They know the difference.

Sevareid: Look at this extraordinary phenomenon of many European and domestic left, liberal, socialists, like the Prime Minister of Sweden—who are all exercised about the cruelties which are very real in right wing dictatorships like Chile. This upsets them terribly. The mass cruelties of Hanoi or Russia or China, or Cuba do not bother them, or they don't attack it.

Moynihan: I want to give some benefit of the doubt to someone like the Prime Minister of Sweden, who must get a lot of benefit of the doubt or else you are led to very ominous suspicions. That is to say, it is possible that a bourgeois mind such as that of Mr. Palme cannot conceive of totalitarian brutality. He can imagine a country with 6,000 people in jail. He can't conceive one with 6 million. That's the kindest thing you could say about him. What you could also say is that he is, I'm afraid, one of a long succession of Swedes who have got along fine with totalitarians, particularly if they were close at hand. They got along well with Hitler, they got along well with Stalin and they will get along well with whomsoever happens to be close at hand—not least because they have their skins to worry about but because of a failure of intellect and moral courage which has made people who perhaps have too much liberty in the world for their own good to underestimate the value of liberty.

Sevareid: It seems to me that philosophical socialists and even democratic countries cannot accept the fact that a great capitalist country like ours can be successful.

Moynihan: So much intellectual capital was bet on the fact that we would fail that in the face of whatever success we have—which is considerable—insistence goes on that no it wasn't a success. This is what it comes to. Look at the behavior of a country like Sweden. I'm sorry, the Swedes have simply, repeatedly, associated themselves with a standard Communist tactic, which is as old as Lenin, which is to find some imperfection in a bourgeois setting and really concentrate on it using Western standards of liberty and justice to indict the Western societies in the name of other societies that have not a smidgen of either liberty or justice. There had been, you know, sixty years of this and we ought to begin to recognize the pattern.

Sevareid: You make a point of the great difference between public diplomacy and private diplomacy. You say the UN is public diplomacy and that you do not use the same approach and the weapons you would negotiating privately with some foreign country.

Moynihan: I experienced that. For two years I was Ambassador to India in not the easiest of circumstances. I had one press conference and that was the day before I left and it was to say goodbye and thank the people for being friendly. I made four public appearances. That was a situation in which private diplomacy was altogether appropriate and it seemed to me that that worked pretty well. The UN is a place where ideological assault either is answered or it is not, and there is a possibility to do better than we might think.

Let me cite a little sequence. After the non-aligned nations decided not to move to expel Israel, in the General Assembly, they thought they would do something else. The General Assembly was just getting set up, and we got word one morning that the Credentials Committee, which is where this expulsion would take place, had hit on a new idea. They were going to refuse to take Chile's credentials because Chile was a military dictatorship and therefore couldn't really be representative of its people.

That was going to get us in a fix because we were expected to go across the street and say, "Well now, Chile's not so bad and Chile's better and Chile's good," or whatever. We were supposed to rise to it. We sat down and in fifteen minutes of going through the list of countries, we came up with a list of 85 countries which either were military dictatorships or had a government installed by a military coup. We went across the street and this thing came up exactly as forecast, and we said, "This is an absorbingly interesting proposition, that military governments cannot be representative of their people, and we, as a matter of fact, came prepared with a list of 85 such governments and perhaps we should consider them all." Bang went the gavel of the Chairman of the Credentials Committee. He said all credentials have been accepted. Then they go out mumbling, "Why'd you do that? Why'd we do that? Because they did it."

Sevareid: You've been very diplomatically quiet about your leaving the UN. Conventional wisdom in Washington has it that the man who put you there, Mr. Kissinger, is the man who in effect put you out. Is there anything you want to say about this?

Moynihan: That's about right. He's Secretary of State and he had the right to do that. I admire and respect Henry Kissinger. He is my friend. He has to make judgments about things in terms of, and including, how he feels about arrangements. And he made this judgment. I could have stayed as long as I wanted. I didn't want to stay in the face of a feeling that I was causing him more grief than otherwise and that he really wasn't very comfortable with the situation. There needn't be any secrets about these things.

Sevareid: Well, he knew your nature. He knew you were combative. He knew you knew how to make a speech. You did the things that he presumably wanted you to do at the UN.

But I thought that the moment you were on page one constantly your time at the UN was finished because I didn't think Kissinger would be upstaged in his own theatre. That may sound harsh but it is a rather widespread conviction.

Moynihan: That wouldn't have troubled me. I would never have left on that ground, because I would have said to my good friend and colleague from this university, "That's unsettling, but it can't be helped. I mean, if I'm going to do what you want me to do, that's going to happen. So, we're just all going to have to suffer that a little bit."

Sevareid: What would you call yourself now in terms of political philosophy? Our friend, Henry Fairlie, the British writer who lives over here, called you a "turncoat liberal." He is a changed Tory himself. How do you react to that kind of criticism?

Moynihan: Changed Tories are like reformed drunks. They should be treated with sympathy, but not very great seriousness when they lecture you on your own tendencies toward the condition from which they have just rescued themselves, or from which some mission has rescued them. I do not give a damn what Henry Fairlie has to say about my politics. I don't tell him about his. He's an Englishman, I'm an American. When I gave a commencement address at Fordham a while ago a few students were heckling in the back. I remember saying that I guess it's the destiny of people of my generation and opinions to have grown up in a time when I was too radical to be invited to Fordham but now to have seen things change to the point where I was not radical enough to be welcomed.

Sevareid: You've served directly with four Presidents, beginning with Kennedy. You were full of praise for Mr. Nixon at one point when you were in Washington. Have you changed your mind about him?

Moynihan: I went to work for Mr. Nixon after working for Robert Kennedy in the 1968 election and, later, for Humphrey. It was a situation of intense crisis. When I arrived in Washington there were sandbag and machine gun emplacements on the White House steps. This country was in a state of extraordinary tension, and it seemed to me that the kind of liberal values that mattered were being threatened by the rise of urban violence. Everybody was getting very upset.

I was the first person ever to be Assistant to the President for Urban Affairs, and I'm the last person, so far, and with any luck I will remain the last person. But there was this crisis and the question was how to deal with it. I think enough time has passed for me to tell you what actually happened. You know, it took a certain amount of fortitude for a President to say, "All right, try it this way . . ." I got down there and I got in the White House, sitting next to Kissinger's office in the basement. I soon found that the mayors and the urban city officials of this country were in a state of panic. Panic is the only way to describe it. I would get phone calls sixteen hours a day and they would say: "this city is about to blow." And I would ask, "well, what's the problem?" "Well, we haven't got this, that or the other things." What could be done? Well, they needed a federal judge or they needed a bridge or they needed a paving contract or a day care center. The widest range of things were at issue but the fact was: If this or that isn't done, the city will blow up. This had obviously been going on for some time and people had been chasing around trying to provide these things and the panic fed on itself. It's not because in a certain sense it was being rewarded, but I mean it was true panic and fear. I felt that there was no way we could respond in these terms, and I began a very blunt thing, which was the biggest risk I've ever taken in my life. It had to be made and I must say the President backed me up.

I would get into a conversation with a Mayor and I would say: "Your situation is perilous?" "Absolutely perilous," he would say. "You think violence, mass violence, is imminent?" "Unavoidable," he would say, "unless you do that or this." And then I would say, "Well, that is very disappointing. You're not the only city that has told us that. We are obviously heading for a disaster. Our resources are very limited, and we are going to have to reserve our resources for those places where there is still hope. Obviously there's no hope for you, and so go ahead, do the best you can when it breaks. When it's all over, if we can be of any help, we will, but there's no way to prevent the outbreak in your place and we are going to use our resources entirely for those places where there is still hope." For two months, I guess, there was disbelief on the other end of the telephone. But by springtime the panic had kind of broken. People stopped calling us up and saying "There's no hope here." They started calling up and saying, "Well, things are going pretty well here, and if we could get a little something out of you they'd probably go even better, but they're going pretty well." We broke it. And, you know, there has in effect not been an urban riot since.

Sevareid: You give Nixon credit for this; is this what you're saying?

Moynihan: I'm saying that I came to the man with a very chancy proposition about what to do with a crisis and he took the chance.

Sevareid: How did a man like you get along with people like Haldeman or Ehrlichman? Were you aware of what was going on in terms of what eventually became the Watergate business, the wiretapping and all that?

Moynihan: Oh, I didn't know anything about that. I don't think many people did. But I got to feel that a kind of a sour and offensive atmosphere was settling in that place, and the time came when I just left. I was asked to stay. I could have stayed. I was asked to go to the United Nations, but I didn't. So you might say I had some sense of what was happening but not much, no, no, not much. I wasn't involved in any political things, and so much of the particular trouble came out of the political side of the operation. I just wouldn't have known about it. Was I acutely perceptive of that situation? No, I was not. And if you want to ask yourself, am I a

man who can always sense when something's going wrong around
him? The answer is no, I'm not.

Sevareid: Patrick Moynihan served for two years as Ambassador
to India. He arrived there just after we chose to side with Pakistan in
the India-Pakistan war. The Indians were angry with us.
The times called for tact, correctness. Moynihan did not comment
either in private or public about the decay of Indian democracy.
He met Indira Ghandi at arms length. It was only in an artist's
fancy that the American Ambassador and the Prime Minister of
India danced together.

Mr. Moynihan were you surprised at what Indira Ghandi has done?

Moynihan: I was not surprised. I was bitterly disappointed. Having been there the last two years before it happened, I saw it building
up. There was a specific in the case of India which is that the court
ruled that Mrs. Ghandi had violated the election law, a trivial
violation—which no doubt she did—and ruled that she had to give
up her seat and couldn't run again. You know, if the court had just
said, "you have lost your seat in parliament," she could have said,
"Well, all right," and turned around and run again and been re-
elected again. But they didn't and that precipated the crisis. On the
other hand, for the whole preceding time there had been this
mounting pressure from the government against the press, against
the unions, against anybody who was resisting her. The people were
protesting the ineffectiveness of government and the more they pro-
tested, the more government did things which made the government
even more ineffective and you got that spiraling down. But when
it happened, you know, half the people in the world who had a
free press lived in India and that disappeared in June of 1975 and
we didn't hardly even notice it. What's the matter with us?

India didn't have to close down the press it had. One of the
glories of Indian democracy was its English language press which
was available throughout the subcontinent. I mean, go to some
dusty little airport in a dinky town in the middle of India at 5:30
in the morning and there wouldn't be anything there you could look
forward to but there'd be a copy of the Indian Express.

Sevareid: Mr. Moynihan, I want to ask you about a facsimile of a
check, that you showed me for sixteen billion, six hundred and forty
million rupees that you gave the Indian government. I understand
it's the biggest check ever written. What was that all about?

Moynihan: That is a check of the largest debt settlement in the history of the world. I negotiated it when I was Ambasador in India in 1973. It represented at the time one quarter of the currency of the Republic of India. Its dollar value would have been about four billion then—a big check. This money came into our possession, as it were, during the 1960's when there were two years in a row that the Indian crop failed and President Johnson sent huge shipments of food under the Public Law-480 program. The Indians paid us in their local currency, and we acquired this enormous debt —a debt which the Indians would have taken five generations to pay off. It was the largest thing between us. I mean, they felt we sort of owned them, as if we were the village money lender owning the peasants from one crop to another. Somehow we had got to get rid of it. It had defied a straight-out solution for a long while, but in 1973, with the help of John McCormick, the old Speaker of the House of Representatives, we got this settlement. It was agreed that this money could only be used for internal purposes in India. It had to be spent as rupees.

I remember coming back from the signing ceremony at the embassy and we had a little champagne broken out for the occasion. I had a photostat of the check, and my son John took a look at it and went scurrying upstairs and got the *Guiness Book of World Records* and came running back and said, "It's the world's largest check!". We wrote off to the Guiness people and they wrote back saying it was. I had finally made an impression on my then 14-year-old son.

There's a little story about this in terms of the ideas Americans had about our role in the world which suggests to me how distant we are from an era which is not in fact very far back—that is 1965. Indira Ghandi as Prime Minister came to the United States and at a White House dinner President Johnson announced and agreed upon a plan whereby we were going to take these rupees and use them to set up and finance the higher education system of India. It would be run, this university system, like the University of California. The regents would be a joint American-Indian board and there would be an American executive director. Somehow we had the idea, and they had the idea, that it would be good for us to be sort of molding the minds of, shaping the professions of, the people of India, and that there wouldn't be any conflict about this. Well, the Indians, when they got back and looked at this thing which they had participated in drawing up, said: "Oh, God, no, no, not that." The suspicion arose: were we trying to run India? No! We were trying to get medical schools and engineering schools and agricultural schools and we did set up a whole series of agricultural universities along the line of those great middle western agricultural technical institutes. Well, there was so much good will and so much simplemindedness.

Sevareid: They denounce us all the time now; at least Mrs. Ghandi does. But isn't it true that the immense amount of grain we shipped to them to keep them alive they then distribued to their people for certain payments and built their whole public sector activities out of that money? In other words, our money built Indian Socialism. Is that a fair statement?

Moynihan: Exactly. We are represented around the world as people who are opposed to experiment in alternative economic arrangements. The hell we are! What we stand for is liberty and we can be pretty sticky about that. There are many economic arrangements, as you can imagine, and our opposition has never been ideological. Really it hasn't. And why do we let ourselves be the ones who think that it is? I mean, there's a specific here in India. If you want to create a large public sector, own steel mills and railroads and build new factories and so forth, you have to have money. Now, how do you get money? Well, you can print it. That doesn't work very long. You have an inflation very quickly. Or you get money by borrowing or by taxation. Borrowing has its limits. Taxation is the normal way. But, the Indian government simply has never been strong enough to tax its people. To this day, the central government does not tax income from agriculture, although most Indians are farmers. It doesn't have the political strength to do it. Well, along we came with this enormous amount of wheat. The Indian government took it. They sold it to the Indian people who paid for it, in effect, as if it were a tax. Suddenly the Indian government had a fortune, by their standards, which they could use to create a public sector, a public sector that in the main has been an economic disaster, but that's not our fault. Certainly we didn't prevent their doing it, and certainly we were not unaware they were doing it. We thought they were doing it and we said good luck to them. It is not very gracious of them to go around depicting us as a bunch of purchasing agents for international capitalism.

Sevareid: Then you get to this whole fuss now about the multinational corporations. They're supposed to have a great power octopus stretching all over the world, beyond national laws, and so on. Yet the tiniest country can throw them out or buy into them or raise their taxes or whatnot.

Moynihan: When I was in India—which is, after all, a country with a population larger than that of Africa and South America combined—I used to go up and down the ministries. I'd go in to see a minister and say: "Minister, remember this company, X or Y, from America, that was here in the 1960's and spent a couple of years negotiating a proposal to build a fertilizer complex over there in Gujurat?" They would say, "Oh yes, we remember them." I said, "Well, you know, they really have gone into a big overseas operation just recently." "Oh, where?" I'd say, "In Siberia." And then there'd be a long "ah hmm." This pattern of American companies being rejected in democratic socialist India and then being grabbed up by totalitarian communist Russia got so embarassing that the Communist Party in India put out a statement about it, which is the only statement of its kind that Indian intellectuals have not found demeaning. They said, "The simple fact is that Indian socialism is not mature enough to take the encounter with these wicked institutions." Well, what the hell is that all about? I'll tell you. I am not of a conspiratorial mind; I don't have the imagination for it maybe, and maybe I don't have the wit for it, but it's not my tendency. But every so often I sense a conspiracy and I'm telling you that the Soviet Union has gone all over the world persuading poor countries that need the kind of capital and technology that comes with multinational companies not to take them. They say, don't you touch that dangerous organization that will corrupt your independence. And the next thing you know those companies show up in Moscow, because the Soviets want them in the worst way.

Do you know why they want American technology? It's rather fascinating and it's sort of a tribute to what a free society can produce. It's also a tribute—I'm not unrelucant to say—to the Soviet sense of their own condition. They know that their technology has just not caught up with us, never will, and they know why. It's because they are not a free society. They know that they're just as smart as we but the restraints in that society are limiting. The technology is not so important that they're going to give up the controls they have in order to get it. So they think they can import it from a free society and get it on the cheap. They're going to turn out to be wrong. Technology is not a secret. It's a system.

Sevareid: Mr. Moynihan is best known in the academic community as a brilliant political scientist and sociologist—a reasonable man with data, a careful man with conclusions. The most famous book he has written is *Beyond the Melting Pot* (with Nathan Glazer). It's a study of ethnic communities, pure and impure, in New York. His mind has been buried in people and numbers. When we talked about youth and crime he talked in figures and reasons.

Moynihan: In the 1960's and now in the 1970's the United States experienced the most extraordinary impact of a population boom that any society in history has ever done. The demographers have a saying which is a wonderful one I think, which is that every society is periodically invaded by barbarians. And who are these barbarians? These barbarians are young males, aged fourteen to twenty-four. They come crashing in and they don't yet know how to behave so you've got to teach them to be a Frenchman or a Japanese or an American or whatever. There's a lot of turbulence. One of the significant ratios in the world is the number of attackers as against the number of defenders. The people fourteen to twenty-four, females too, but males mostly, they're the people that cause all the trouble. Before 14 they're children. After 24 they've got children and the children are causing trouble for them. Those are the years that people run the fastest, sing the best, make love most enthusiastically. It's a wonderful age but also a turbulent one. Well, from 1890 to 1960 the number of persons aged fourteen to twenty-four in this country grew by 10.6 million. In seventy years it grew by 10.6 million. Then in one decade, in the 1960's, it grew by 11.5 million. But during the 1970's, it will increase by only 600,000 and in the 1980's it will increase even less.

Sevareid: So are you saying we might have a quieter period beginning in a few years from now because there won't be so many hell-raisers age 14 to 24?

Moynihan: That's right. They raise hell anytime in history and any place and they are here in large numbers right now. They are no longer dropping out of school as it were but they are dropping into local candy stores. It's been described like the process of a python swallowing an ox. You know, the ox just slowly, slowly diminishes after a while. That's point one. And that's the most important thing. The second thing is, don't underestimate the role of social disorganization in the cities. Young people are not growing up with the kind of watchful attention by adults that diminishes this impulse to raise hell and get into trouble. I could have gone to jail for God knows how many little things. Well, I didn't. I was lucky and I also had some people watching. There are great ranges of American cities where no one watches these kids and God have mercy. I mean, they're going to get in trouble and they do.

Sevareid: About ten years ago I think you said that a great many of these social problems might be more conducive to solution by the conservative approach rather than the traditional liberal one. Which ones? Crime, I would think.

Moynihan: Well, let me go back. I was a member of the national board of Americans for Democratic Action, which is sort of liberalism incarnate. I spoke to a meeting of the board and said that somehow liberals have got to learn from life what conservatives seem to be born knowing which is that there are limits to the kinds of things government can effectively do.

Sevareid: You know, when President Ford gave his last State of the Union speech he said let's build four more federal prisons. Some liberal writers thought that was a harsh, fascist kind of thing to do, no solution to anything. But what can be done?

Moynihan: All kinds of liberal politicians thought it was a sensible thing to do. I think liberals particularly (and I would think of myself as one) ought to be very careful about the words we use to responses such as, "If you commit a crime you should be put in prison." I mean, are we not saying that liberty is the most important thing society provides its people? The most important thing a free society can do is to deprive someone of his freedom for a period. It speaks to that thing which we value most. It doesn't bother me one bit that we say, "If you do something wrong, we will do the harshest thing we can do to you which is to take away your freedom for a bit, not forever," and so forth. Remember in the 1960's when there was an enormous increase in crime, the population of our jails and prisons went down, not up. We shouldn't see ourselves as going through some orgy of recrimination. We may just be getting back to the ratio of crime and punishment of earlier eras.

Sevareid: Still, the first function of government is to protect the citizen, his personal safety and his property.

Moynihan: You know, in that wonderful Saul Bellow book, *Mr. Sammler's Planet,* in which an old European gentleman wandered around New York and what he saw was an elite that will not defend itself. And here at my university, Harvard, it is astounding how in the last decade we've taken on the air of a besieged garrison, a

kind of garrison state of mind with respect to crime. We have
light, we have chains, we have guards, we have buses. About two
years ago there was a series of robberies at knifepoint in one of the
nearby streets and the Harvard police put out a statement that said
there are two people who are doing this. They seem to operate
along Bow Street and if any student wants to take a walk at night,
call the Harvard Police Department and we will send a cop to go
for a walk with you. Well, that was decent but I wonder if it wouldn't
have been more sensible to go out and get those two sons of bitches
on Bow Street and get them off that street.

Sevareid: Mr. Moynihan, you've written quite a lot about the
national ethnic condition and the eminent problem of the melting
pot that doesn't now seem to be melting.

Moynihan: Ethnicity is not just an American phenomenon. This
is a worldwide phenomenon. Formerly ethnicity, the attachment to
other people in terms of some sort of kinship relationship was
thought to be a kind of residual carry-over from pre-industrial times.
One of the great and central propositions of the Marxists was that
it would disappear, that the workers would cease to be Czechs or
Poles or Russians or Englishmen or Frenchmen, that they would all
be workers, that class would be the thing that held people together.
Well, they were wrong. They were just dead wrong. It's a problem
they cannot explain to themselves. They struggle with it and dig up
rather obscure, sometimes learned men from Vienna, (Otto Bauer is
one such) who try to interpret it. But it is almost the central
theoretical problem of Marxism in its own societies.

Sevareid: It's odd that in Russia itself ethnicity is formally recognized and people put in categories.

Moynihan: Right, and ethnicity doesn't get weaker; it gets stronger.
As the world gets more politicized, groups become more important.
The ethnic group is a great organizing principle by which to make
claims on government. You see it everywhere. There is no place in
the world, with one or two exceptions, where this doesn't happen.
But there's something else to be said about ethnicity, and that is,
it's got a cruel side to it. Sigmund Freud says in *Civilization and Its
Discontents* that it is possible to organize a society based on love,
as long as there is an external group to hate.

Sevareid: It seems unfair to end with the pessimistic thoughts of
Sigmund Freud. It also seems unlikely that Mr. Moynihan will end
his career as a professor, even at Harvard. He has been on the

forward edge of so many of the ideas that have cut through American thought. There's been talk of him as a candidate for the Senate from New York or as a Secretary of State if the Democrats win. We certainly haven't heard the last from Patrick Moynihan.